*Hundreds of Heavenly
Ways to Care for Yourself—
According to the Stars*

THE
ASTROLOGICAL
— GUIDE TO —
SELF-CARE

Features Advice for All Twelve Zodiac Signs!

CONSTANCE STELLAS

* ** *

Adams Media
New York   London   Toronto   Sydney   New Delhi

Dedication

To my Greek Grandmother. I am her namesake and loved
her Taurus view of life: No Monkey Business!

Adams Media
An Imprint of Simon & Schuster, Inc.
100 Technology Center Drive
Stoughton, MA 02072

First Adams Media hardcover edition December 2019

ADAMS MEDIA and colophon are trademarks of Simon &
Schuster.

For information about special discounts for bulk purchases,
please contact Simon & Schuster Special Sales at 1-866-506-
1949 or business@simonandschuster.com.

The Simon & Schuster Speakers Bureau can bring authors
to your live event. For more information or to book an event
contact the Simon & Schuster Speakers Bureau at 1-866-248-
3049 or visit our website at www.simonspeakers.com.

Interior design by Michelle Kelly
Interior images © 123RF, Getty Images, and
Clipart.com

Manufactured in the United States of America

4 2022

Library of Congress Cataloging-in-Publication Data
Names: Stellas, Constance, author.
Title: The astrological guide to self-care / Constance Stellas.
Description: Avon, Massachusetts: Adams Media, 2019.
Identifiers: LCCN 2019030430 | ISBN 9781507212349 (hc) | ISBN
9781507212356 (ebook)
Subjects: LCSH: Astrology. | Self-care, Health--Miscellanea.
Classification: LCC BF1711 .S785 2019 | DDC 133.5--dc23
LC record available at https://lccn.loc.gov/2019030430

ISBN 978-1-5072-1234-9
ISBN 978-1-5072-1235-6 (ebook)

Contains material adapted from the following titles published
by Adams Media, an Imprint of Simon & Schuster, Inc.: *The
Little Book of Self-Care for Aquarius* by Constance Stellas,
copyright © 2019, ISBN 978-1-5072-0984-4; *The Little Book
of Self-Care for Aries* by Constance Stellas, copyright © 2019,
ISBN 978-1-5072-0964-6; *The Little Book of Self-Care for
Cancer* by Constance Stellas, copyright © 2019, ISBN 978-
1-5072-0970-7; *The Little Book of Self-Care for Capricorn*
by Constance Stellas, copyright © 2019, ISBN 978-1-5072-
0982-0; *The Little Book of Self-Care for Gemini* by Constance
Stellas, copyright © 2019, ISBN 978-1-5072-0968-4; *The Little
Book of Self-Care for Leo* by Constance Stellas, copyright ©
2019, ISBN 978-1-5072- 0972-1; *The Little Book of Self-Care
for Libra* by Constance Stellas, copyright © 2019, ISBN 978-
1-5072-0976-9; *The Little Book of Self-Care for Pisces* by
Constance Stellas, copyright © 2019, ISBN 978-1-5072-0986-
8; *The Little Book of Self-Care for Sagittarius* by Constance
Stellas, copyright © 2019, ISBN 978-1-5072-0980-6; *The
Little Book of Self-Care for Scorpio* by Constance Stellas,
copyright © 2019, ISBN 978-1-5072-0978-3; *The Little Book
of Self-Care for Taurus* by Constance Stellas, copyright
© 2019, ISBN 978-1-5072-0966-0; *The Little Book of Self-
Care for Virgo* by Constance Stellas, copyright © 2019, ISBN
978-1-5072-0974-5.

Acknowledgments

I would like to thank Karen Cooper and everyone at Adams Media who helped with this book: Brendan O'Neill, Katie Corcoran Lytle, Laura Daly, Sarah Doughty, Leah D'Sa, Julia Jacques, Eileen Mullan, Casey Ebert, Sylvia Davis, and everyone else. Thanks as well to Frank Rivera and the design team for their work on the book's cover and interior. I appreciated your team spirit and eagerness to dive into the riches of astrology.

Contents

Introduction

Looking for a little "me time"? Want to feel more relaxed while deepening your connection to the world around you? Look to the stars! For thousands of years, the zodiac has guided humans to their highest purpose. And now, it can provide unique suggestions for your self-care—and the self-care of your loved ones.

In *The Astrological Guide to Self-Care*, you'll find heavenly ways to focus on your true self. Discover how to incorporate self-care into your life, while learning just how important astrology is to your overall self-care routine. Strengthen your understanding of yourself and the world around you, with the zodiac as your map. Then, relax, rejuvenate, and stay balanced with nearly one thousand self-care rituals, organized by the four governing astrological elements and twelve astrological signs.

With a brief history on the ancient mythologies and deities portrayed in the twelve signs, you'll recognize your unique personality reflected in the stars based on your Sun sign and sign element. You may also dive deeper into your astrological self-care by looking into sign-specific ideas for your Moon sign or Rising sign. And all the information on signs and elements that don't directly pertain to you in this self-care guide is all the more advice, insight, and knowledge you'll be able to offer your family and friends.

As you delve into what self-care means to you, you'll learn how to harness the full potential of your horoscope and take advantage of the celestial energies affecting your life. After just a few astrologically guided self-care activities, you'll feel more calm, balanced, and in sync with the universe. Wherever your self-care journey takes you, let the stars be your guide.

PART 1

Signs, Elements, and Self-Care

✦ ✹ ✦

CHAPTER 1

What Is Self-Care?

Astrology gives insights into whom to love, when to charge forward into new beginnings, and how to succeed in whatever you put your mind to. When paired with self-care, astrology can also help you relax and reclaim that part of yourself that tends to get lost in the bustle of the day. In this chapter you'll learn what self-care is—for you (and your loved ones). No matter your sign, self-care is more than just lit candles and quiet reflection, though these activities may certainly help you find the renewal that you seek. You'll also learn how making a priority of personalized self-care activities can benefit you in ways you may not even have thought of. Whether you're a Capricorn, a Pisces, a Leo, or any other sign, you deserve rejuvenation and renewal that's customized to your sign—this chapter reveals where to begin.

What Self-Care Is

Self-care is any activity that you do to take care of yourself. It rejuvenates your body, refreshes your mind, or realigns your spirit. It relaxes and refuels you. It gets you ready for a new day or a fresh start. It's the practices, rituals, and meaningful activities that you do, just for you, that help you feel safe, grounded, happy, and fulfilled. The activities that qualify as self-care are amazingly unique and personalized to who you are, what you like, and, in large part, what your astrological sign is. If you're asking questions about what self-care practices are best for your particular sign and element, or those of your friends and loved ones, you'll find answers—and restoration—in Parts 2 and 3. But, no matter which of those self-care activities speak to you and your unique place in the universe on any given day, it will fall into one of the following self-care categories—each of which pertains to a different aspect of your life:

- Physical self-care
- Emotional self-care
- Social self-care
- Mental self-care
- Spiritual self-care
- Practical self-care

When you practice all of these unique types of self-care—and prioritize your practice to ensure you are choosing the best options for your unique sign and governing element—know that you are actively working to create the version of yourself that the universe intends you to be.

Physical Self-Care

When you practice physical self-care, you make the decision to look after and restore the one physical body that has been bestowed upon you. Care for it. Use it in the best way you can imagine, for that is what the universe wishes you to do. You can't light the world on fire or move mountains if you're not doing everything you can to take care of your physical health.

Emotional Self-Care

Emotional self-care is when you take the time to acknowledge and care for your inner self, your emotional well-being. Whether you're angry or frustrated, happy or joyful, or somewhere in between, emotional self-care happens when you choose to sit with your feelings: when you step away from the noise of daily life that often drowns out or tamps down your authentic self. Emotional self-care lets you see your inner you as the cosmos intended. Once you identify your true emotions, you can either accept them and continue to move forward on your journey or you can try to change any negative emotions for the better. The more you acknowledge your feelings and practice emotional self-care, the more you'll feel the positivity that the universe and your life holds for you.

Social Self-Care

You practice social self-care when you nurture your relationships with others, be they friends, coworkers, or family members. In today's hectic world, it's easy to let relationships fall to the wayside, but it's so important to share your life with others—and let others share their lives with you. Social self-care is reciprocal and often karmic. The support and love that you put out into the universe through social self-care is given back to you by those you socialize with—often tenfold.

Mental Self-Care

Mental self-care is anything that keeps your mind working quickly and critically. It helps you cut through the fog of the day, week, or year, and it ensures that your quick wit and sharp mind are intact and working the way the cosmos intended. Making sure your mind is fit helps you problem-solve, decreases stress since you're not feeling overwhelmed, and keeps you feeling on top of your mental game—no matter your sign or your situation.

Spiritual Self-Care

Spiritual self-care is self-care that allows you to tap into your soul—and the soul of the universe—and uncover its secrets. Rather than focusing on a particular religion or set of religious beliefs, these types of self-care activities reconnect you with a higher power: the sense that something out there is bigger than you. When you meditate, you connect. When you pray, you connect. Whenever you do something that allows you to experience and marry yourself to the vastness that is the cosmos, you practice spiritual self-care.

Practical Self-Care

Self-care is what you do to take care of yourself, and practical self-care, while not as expansive as the other types, is made up of the seemingly small day-to-day tasks that bring you peace and accomplishment. These practical self-care rituals are important, but are often overlooked. Scheduling a doctor's appointment that you've been putting off is practical self-care. Getting your hair cut is practical self-care. Anything you can check off your list of things to be accomplished gives you a sacred space to breathe and allows the universe more room to bring a beautiful sense of cosmic fulfillment your way.

What Self-Care Isn't

Self-care is restorative. Self-care is clarifying. Self-care is whatever you need to do to make yourself feel secure in the universe.

Now that you know what self-care *is*, it's also important that you're able to see what self-care *isn't*. Self-care is not something that you force yourself to do because you think it will be good for you. Some signs are energy in motion, and sitting still goes against their place in the universe. Those signs won't feel refreshed by lying in a hammock or sitting down to meditate. Other signs aren't able to ground themselves unless they've found a self-care practice that protects their cosmic need for peace and quiet. Those signs won't find parties, concerts, and loud venues soothing or satisfying. If a certain ritual doesn't bring you peace, clarity, or satisfaction, then it's not right for your sign and you should find something that speaks to you more clearly.

There's a difference though between not finding satisfaction in a ritual that you've tried and not wanting to try a self-care activity because you're tired or stuck in a comfort zone. Sometimes going to the gym or meeting up with friends is the self-care practice that you need to experience—whether engaging in it feels like a downer or not. So consider how you feel when you're actually doing the activity. If it feels invigorating to get on the treadmill or you feel delight when you actually catch up with your friend, the ritual is doing what it should be doing and clearing space for you—among other benefits...

The Benefits of Self-Care

The benefits of self-care are boundless and there's none that's superior to helping you put rituals in place to feel more at home in your body, in your spirit, and in your unique place in the cosmos. There are, however, other benefits to engaging in the practice of self-care that you should know.

Rejuvenates Your Immune System

No matter which rituals are designated for you by the stars, your sign, and its governing element, self-care helps both your body and mind rest, relax, and recuperate. The practice of self-care activates the parasympathetic nervous system (often called the rest and digest system), which slows your heart rate, calms the body, and overall helps your body relax and release tension. This act of decompression gives your body the space it needs to build up and strengthen your immune system, which protects you from illness.

Helps You Reconnect—with Yourself

When you practice the ritual of self-care—especially when you customize this practice based on your personal sign and governing element—you learn what you like to do and what you need to do to replenish yourself. Knowing yourself better, and allowing yourself the time and space that you need to focus on your personal needs and desires, gives you the gifts of self-confidence and self-knowledge. Setting time aside to focus on your needs also helps you put busy, must-do things aside, which gives you time to reconnect with yourself—and who you are deep inside.

Increases Compassion

Perhaps one of the most important benefits of creating a self-care ritual is that, by focusing on yourself, you become more compassionate to others as well. When you truly take the time to care for yourself and make yourself and your importance in the universe a priority in your own life, you're then able to care for others and see their needs and desires in a new way. You can't pour from an empty dipper, and self-care allows you the space and clarity to do what you can to send compassion out into the world.

Starting a Self-Care Routine

Self-care should be treated as a ritual in your life, something you make the time to pause for, no matter what. You are important. You deserve rejuvenation and a sense of relaxation. You need to open your soul to the gifts that the universe is giving you, and self-care provides you with a way to ensure you're ready to receive those gifts.

To begin a self-care routine, start by making yourself the priority. Do the customized rituals in Parts 2 and 3 with intention, knowing the universe has already given them to you, by virtue of your sign and your governing element.

Then, turn to your friends and family members and share the gifts of astrological self-care with them. Now that you understand the role that self-care will hold in your life, let's take a closer look at the connection between self-care and astrology.

CHAPTER 2

Self-Care and Astrology

Astrology is the study of the connection between the objects in the heavens (the planets, the stars) and what happens here on earth. Just as the movements of the planets and other heavenly bodies influence the ebb and flow of the tides, so do they influence you—your body, your mind, your spirit. This relationship is ever present and is never more important—or personal—than when viewed through the lens of self-care.

In this chapter you'll learn how, no matter your star sign, the locations of these celestial bodies at the time of your birth affect you and define the self-care activities that will speak directly to you. You can also deepen your understanding of who you are and reap the additional benefits of astrological self-care by viewing the sign-specific rituals through the lens of your Moon sign—the sign the Moon was passing through when you were born—or your Rising sign, the sign that was rising over the eastern horizon when you were born.

(Learn more about both your Moon sign and your Rising sign by going online or consulting an astrologer.) You'll see how the zodiac influences every part of your being and why ignoring its lessons can leave you feeling frustrated and unfulfilled. You'll also realize that when you perform the rituals of self-care based on your sign, the wisdom of the cosmos will lead you down a path of fulfillment and restoration—to the return of who you really are, deep inside. And if you share the appropriate sign-specific rituals with your loved ones, they, too, can discover their best selves.

Zodiac Polarities

In astrology, all signs are mirrored by other signs that are on the opposite side of the zodiac. This polarity ensures that the zodiac is balanced and continues to flow with an unbreakable, even stream of energy. There are two different polarities in the zodiac and each is called by a number of different names:

- Yang/masculine/positive polarity
- Yin/feminine/negative polarity

Each polar opposite embodies a number of opposing traits, qualities, and attributes that will influence which self-care practices will work for or against your sign, and which will restore your own personal sense of cosmic balance.

Yang

Whether male or female, those who fall under yang, or masculine, signs are extroverted and radiate their energy outward. They are spontaneous, active, bold, and fearless. They move forward in life with the desire to enjoy everything the world has to offer to them, and they work hard to transfer their inspiration and positivity to others so that those individuals may experience the same gifts that the universe offers them. All signs governed by the fire and air elements are yang and hold the potential for these dominant qualities. We will refer to them with masculine pronouns. These signs are:

- Aries
- Leo
- Sagittarius
- Gemini
- Libra
- Aquarius

There are people who hold yang energy who are introverted and retiring. You—or a loved one—might fall into this category. However, by practicing self-care that is customized for your sign and understanding the potential ways to use your energy, you can find a way—perhaps one that's unique to you—to claim your native buoyancy and dominance and engage with the path that the universe opens for you.

Yin

Whether male or female, those who fall under yin, or feminine, signs are introverted and radiate inwardly. They draw people and experiences to them rather than seeking people and experiences in an extroverted way. They move forward in life with an energy that is contemplative and receptive, as well as focused on communication and the achievement of shared goals. All signs governed by the earth and water elements are yin and hold the potential for these reflective qualities. We will refer to them with feminine pronouns. These signs are:

- Taurus
- Virgo
- Capricorn
- Cancer
- Scorpio
- Pisces

As there are people with yang energy who are introverted and retiring, there are also people with yin energy who are outgoing and extroverted. You—or a loved one—might fall into this group. And by practicing self-care rituals that speak to your particular sign, energy, and governing body, you will reveal your true self and the balance of energy will be maintained.

Governing Elements

Each astrological sign has a governing element that defines its energy orientation and influences both the way the sign moves through the universe and the way that sign relates to self-care. The elements are fire, earth, air, and water. All the signs in each element share certain characteristics, along with having their own sign-specific qualities:

- **Fire:** Fire signs are adventurous, bold, and energetic. They enjoy the heat and warm environments and look to the sun and fire as a means to recharge their depleted batteries. They're competitive, outgoing, and passionate. The fire signs are Aries, Leo, and Sagittarius.
- **Earth:** Earth signs all share a common love of and tendency toward a practical, material, sensual, and economic orientation. The earth signs are Taurus, Virgo, and Capricorn.
- **Air:** Air is the most ephemeral element, and those born under this element are thinkers, innovators, and communicators. The air signs are Gemini, Libra, and Aquarius.
- **Water:** Water signs are instinctual, compassionate, sensitive, and emotional. The water signs are Cancer, Scorpio, and Pisces.

Part 2 will teach you all about the ways specific governing elements influence and drive connections to cosmically chosen self-care rituals, but, for now, it's important that you realize how relevant these elemental influences are to self-care practice and to the activities that will help restore and reveal.

Sign Qualities

Each of the astrological elements governs three signs. Each of these three signs is also given its own quality or mode, which corresponds to a different part of each season: the beginning, the middle, or the end.

- **Cardinal signs:** The cardinal signs initiate and lead in each season. Like something that is just starting out, they are action-driven, enterprising, and assertive, and are born leaders. The cardinal signs are Aries, Cancer, Libra, and Capricorn.
- **Fixed signs:** The fixed signs come into play when the season is well established. They are definite, consistent, reliable, principled, and powerfully stubborn. The fixed signs are Taurus, Leo, Scorpio, and Aquarius.
- **Mutable signs:** The mutable signs come to the forefront when the seasons are changing. They are part of one season, but also part of the next. They are adaptable, versatile, and flexible. The mutable signs are Gemini, Virgo, Sagittarius, and Pisces.

Each of these qualities tells you a lot about yourself and who you are. They also give you invaluable information about the types of self-care rituals that each sign will find the most intuitive and helpful.

Ruling Planets

In addition to qualities and elements, each specific sign is ruled by a particular planet that lends its personality to those born under that sign. Again, these sign-specific traits give you valuable insight into the personality of the signs and the self-care rituals that may best rejuvenate them. The signs that correspond to each planet—and the ways that those planetary influences determine your self-care options—are as follows:

- **Aries:** Ruled by Mars, Aries is passionate, energetic, and determined.
- **Taurus:** Ruled by Venus, Taurus is sensual, romantic, and fertile.
- **Gemini:** Ruled by Mercury, Gemini is intellectual, changeable, and talkative.
- **Cancer:** Ruled by the Moon, Cancer is nostalgic, emotional, and home-loving.
- **Leo:** Ruled by the Sun, Leo is fiery, dramatic, and confident.

- **Virgo:** Ruled by Mercury, Virgo is intellectual, analytical, and responsive.
- **Libra:** Ruled by Venus, Libra is harmonious, romantic, and graceful.
- **Scorpio:** Ruled by Mars and Pluto, Scorpio is intense, powerful, and magnetic.
- **Sagittarius:** Ruled by Jupiter, Sagittarius is optimistic, boundless, and larger than life.
- **Capricorn:** Ruled by Saturn, Capricorn is wise, patient, and disciplined.
- **Aquarius:** Ruled by Uranus and Saturn, Aquarius is independent, unique, and eccentric.
- **Pisces:** Ruled by Jupiter and Neptune, Pisces is dreamy, sympathetic, and idealistic.

A Word on Sun Signs

When someone is an Aries, a Leo, a Sagittarius, or any of the other zodiac signs, it means that the Sun was positioned in this constellation in the heavens when they were born. Your Sun sign is a dominant factor in defining your personality, your best self-care practices, and your soul nature. Every person also has the position of the Moon, Mercury, Venus, Mars, Jupiter, Saturn, Uranus, Neptune, and Pluto in their chart. These planets can be in any of the elements: fire signs, earth signs, air signs, or water signs. If you have your entire chart calculated by an astrologer or on an Internet site, you can see the whole picture and learn about all your elements. Someone born under Leo with many signs in another element will not be as concentrated in the fire element as someone with five or six planets in Leo. Someone born in Pisces with many signs in another element will not be as concentrated in the water element as someone with five or six planets in Pisces. And so on. Astrology is a complex system and has many shades of meaning. For our purposes, looking at the self-care practices designated by Sun signs, or what most people consider their sign, will give you the information you need to move forward and find fulfillment and restoration for yourself and others.

PART 2

Self-Care Rituals by Element

* ** *

CHAPTER 3

Essential Elements: Fire

Fire gives us heat, warmth, and light. And those who have fire as their governing element—Aries, Leo, and Sagittarius—all have a special energy signature and connection with fire that guides all aspects of their lives. Fire signs are drawn to the flames in all varied forms and environments, whether this gift comes from the sun, an outdoor campfire, or a cozy fireplace fire, and their approach to self-care reflects their relationship with this fiery element. Let's take a look at the mythological importance of the sun, as well as the basic characteristics of the three fire signs, and what they all have in common when it comes to self-care.

The Mythology of Fire

In astrology, fire is considered the first element of creation. Perhaps it was primitive humans' way of understanding the big bang, or maybe fire just made a clear-cut difference between living in the wild and gathering together in human communities. In Greek mythology, the immortal Prometheus angered the gods by stealing fire for the mortals he had such affection for down on earth. As punishment he was chained to a rock and Zeus sent an eagle to eat his liver. Magically, this liver regenerated every day and the eagle kept devouring it. Prometheus was later released from this curse, but the gift of fire that he gave to humankind was not completely free of conflict.

Fire was—and remains—an essential part of civilized life, but it also gives humans the ability to forge weapons of war. Fire warms a home, cooks a meal, and restores and enlivens the spirit, but too much fire can destroy. All fire signs feel this duality between the creative and destructive force of their fire power energy, and this duality drives their likes and dislikes, personality traits, and approaches to self-care.

The Element of Fire

The fire signs are known as the inspirational signs, because their enthusiasm and buoyant personalities help them to cheer themselves and others on to great success. They also represent the spiritual side of human nature, and their sense of intuition is strong: Fire signs often have hunches about themselves and others, and if they follow these hunches, they typically achieve whatever they set out to do. For example, Aries inspires the spark that pioneers a project or endeavor. Leo is a leader who inspires his circle of friends, family, or colleagues to keep their eyes on the goal at hand, even when things get tough. And Sagittarius is an idealist and searches (and helps others search) for truth.

Astrological Symbols

The astrological symbols (also called the zodiacal symbols) of the fire signs also give you hints as to how the fire signs move through the world. All of the fire signs are represented by animals of power and determination, which ties right back to their shared fiery element:

- Aries is the Ram
- Leo is the Lion
- Sagittarius is the Centaur (half horse/half man)

Each fire sign's personality and subsequent approaches to self-care connect to the qualities of these representative animals. For example, the Ram is determined and confident. The Lion is king of the jungle and boldly defends his turf. And the Centaur, also called the Archer, shoots his arrows of truth and moves powerfully against any attempts to rein him in.

Signs and Seasonal Modes

Each of the elements in astrology has a sign that corresponds to a different part of each season.

- **Cardinal:** Aries, as the first fire sign, is the harbinger of spring, and the spring equinox begins the astrological year. Aries is called a cardinal fire sign because he leads the season.
- **Fixed:** Leo, the second fire sign, occurs in midsummer when summer is well established. Leo is a fixed fire sign. The fixed signs are definite, principled, and powerfully stubborn.
- **Mutable:** Sagittarius is the sign that brings us from one season to the next. Sagittarius moves us from autumn to winter. Such signs are called mutable. In terms of character the mutable signs are changeable and flexible.

If you know your element and whether you are a cardinal, fixed, or mutable sign, you know a lot about yourself and your loved ones. This is invaluable for self-care and is reflected in the customized fire sign self-care rituals found later in this chapter.

Fire Signs and Self-Care

Self-care is incredibly important for fire signs. But learning how to set aside time for self-care takes discipline, because fire doesn't want to stop. Fire elements have a wonderful spark that lights up their minds, bodies, and spirits, but, as with fire, those born under this element frequently burn out. When this happens, making frequent pit stops to refuel, rest, and engage in self-care activities that are personalized for their element are what fire signs require to be stoked back to life.

Fire signs need to keep in mind that their self-care activities should be fun and varied; they don't want to get bored doing the same thing over and over again when there are so many different self-care options to try! The fire element crackles with enthusiasm and good spirits, and the more activity, socializing, and fun fire signs can have, the better they like it and the easier it is for people born under this element to get fired up. Fire signs will easily follow any practice or activity that enhances playfulness. Variety in exercise, diet, décor, fashion, friendship, vacations, and socializing gives all fire elements the motivation to enjoy life—and without a good time, life is a misery for these bold personalities.

For fire signs, the best way to approach self-care is to make it a game. The fire signs will have the willpower to follow through on a plan if they decide something is worthwhile and they can enjoy it. The rules of the "game" don't matter as much as the sense of achieving a good score, beating the competition, or enjoying the process. For example, if a fire sign decides to do 10,000 steps in a day and finds at 5 p.m. that he is 1,000 steps short, his motivation to reach his goal would help him find a fun way to complete the program. Perhaps he will decide to march to music, skip, or hop his way to 10,000. A fire sign will get what he needs in two different ways through this type of self-care: He both wins the game and has fun doing it!

Maintaining that flame and steady inspiration is the goal of any fire sign self-care program: If a fire sign plays the game of taking care of his body, mind, and spirit, not only will he benefit from his efforts, but he will inspire others to follow him. So now that you know what fire signs need to practice self-care, let's take a look at the activities that will help those born under this element to flourish.

Sweat Your Way to Relaxation

While we often think of heat as linked to passion and intensity, it can also be incredibly restorative and relaxing for fire signs. Embrace the calming effect of heat by seeking out a sauna at your local gym or spa. Take time to lounge in the warmth, allowing the sweat to cleanse your body of impurities. Breathe in the heat and feel it soften your muscles and increase your circulation. As the warmth envelops your body, any pain and stress will melt away.

Can't find a sauna nearby? No problem. Turn on your shower to hot and let the water run for a few minutes. Be sure to close your windows and bathroom doors. Then get a comfy seat and kick back in your own at-home sauna for some rest and recuperation.

Try a Sports Massage for Ultimate Relief

Do your sore muscles need a little TLC? Have you sustained an injury from all the running around you do? Soothing touch is a great way to alleviate stress in your body. As a fire sign, you can ignite a different type of heat inside you by turning to the therapeutic benefits of a sports massage. The warmth created by kneading muscle tissue and improved blood circulation can ease chronic tension, pain, and stiffness.

Place your trust in an experienced massage therapist. Before your massage starts, tell them exactly how your body feels and what it needs to get better. Don't be afraid to speak up at any point during your massage. Communication is key.

Burn Up the Competition

Fire signs thrive off of a little friendly competition—the key word being *friendly*! Engage your fiery competitive side in a healthy way by joining a community sports league of your choosing. You may find that team sports, like soccer, kickball, basketball, volleyball, or even a running group, suit you best. The sense of comradery can jump-start that passion inside you for action. Use the energy and excitement coming from your teammates as fuel. Just remember, it's only a game. No matter if your team wins or loses, the primary goal is to have fun and get your body moving.

Teach That Learning Is Power

It's as simple as ABC....As a fire sign, your ambition and passion for adventure has given you a lot of life experiences. Bring that passion and spirit you have for life to others by volunteering as a teacher in one capacity or another. This may mean becoming a mentor at a local after-school program, reading to children at the library, or teaching adults a special skill like painting or accounting at a community center. The choice is yours. However you choose to go about it, know that instilling knowledge in others is an act of love and patience. A good teacher can inspire and motivate their students. And the benefit isn't just theirs. As a fire sign, you find engaging with a group to be incredibly fulfilling for you too. Take a survey of your many talents and see where you can help.

Soak Up the Sun

It's time to turn up the heat! Fire signs need vacations just like everyone else, but when planning yours, stick to warm, sunny destinations. You need the warmth to feed your soul. Ditch your coat and look for vacation spots on the beach, where the sun is strong and the temperatures soar. Fire signs are nourished by the heat, so soak up the rays for ultimate replenishment.

Keep your body and mind challenged with tons of adventures and new experiences. While taking some time to lounge and relax is totally fine, you need something to get your fire burning. Try to schedule at least one activity each day you are on vacation, whether that means going for a hike through canyons or learning to surf. The more out of your comfort zone you are, the more alive you'll feel.

Make 'Em Laugh

There's nothing quite like the power of a good belly laugh. Fire signs are extroverts by nature and love to entertain people with stories, songs, and even jokes. While you may not have an entire stand-up comedy set ready to go yet, all it takes is one simple joke to get someone laughing and improve their day. And that rush of joy coursing through your veins as your audience laughs is enough to raise any fire sign's temperature. Don't know any good jokes off the top of your head? Go for the classics or search online for some new material. And remember, it's all in the delivery!

Focus On the Flame

Fire signs are drawn to the sacred element inside them: the flame. From the blue center to the red-hot aura glowing outward, the flame calls you on an instinctual level. Use the power of fire to keep yourself balanced when you need it most. At times of high stress, find a quiet respite. Light a candle of your choosing and sit in front of it. Watch as the flame dances, softly flickering as it burns slowly. Take solace in the beauty of the glow before you, allowing the whole world to fall away around you. It is just you and the flame. Fix your gaze on the flame as it flares and sways, and try to quiet your mind as best as possible. If you find your mind wandering, don't worry. Gently return your focus to the light in front of you. Repeat for as long as you wish or until the flame has safely extinguished.

Find Your Passion

Discovering what kindles the passion inside you usually comes naturally for fire signs. After all, you are full of strong emotions and big ideas, all of which drive your sense of self-knowledge and well-being. Maybe it's a hobby that makes your heart sing, or a political cause, or a person. Home in on those things and make them a prominent part of your life if they aren't already. Indulge in the passion you feel for them, and let it fill you with meaning and support. If you are unsure about what lights your fire,

it's time to start learning about yourself. Try a new meal, make a new friend, or read a new book. Your journey of self-discovery will lead you to your true passions.

Flirt

Intimacy and sexual connection are key components in a relationship, especially for fire signs. You live to feel close to others and make your passion for them known in one way or another. When the mood strikes, unleash your inner flirt and have some fun with the person you are smitten with. Bat your eyes. Whisper sweet nothings. Tell them a corny joke. Let loose and show your unique personality.

Combine Earth and Fire

Stone is one of the earth's most sacred elements, and with a touch of heat, it becomes the ultimate healing tool. You can benefit from the combination of these two elements by indulging in a hot stone massage.

Fire signs are naturally active beings, often pushing their bodies to the limit with exercise and adventure. Take time to let your body relax and heal after strenuous activity. And why not do so with a soothing hot stone massage? Not only do the stones connect with the primal fire inside you, but they expand your blood vessels, improving circulation and flushing your skin, all while relaxing sore muscles.

Try Spontaneity

When was the last time you did something completely on impulse? Hopefully not too long ago, because enthusiastic spontaneity is the ruling philosophy for all fire signs. Have you been feeling a little trapped lately? Stuck in a rut you just can't break free from? Don't ignore that little voice inside you urging you to do something a little out of your comfort zone. Being impulsive and spontaneous ignites the fire sign's soul and feeds the energy within. Without it, you'll suffocate under the weight of predictability.

Watch a Comedy

When you're in need of emotional release, turn to your favorite laugh-out-loud comedy. It may seem counterintuitive, but a funny movie is actually one of the best ways a fire sign can let go of any nasty emotions that have been building up over time. You have so much passion swirling inside you that you need a positive way to let it all out. If you have a favorite comedy, turn it on—or if you want to try something new, check out what's playing at your local theater. Need more of a reason to laugh? Not only does laughter help reduce stress hormones in your body, but also it helps increase immune cells and releases endorphins, the body's feel-good chemical. Win-win!

Make a Priority List

Fire signs often have a lot of great ideas and like to start a variety of projects when inspiration strikes. It's just part of the territory—you are naturally creative and dream big. The hurdle is completing these projects.

Take a survey of your life and make note of different projects or plans that are sitting around half-finished. Make a priority list of the tasks you want to complete and when you want to complete them by. You can be as specific or as vague as you want.

Maybe that wine rack you are building doesn't need to be finished for another year or so, or maybe you want to show off your favorite bottles by next month. The ultimate goal is committing to expectations and following through on your plans. And just imagine how much better you'll feel once you've checked off a few of those projects from your list.

Burn, Baby, Burn

Fire is cathartic for fire signs. It can cleanse and purify your energy, and it helps you let go of emotional burdens. From destruction comes regrowth, better and stronger than before.

Use the natural destruction inherent with fire to your advantage. Write down your feelings on a few pieces of paper. Light a candle and place it in a firesafe bowl or in the sink. Carefully hold each piece of paper to the flame and allow it to catch fire. Watch as fire consumes your words and emotions. Drop the piece of paper into the sink or bowl to continue burning. As each emotion goes up in flames, feel the weight on your heart lessen. You are free, ready to rise from the ashes more resilient and determined.

Sleep It Off

A good night's sleep can be transformative, but unfortunately, fire signs often have a hard time getting enough sleep. As a fire sign, you naturally need less sleep than others, but that doesn't mean you are invincible. It just means you have to work a little harder at giving yourself the best chance possible for restorative sleep.

Creating a good sleep routine is key. Do you already have a routine, or does it change from night to night? Do you have a specific bedtime you shoot for, or do you stay up until different times depending on your mood?

To help stabilize your sleep schedule, try implementing a few easy, enjoyable activities you can do right before bed, anything from reading for a few minutes to taking a long bath, or even meditating. Aim to get into bed at around the same time every night. Fire signs love spontaneity, but when it comes to good sleep hygiene, predictability is paramount.

Avoid Burnout

With all the complicated emotions you hold onto as a fire sign, it can sometimes be helpful to seek out a professional therapist to work through your thoughts. Talking to a professional is often a therapeutic experience and can promote overall wellness in your life. Fire signs are prone to emotional fatigue and burnout because their emotions run intensely for extended periods of time. It can drain your system to keep your feelings bottled up. Eventually, you'll run out of gas. Turning to a trained professional who can help you understand and sort your stressors can save your emotional well-being and give you a healthy outlet to better yourself.

Change It Up

Predictability is the fire sign's ultimate enemy. How do you avoid getting stuck in the same humdrum pattern? Change things up. Start in your home, where you spend the majority of your time and where you feel the most comfortable.

To get the winds of change blowing, open your windows (if you can) and move your furniture around into different arrangements in all of your major spaces. This could mean moving your bed from one wall to the other or changing which direction your couch faces. It could also mean doing something as small as adding a piece of furniture to a room. Whatever feels right to you! Sometimes just changing your perspective can make all the difference in the world.

Try Minimalism

Clutter can do more than just cause a mess in your home. It can overwhelm your mind and make you feel trapped. Fire signs love big spaces with a lot of room to move around. If you find that you are feeling claustrophobic in your own living space, it might be time to streamline your belongings.

Start by going through your closets and cabinets and throw out anything you don't need. Next, move on to your furniture. Many fire signs find the minimalist design aesthetic a pleasing choice. Look for furniture that does double duty, like a combination desk and dining table. The most important thing is to give yourself space to feel free.

Follow Your Intuition

Your intuition is invaluable when it comes to decision-making. Fire signs often move from one idea to the next rather quickly, but your gut reaction to an idea can help inform whether you should pursue it or not. You don't have the time to sit and weigh the pros and cons, using your mind to decide. You use your heart and that feeling pulsing inside either urging you forward or calling out warnings to stop. Listen to that voice. It tells the most primal truths about your journey as a person, and its only purpose is to help you navigate through life's confusing moments.

Still aren't sure what your intuition is telling you? Sometimes, it can even be a physical feeling. Do you get a warm rush in your veins when you think of something? Or is it more of a stomachache? Our bodies have different ways of speaking to us. Listen for yours.

Don't Test Your Limits

Fire signs tend to overexert themselves, physically and emotionally. Because of this, it's important to recognize your limits, and to try not to push them too much. If you find you have a propensity for going too far emotionally, it might be time to create a list of warning signs that you can flag for yourself. When you see those warning signs popping up in your thought pattern and behavior, or if you feel yourself getting too stressed and overwhelmed, schedule a self-care activity to help find equilibrium once again. It can be as simple as taking a bath or visiting an old friend.

If you push yourself athletically, always give your body time to recuperate. While fire signs always want to go farther and be better physically, not allowing your body rest after physical exertion can increase your risk for serious injury. Don't let your fire burn too bright—you are your own best advocate for balance and well-being.

Embrace H₂O When Working Out

Water and fire are opposites. And while water can extinguish fire, those born as fire signs need water to keep them thriving and succeeding. With all the strenuous activities you do as a fire sign, don't forget to keep hydrated. It can be easy to forget to stop and drink water when you are focused on achieving a physical goal. Make it a priority to drink the recommended number of cups of water a day, and more if you are engaging in demanding physical workouts. Remember that water will not smother the flame burning inside of you.

Beat the Heat

Balance can be the key to a happy life. As a fire sign, you must learn to offset your heat and passion with coolness. Begin with how you nourish your body. If it feels like your inner fire is burning too hot, put away the spices and try to balance the heat by eating cooling foods. Turn to foods such as watermelon, cucumber, yogurt, and, if you are feeling really indulgent, ice cream. The cool contrast will help keep your inner fire from burning out of control.

Try the Ancient Power of Hot Yoga

Bikram yoga is a form of yoga done in an environment where the temperature is about 104°F (40°C). Heat is a vital element of this exercise. Practicing yoga in a heated room is a great way to potentially increase your metabolism and your heart rate, which in turn allows your blood vessels to expand and your muscles to become more flexible. Check with your doctor first if you have any health conditions.

This form of hot yoga is perfect for fire signs. Fire signs feed off of the heat around them, and use it to find equilibrium and balance. Look for hot yoga classes near you to challenge yourself and your body. If you've never tried a hot yoga class before, be sure to hydrate your body beforehand and to bring a small towel with you to class. Get ready to sweat!

Draw a Bath

As a fire sign, you already have a special affinity to heat and its galvanizing power. But it is also a wonderful relaxation tool. Warm water can be incredibly soothing for a weary fire sign. If your mind is cluttered from the demands of day-to-day life, and your muscles are sore from all of the physical activities you do, climb into a warm bath and let the water alleviate your ailments.

You can even add a special bath bomb or bubbles to the bath to make it more relaxing; go for scents like lavender, jasmine, or even rose to ease your mind. Adding Epsom salts to the warm water can help take the ache out of overused muscles. Start by adding 1 cup (8 ounces) of Epsom salts to the bath as the water runs.

Enlist in Boot Camp

Boot camp–style exercise classes are popular fitness options for fire signs looking to add a little heat to their typical workout regime. These boot camps attract a wide variety of people, and the group atmosphere can really ignite a spark for fire signs who love a little friendly competition. You'll learn to encourage others to push their physical limit, and to push your own limit as well. The combination of intense cardiovascular or strength-training exercises with a supportive team dynamic can be a rewarding experience for many fire signs. Make friends, build muscle, and tone your heart, all at the same time.

Enjoy Fireside Chats

The fireplace is often the center of the home. It's where people gather together to keep warm and to share stories. As a fire sign, you have an innate connection to fireplaces—they feel comfortable to you, like old friends. If you have a fireplace in your home, make it the center of your space. Arrange seating around the fireplace so it becomes the focal point. Use it as often as you can to take advantage of your sacred connection to the fire it contains.

If you don't have a fireplace already, you can often buy a decorative, portable fireplace from many home goods stores. Just the look of fire dancing can pacify a stressed-out fire sign. If you can't have any sort of fireplace, decorative or not, in your home, look for a restaurant or bar nearby that has one and make that your new go-to spot for drinks, dinner, and cozy relaxation.

Go on a Digital Detox

Fire signs are always moving from one thing to the next. That's because they are ambitious and motivated, traits that can sometimes lead to some serious burnout if you aren't careful.

One way to purposefully give yourself a break from the fast pace of the world around you is to unplug digitally as often as possible. Try and put your phone or tablet away at the same time every night, approximately an hour before bedtime. This gives your mind time to unwind before sleep.

If you go on vacation, consider switching your phone on just once a day to check for urgent messages. At home, designate a basket for devices, and ask that family members place their phones and tablets in it before time meant to be spent together. And when going to dinner with friends, focus on enjoying your food and company—not keeping one eye on your phone at all times.

Catch Some Rays

Spending time outside soaking up the sun can lift any fire sign's mood. Think of yourself as a solar panel. You need the sunlight to reenergize your soul when you are feeling depleted. Lucky for fire signs, sunlight can help increase your levels of serotonin—those feel-good chemicals in your brain—thus boosting your happy mood.

Take some time to bathe in the sun, letting the rays wash over you. Feel the warmth on your skin, and imagine the sunshine penetrating down into your heart, lighting you up on the inside. Bask in the warmth around you.

While sun exposure, at the right times and intensity, can be beneficial for anyone, too much sun can be dangerous, even if you are a fire sign. While you're recharging in the sun, always take the proper precautions, like wearing sunscreen and remembering to reapply.

Get Creative

Being creative comes naturally to fire signs. They are often temperamental and passionate, and need a healthy way to release the emotions inside of them. While many fire signs turn to physical activities like athletics to help control the blaze within, flexing your creative muscles can be just as beneficial. Try indulging in the creative arts as inspiration. Hobbies such as painting, pottery, coloring, writing, or even knitting or scrapbooking can fuel your creative spark. Get a friend to join you as well. There are tons of ways to let your creativity run free. The only limit is your own imagination.

Take a Last-Minute Trip

Fire signs are drawn to impulse and improvisation. If they don't feed their desire for adventure on a regular basis, fire signs can sometimes get cranky and start feeling stuck. To remedy this, cash in your airplane miles and take a last-minute trip to somewhere you've always wanted to visit. Even an unplanned weekend trip to another town nearby can satisfy a fire sign's need for fresh scenery. Your desire to explore unfamiliar territory can lead you to great discoveries about yourself and the world around you. Don't let the fear of the unknown stop you. Be spontaneous!

Get Physical

Making time for yourself can be difficult when you are a fire sign. You are always going, going, going, with very little downtime. There's always so much to do, and so little time to do it. Who wants to spend their free time going to the doctor? But, as a fire sign, it's important to make your health a priority; you tend to push yourself both physically and mentally, striving for the next success benchmark. Make sure you keep tabs on your health, and schedule an annual physical checkup with your doctor to make sure you are healthy and strong. Your wellness should never be put on the back burner.

Greet the Day

Whether you are an early bird or a night owl, as a fire sign you have a natural attraction to the sun. You are drawn to its power and heat, and can often generate strength from its rays. Don't ignore this special connection you have with the sun. Embrace its energy and start your day by going for a long morning walk. Beginning the day by communing with the element that speaks to you the most will help set the stage for a positive afternoon, evening, and night ahead.

Check In on Your Emotions

Your emotional health is often overlooked when you're a fire sign. You are constantly moving from one thing to the next, so you may not make time to take your emotional temperature. Fire signs also spend a lot of time supporting and entertaining others. You are the first to step up and help a friend in need, but that concern doesn't transfer to your own well-being. Check in with yourself as often as possible. Are you stressed? Tired? Overwhelmed? Take stock of what you are feeling. If any of those feelings intensify, take some time to practice self-care in whatever form that suits you best.

Just Say No

Fire signs are prone to saying yes to everything, almost to a fault. You tend to move from one activity to the next, accepting the latest invite and helping friends whenever they need. That's wonderful for everyone else, but it also means you burn both ends of your candle, until sometimes the only thing left is ashes. To help keep your fire from going out, practice saying no when you are feeling overextended. This may happen at work, with friends, with your family, or even with yourself. Prioritize your own needs over the needs of others. Know there is nothing wrong with taking time to stoke your own flame.

Keep Your Cool

Fire signs can be temperamental at times. It's not your fault. You are naturally feisty and passionate, both positive traits that make you loyal and hardworking. Sometimes, though, you can get a little too overheated. At that point it's important to take a step back before you lose your cool too much. One trick you can try is to count to five in your head, or out loud. An alternate option is to exhale first and then inhale, and repeat three times. Either way, you'll give yourself a moment to curtail the strong emotions that are driving you. Practice tamping down the fire within you without letting it go out.

Enjoy the Sunset

The sun is very symbolic for fire signs. Its energy sustains and comforts you, so it's no surprise that watching the sun set after a long day can help you relax and find peace. Find a local spot with a great view if you can, and settle in for a show. Find solace in watching the different colors that emanate across the sky as the sun dips below the horizon: from bright orange, to light pink, soft periwinkle to, finally, a deep blue. Let the phases of its descent remind you that with every ending comes a beginning. The sun goes down, and the sun comes up.

Go for a Ride

Satisfy your fiery sense of adventure with a spontaneous mini–road trip. Take the back roads, avoid the highways, and make this a leisurely trip to clear your mind, ease your spirit, and reignite your wanderlust. You don't necessarily need to have a final destination in mind; just embrace the journey and the open road. As you're driving, you can sing along to your favorite playlist or put on a podcast or audiobook. Take the time alone in your car to enjoy yourself and your surroundings. It does not need to be a lengthy drive in order to experience its benefits—you just need to relax and enjoy the ride.

Take a Break from Social Media

Fire signs love to live in the moment, but don't ruin that moment by feeling the need to update your social media accounts. By taking a step back from your online presence, you allow yourself to be present and fully experience the world around you. Rather than fearing missing out on the things you see people post about, go out into the world and enjoy them yourself.

Social media can be a great way to stay in touch with friends and family; however, don't let it be the only way you communicate and tend to your relationships. A social media detox allows you to rekindle these connections and share your stories in person.

Strike a Work-Life Balance

As a fire sign, you have a passion to succeed in every aspect of your life. While this burning desire to achieve greatness powers your professional performance, it can also cause your work life to take over your whole life. It's important for your overall well-being that you keep your life inside the office balanced with your life outside the office. If you set boundaries between your professional and personal lives, you will be more productive at work and more fulfilled outside of it. You don't want to neglect your work responsibilities, but it's important to disconnect and recharge. By striking this work-life balance, you'll continue to succeed without burning out.

Find Meaning in Your Breath

Oxygen feeds fire, so when you feel your spark starting to dim, grab 10 minutes to take some deep, meaningful breaths. Whether you're at work or at home, it's the perfect way to take some time for yourself and recharge. Open a window, step out your front door, or even just turn on a desk fan. As long as you can feel the air moving, you're in good shape. As you're enjoying the air, allow yourself to live in that moment. Take a breath in through your nose, hold for 5 seconds, and breathe out through your mouth. Feel the air fill your lungs and circulate through your body. This simple mindful breathing exercise feeds your internal flame, calms your mind, and reenergizes your spirit.

Forgive Yourself

As a fire sign, you find it easy to go from passionate to incensed. Usually, these feelings are reserved for people who aren't able to keep up with your fiery spirit. However, what happens when you are the one you're upset with? If you've done something that's created your own mental hang-up, you need to extinguish those feelings sooner rather than later. You don't want to be your own worst enemy. While it's important to keep yourself accountable, you also need to be able to forgive yourself for any missteps or mistakes you've made. Release those feelings that have been burning you up inside and channel your energy into positive thoughts and actions.

Freewrite

Fire signs are known for following their gut instincts, but with all the background noise buzzing around you, it can be hard to home in on what your gut is saying. Try a stream of consciousness writing exercise to amplify your inner monologue. First, clear your mind. Next, think about something you feel you need guidance on: anything from a career question, to relationships, to personal development. Then just start writing. Don't think about what you are writing; just allow the words to flow. Write for as long as you want. In the end you may find the answer you were looking for all along buried within your words.

Don't Skimp on the SPF

Just because fire signs have a unique connection to the sun doesn't mean they still can't get burned by its power. Given the amount of time you spend outside keeping active, make sure to wear sunscreen and/or protect your skin with UV blocking clothing. Hats are particularly important, as is reapplying sunscreen every hour or so when you are in the sun. If you've already spent too much time outside and gotten burned, a bottle of aloe gel can soothe the sting and help your skin heal more quickly.

Inspire Others

You are lucky to have such a powerful flame burning inside you. Fire signs may forget that not everyone possesses their same ambition and fervor. Use your natural fire for good and inspire someone else in your life.

Try sending a friend or a loved one a card of encouragement. The small gesture can help light a fire under them and give them the strength to take a risk. If sending a card isn't your cup of tea, a text, email, or phone call can offer the same sentiment. The goal is to reach out and share your own fire with someone else who needs it.

Let It Go

Holding on to negative emotions can do long-term damage to your well-being. Because of how passionate you can be as a fire sign, you may find you let resentment or other destructive feelings boil inside you. Let those feelings go. Don't allow them to fester and build inside of you until they get to an unmanageable point. Release any grudges you have against a person who has wronged you, and forgive them for their wrongdoing. Once you let these emotions loose into the universe, you'll begin to heal and open up to more positivity and light.

Take a Risk

You already know that, as a fire sign, you have great instincts, but you may struggle with acting on them. Trust your gut and take a risk. Ask someone out on a date, apply for a new job, or make a large purchase that you've been eyeing for a while. Do something risky for yourself. It's easy to tell yourself "I'll do it later" or "It's not the right time." There's no time like the present. It might seem scary when you are in the moment, but big risks often mean big rewards. Tap into that passion churning inside you and take a leap of faith.

Play a Board Game

Fire signs are competitive when it comes to just about anything. Even the most mundane of tasks can become a game for you, one that you absolutely must win. To feed your competitive spirit in a healthy manner, try playing a board game. You're already used to being active outside, taking on one athletic challenge and then the next. Now train your mind. There are so many options to help you start flexing your brain muscles, from classic games like Monopoly and Scrabble to team games like charades, and even strategy and role-playing games.

Seek Your Fire Totem

Your fire is unique to you. To remind yourself of this, seek out a personal totem that symbolizes your fire and flame that you can keep with you at all times. A totem is a sacred object that serves as an emblem for a group of people. In your case, this totem will symbolize your connection to the fire burning within. It could be a piece of jewelry such as a bracelet, necklace, cuff, or amulet, or even a small desk trinket that you can keep by your side at work. There's no right or wrong when it comes to choosing your totem. Focus on something that calls to you and makes you feel brave and powerful when it is in your presence.

Make a Game of It

Fire signs can get bored easily. They are drawn to adventure and spontaneity, so the last thing they want is to get stuck in a pattern of tedium. Unfortunately, everyone has responsibilities they would rather not do, but how you react to those responsibilities is your choice. Tap into your fun-loving nature and make things more playful. Whether it's at work or around the house, turn your chores and responsibilities into a game. Even something as mundane as vacuuming the living room becomes a game when you set a timer for yourself. It makes things fun, feeds your competitive nature, and gets finished what needs to be done. In the end, changing how you think about a task can change how you complete it.

Smile at a Stranger

Smiling can change how you see the world, and how the world sees you. In fact, some studies suggest that the physical act of smiling can trick your brain into being happy even when you are in a bad mood. As a fire sign, you have so much love and happiness inside you—let it shine through and catch on like wildfire. Make a deal with yourself to smile at one stranger a day. Because your happy energy is contagious as a fire sign, this small act of kindness could do wonders for boosting someone's mood.

Treat Yourself

You spend a lot of time entertaining those around you. The energy you have as a fire sign is infectious, so it's no wonder that people are drawn to you. You also love making people smile and laugh—it comes naturally and boosts your mood. But, despite your penchant for entertaining, it's important to give yourself a break every once in a while. Alone time can be just as beneficial as time spent with large groups. Take yourself out to dinner once a month as a treat. To keep things lively, sit at the bar and people-watch. Keep yourself open to new conversation with other bar patrons. Allowing someone else—your server—to wait on you for once will help rejuvenate your spirit.

Try a Fire Craft

Fuel your creative spark by taking up a craft that is powered by fire. While regular crafting activities such as painting, drawing, and sculpting are all wonderful ways to unwind and explore your artistic side, as a fire sign you crave something with a little more heat. Try pottery making, glassblowing, or woodburning classes to satisfy your appetite. Your innate connection to fire will only deepen your creative reach and encourage your imagination. Find inspiration in how the heat transforms different materials—how it hardens clay, melts glass, and singes wood. Honor the power of fire through the creative process.

Binge a New Show

There's nothing quite like snuggling up on the couch in front of your TV (or laptop) after a long day. As a fire sign, you've probably been jumping from one activity to the next, trying to keep active and keep yourself moving. But there's nothing wrong with slowing down for a bit. Binge-watching a new show can be the perfect break you need from your hectic schedule. Make a night of it, and burn through every episode you can find. Make a bowl of popcorn, open a bottle of wine, and kick off your shoes. Let yourself become obsessed with knowing what happens next.

Become More Patient

Fire signs have so many wonderful personality traits. Your level of loyalty, ambition, and passion is something to be envied. But you also have some unfavorable traits that you can work on. For example, your

fieriness can often be interpreted by others as impatience. As a fire sign, your emotions tend to escalate very quickly, and your intensity can sometimes get the best of you.

Patience is a skill that often takes practice. Make it a personal goal to become more patient with others, situations, and yourself. When you feel that you are losing your patience, take a few deep breaths to de-escalate your emotions before they go too far. You have the power to control how you react to what you are feeling inside.

Start an Idea Book

Fire signs are known for their creativity and great ideas. Don't risk letting those good ideas slip away by not taking the time to write them down. Consider buying an idea journal where you can keep track of all the cool things that you come up with on a daily basis. Similar to a dream journal, an idea journal is the perfect place to house your million-dollar thoughts. These journals are specifically created to help you tease out and capture your next great idea, and many even have prompts to inspire and challenge you. Never forget another genius idea again!

Fight for Your Rights

Use your passion to change the world. Fire signs have a lot of strong opinions and personal beliefs. Identify those causes that mean the most to you and put all of your energy into fighting for them. Whether it's environmental issues, animal welfare, women's and LGBTQ+ rights, veterans' affairs, or anything else that lights your fire, know that you can make a difference just by showing up and being present. Start by joining a social media group that gives updates about organized protests near you. Volunteer on weekends at local shelters. Make signs for rallies. Whatever it takes. Fight for what you believe, and inspire and motivate others to do the same.

Make Your Own Rose Mist

Self-care may not come easy to a fire sign. You are used to caring for others, and can sometimes forget to tend your own fire. Before you know it, your flame is burning out of control. A refreshing mist is a quick and easy way to balance the fire inside you.

Rose water is especially therapeutic for irritated skin. Rose water is a hydrating blend made by steeping rose petals in water. Spritz it over clean skin and breathe in the calming scent of roses. Take a moment to pause and enjoy the sensations around you.

While you can find rose water in many grocery and health stores, you can also make your own. First, boil a large pot of distilled water, and remove the petals from a few (washed) organic roses. Add the petals to the water, and allow to simmer on low heat for 20–30 minutes, or until the petals have lost the majority of their color. Cool, strain the petals, and add the water to a clean spray bottle. Store in the refrigerator.

Have a Solo Dance Party

Break out your dancing shoes and turn on your favorite jam. It's time for a solo dance party! Dancing is a wonderful way for fire signs to expel built-up energy that they haven't been able to let go of yet. It gets your heart pumping and your endorphins flowing. Plus, it's just plain fun. Let loose and really go for it. There's no one there to judge your dance moves or the song you pick to boogie down to. Let the music take control and just go with it. Feel like doing the electric slide? Do it. Want to practice your running man? There's no time like the present!

Take Your Vitamins

Your body is a temple, and it needs the proper nourishment to stay strong and healthy. Fire signs are constantly pushing their physical limits by taking on new athletic challenges. To keep your body from getting run-down, it's important to stick to a vitamin regimen every day. Talk to your doctor about which vitamins are best for you. There are even companies that offer personalized vitamin packs based on your individual needs. Even just a simple multivitamin made for your age group or gender can give your body the boost it needs.

Stargaze

The universe is expansive. Just look up at the sky on a pitch-black night. There are tiny suns and balls of flaming gas millions of miles away. Some estimates suggest there are approximately one hundred billion stars in just the Milky Way alone. Imagine how many more there are in the billions of other galaxies in the universe.

Your presence in this universe is important. Never lose the passion and heat you have burning inside you as a fire sign. It can be easy to feel small sometimes. When you are feeling lost, look up at the stars. They can help you find your way. And if you are lucky, you may even discover the constellations of one of the fire signs—Aries, Leo, or Sagittarius—to guide you.

CHAPTER 4

Essential Elements: Earth

The earth element is the most familiar to all of us, for the earth is our home. We are born on this planet and are the custodians of her beauty, natural resources, health, and well-being. There is an intimate connection between human beings and the balance of the earth's conditions. The earth signs (Taurus, Virgo, and Capricorn) feel this connection more than other signs do, and their approach to self-care reflects their relationship with this natural element. They are practical and realistic, and they need self-care techniques that match their disposition. More so, earth signs are rooted in the material, physical world. They are—at their best—pragmatic, sensual, patient, and grounded. At their worst, they can be greedy, lascivious, and materialistic.

Most humans face the polarity of balancing the need and competition of making a living, with the dreams and desires of their heart. Earth signs accept this as reality instead of fighting against it. Becoming successful in the material world is their natural inclination. Any self-care they do must reflect that ultimate goal as well. Let's take a look at the mythological importance of the earth and its counterparts, the basic characteristics of the three earth signs, and the things they all have in common when it comes to self-care.

The Mythology of Earth

There are many creation myths from all over the world. Most of these myths feature a Mother Earth figure. In Greek mythology, which forms the basis for much of astrology, Gaia was the Earth Mother. She represented the circle of life. Gaia came out of chaos and gave birth to Ouranos, the sky god, who also happened to be her husband. (The Greeks liked to keep things in the family.) The relationship between Gaia and Ouranos was so passionate that their children could not emerge from Gaia's womb. One of these unborn children was Cronos, who in Roman astrology was called Saturn. Cronos decided to overthrow Ouranos and in the womb emasculated his father. And the sky separated from the earth. Cronos, the lord of time, ruled the universe for

a period but later got his comeuppance as Zeus/Jupiter displaced him and became the chief god and ruler of all. These myths regarding the separation of earth and sky (or heaven and earth) abound in ancient world cultures.

Earth signs strive for measured success, and often seek worldly possessions to solidify their self-worth. This need for stability is indicative of their element. Earth, after all, is the foundation for life. It is tangible, solid, and defined. Many earth signs are so grounded in reality they can lose track of their emotional well-being. Self-care rituals that cater to both mind and soul are key for earth signs. Simplicity and practicality are often paramount.

The Element of Earth

Earth signs are known for their measured approach to life. They are typically patient, reliable, and disciplined, traits that often lead to prosperity. Because of this, earth signs are often viewed as well balanced and levelheaded, hence the saying *down-to-earth*. Earth signs are known as the sensible, pragmatic signs, choosing to focus on practical solutions over emotions. They are not light and buoyant like air signs, passionate and fiery like fire signs, nor empathetic and fluid like water signs. Instead, they are committed, strong, and trustworthy. For example, Taurus is loyal and always ready to help friends and family in need. Virgo is hardworking and will never back down from a challenge. And Capricorn is responsible and will help others stick to their responsibilities as well.

Astrological Symbols

The astrological symbols (also called the zodiacal symbols) of the earth signs also give hints as to how earth signs move through the world. Each symbol ties back to the nature associated with earth signs:

- Taurus is the Bull
- Virgo is the Maiden gathering the harvest
- Capricorn is the Goat

All these signs show steadfast and intimate harmony with the cycles of the seasons and a personal connection with the earth: the meadows, green fields, and rocks. Taurus comes from ancient myths about the cults that worshipped the bull as a fertility symbol. She represents coiled power not yet unleashed. Virgo is the only earth sign that has a human symbol. She is a mutable sign and like a junior Mother Earth. Capricorn is of the earth but climbs the mountains of ambition and spiritual ascent. Each earth sign's personality and subsequent approach to self-care connect to the qualities of these representative symbols.

Signs and Seasonal Modes

Each of the elements in astrology also has a sign that corresponds to a different part of each season.

- **Cardinal:** Capricorn is the leader of the earth signs because she marks the beginning of winter and the time of the winter solstice.
- **Fixed:** Taurus, the first earth sign, comes when spring is in full bloom. Taurus is called a fixed earth sign because she comes when the season is well established. The fixed signs are definite, principled, and powerfully stubborn.
- **Mutable:** Virgo, the second earth sign, moves us from summer to autumn. She is a mutable sign. In terms of character the mutable signs are changeable and flexible.

If you know your element and whether you are a cardinal, fixed, or mutable sign, you know a lot about yourself and your loved ones. This is invaluable for self-care and is reflected in the customized earth sign self-care rituals found later in this chapter.

Earth Signs and Self-Care

The earth signs' first motivation in life is to feel comfortable in their physical surroundings. For physical self-care their most important motivation is routine and diligence. Earth signs don't require a lot of variety. Their motto is "If something works, keep it." The downside to this attitude is that earth signs can get stuck in a rut, but the benefits of continuous physical exercise, self-care, and good diet at all ages are the cornerstones of comfort for earth signs.

Earth signs may casually touch other people more frequently than other elements do. They pat, reach out, hug, and extend themselves physically to others. They also have an intimate and close sense of personal space and will be up-front and personal in encountering new people or old friends. They want and need to sense the whole person.

Earth signs take self-care actions in a very practical way. For example, if an earth sign wants to exercise more, they may think the following: "If I can exercise more, I will lose weight and be healthier, so I will have more years to build my business, enjoy my family, and do what I want."

Spiritually, earth signs feel little division between body and soul. If they feel comfortable and well physically, then their soul qualities can evolve and blossom. Some people may feel that the high-minded notions of spiritual retreat and meditation define a spiritual person, and they therefore look down on an earth sign's practical thoughts, such as "How much will it cost to go on this retreat, and how much time will it take?" Earth signs don't consider this

to be materialism at the expense of spirituality. Instead, to them, it is a clear recognition of the practical and sensible way the world works. Ashrams, well-being programs, herbs, and health practices cost money, and it is a reasonable question to ask if the practice is worth it.

The most important "rule" for earth signs is that self-care should feed the senses. Whatever the plan is, it should include every sense. The activity must look appealing, smell good, taste good, sound good, and feel good. The more all the senses are involved, the happier the earth signs will be and the more likely they will be to follow the program. If the price is reasonable, so much the better. But too much sensual input can cause earth signs to overindulge and become lethargic. This is a potential pitfall for all the earth signs.

The overall purpose and meaning of the earth signs is to offer practical solutions to maintain personal self-care and the health of the planet. The earth signs have a lot to teach the people around them. Modern life is increasingly jagged. The earth signs demonstrate the value of solid measured progress. Walk don't run, and take things as they come. This attitude can preserve each of us as well as planet earth.

So now that you know what earth signs need to practice self-care, let's take a look at the activities that will help those born under this element flourish.

Break Free from Your Comfort Zone—Today!

As an earth sign, you tend to be organized, ritualistic, and highly structured. However, because you like structure and rituals so much, you can easily fall into the routine of repeating patterns, and even if that pattern is not particularly healthy, you'll stay with it. Once you're in a comfortable place, it's hard for you to change your habits. But being afraid to change something can hold you back from making life-changing decisions or improving yourself. Getting out of your regular rituals will boost your confidence and open up new doors in your life. Make a choice to break out of your routine and try something new. Do it today! Change one thing, no matter how big or small, and note the difference.

Get Stepping

In terms of fitness, earth signs like measurable results. They like to be able to calculate situations and use concrete facts to do so. This is why a pedometer, smart watch, or fitness tracker would be perfect for you. You like to be able to know the exact number of steps you have taken so you can use that information to plan, to calculate further exercise or meals, or just to motivate yourself. Those folks who go willy-nilly into exercise are not for you; hard facts and organization will get the job done for an earth sign.

Do Some Heavy Lifting

Earth signs are incredibly strong people, mentally and physically. With that in mind, make sure you emphasize weight and strength training in your workouts. Develop your lifting muscles by exercising with weights and concentrating on weight-bearing exercises throughout your life. There are so many variations of weight and strength training that you can easily find a routine that suits your age, strength, general health, and energy level. Ask your weight trainer for guidance. Strength training will help you fight the loss of muscle, bone mass, and strength that occurs naturally with aging. It is also great for your joints, an area of concern for a lot of earth signs.

Heal Your Spirit with the Soil

You *are* an earth sign, after all. What could be more in tune with your nature than to work with the earth? As an earth sign, you tend to hold on to stress and have trouble releasing it, but working with the soil—in whichever way feels right—will bring you into a state of calmness. When you are connected to an element, just being near it and working with it can help realign your energy and bring peace.

So go out and till your soil, buy seeds or plants, and then plant them in precise and organized rows. As you watch your plants grow and tend to them, you will discover your stress will wash away. Even if you don't have space to plant a garden where you live, just getting your hands in the soil will help heal your spirit.

Give Yourself Some Time

Earth signs are grounded, logical, and reliable, so it goes without saying that you hate to be late. In fact, punctuality is an admired quality of the earth signs. If a situation occurs that causes you to be late, it can fill you with stress and cause anxiety. So, with that in mind, make a point of giving yourself some extra time to get where you need to be. This will give a cushion in case some unexpected events pop up and delay you. You know being late will stress you out, so do your mind and spirit a favor and try to eliminate anything that might interfere with your timeliness.

Keep Things Slow and Steady

Earth signs know that nothing great ever comes easily or quickly. In fact, their combined patience and discipline is one of their most admirable traits and allows them to stick things out for the long run. Earth signs like to meticulously plan and hate to rush. Actually, rushing through a task will cause you stress and may lead to mistakes (something you don't tolerate well). Whether working or playing, you should take a slow and steady approach, and your final results will be better quality and

more long-lasting than those of the hurried competition. Keep a steady pace when at home and at work and you'll produce your best results.

Learn at Your Own Pace

As an earth sign, you love to learn new things and are not dissuaded when the subject seems difficult or arduous. Persistence is definitely an earth sign characteristic! But while you love to discover new skills, you don't like being monitored while you do so. You learn better while working solo and do not like to have someone looking over your shoulder. Often methodical and meticulous, you have no patience for those who want to just jump in and go with it. So don't put yourself through that! If you are part of a group for work or school, try suggesting that everyone work on ideas separately and then reconvene to discuss them. That way you can have your solo learning time while still being a team player!

Eat What You Love

Earth signs love their foods, and they especially like to be relaxed and savor their food when they eat it. However, many earth signs have sensitive palates and have to be choosy about what they eat. You need to listen to your body about what it needs and what it can tolerate, and when you find a food you like, enjoy it! Also, being conscious about what foods you are putting in your body is important for earth signs. When you can, try to choose foods grown without pesticides, added hormones, or artificial fertilizers, as many of these things can irritate your body. Go with natural and organic versions of the foods you love.

Take It Slow with Your Workouts

Exercise is proven to be one of the best forms of self-care you can do for your body and mind. But what if you are new to working out or just feel like it isn't your thing? Fortunately for you, as an earth sign, the slow and steady approach also relates to how you should be working out. Earth signs are disciplined, dependable, and committed. So, when they exercise, they should choose workouts that require patience, precision, and a set routine.

Workouts that work your muscles at a slower pace will build your endurance and muscle strength without making you feel like your regimen is hectic and out of your control. Training for races that require preciseness and problem-solving like a Tough Mudder, which is more about endurance than speed, is also a hit with earth signs.

Indulge In the Warmth of Cinnamon

Nothing conjures up feelings of warmth like the smell of cinnamon. It brings back memories of warm, comforting foods on cool, crisp fall days. But cinnamon is not just for autumn time; in fact, it is perfect for earth signs to use all year round. When you're cooking, choose warm spices like cinnamon over sharp and peppery spices, as these tend not to agree with an earth sign's delicate palate. As an added bonus, cinnamon is good for your heart health, helps regulate your blood sugar, boosts your brain function, and offers your body protection from diabetes.

Cinnamon is a marvelous addition to both sweet and savory meals and will add the hint of spice you crave without the burning aftereffects of other spices. Add cinnamon to your favorite foods including oatmeal, pancakes, yogurt, peanut or almond butter, chilis and soups, and even your coffee!

Treat Yourself to Chocolate

Earth signs love chocolate, and it's a wonderful way to treat yourself. Some earth signs may have trouble with dairy though, so try a good-quality rich dark chocolate to indulge in. Not only does dark chocolate taste heavenly, but it benefits your health too. Dark chocolate helps lower blood pressure, is a powerful source of antioxidants, and reduces your heart disease risk. Eat your dark chocolate straight—or melt some in a double boiler, pour into a silicone mold ice cube tray, sprinkle on some healthy nuts and dried fruits, and allow to set for a mouthwatering treat you can feel good about.

Stick with the Classics

Treat yourself to a little shopping trip, but rather than buying the latest fad, shop for your sign. Style magazines and experts may tell you what's all the rage in fashion, but as an earth sign, you won't necessarily feel comfortable or strong—both things earth signs need in their lives—with what is trendy. Earth signs are all about the simple yet elegant look when it comes to fashion, as well as décor. You like things that are classic, well made, neat, and polished— think Audrey Hepburn (who is also an earth sign!) and George Clooney.

In terms of clothing, you feel more comfortable in the elegant and sophisticated and stay clear of the flashy, too tight, or too revealing. You value comfort, but that doesn't mean you don't look suave or glamorous; you like to make a statement without seeming like you are making a statement. So stick with the classics and you'll always exude an understated elegance.

Protect Your Throat

Earth signs are connected to several parts of the body, including the throat. Communication is key to earth signs, and when something interferes with that communication, whether it be a blocked throat chakra or even a sore throat, earth signs' confidence and strength can suffer. So protect your throat! In the colder months, wear a scarf or muffler around your throat. Try meditating with turquoise to open up your throat chakra. If you do get a sore throat, treat it quickly and naturally with a saltwater gargle, honey, lemon water, or ginger tea.

Reach for Your Goals

Once earth signs know what they want, they will stay the course until they get it. Earth signs are strong and disciplined people, so use that tenacity to achieve the things you want most in life. Use your detail-oriented, driven brain and create a goal board. List the things you have been wanting to accomplish—especially those long-term goals you have had for years— and post them up where you can see them every day. This way you can be sure to keep your goals fresh in your mind and on the top of your to-do list. Also make sure the goals you write on your board are clear and actionable. Whatever your goal is, this visual reminder is key to helping you stay focused and on track.

Create a Room of Comfort— Earth-Sign Style

Everyone needs a space, even if it is just one room in your house or apartment, where you can just get away and relax in comfort. Comfortable surroundings are important for earth signs in particular; not only do they crave them, but they feel the most at peace there.

So make sure at least one room in your home is filled with plush, cushy furniture. Big pieces of furniture are important for comfort, too, because they give you a sense of security and a feeling that you are staying put. Overstuffed pillows and soft blankets would make nice accents here as well. Create a room that makes you feel safe and snug, a place you can go to find relaxation and peace and forget the stresses of your life, and you will be a truly happy earth sign.

Wrap Yourself in Warmth

There is something so special and nurturing about being wrapped in something cuddly. Earth signs especially like to feel warm, protected, and comfortable. A good way to accomplish this feeling in your home is to find a thick, warm comforter for your bed. Bonus points if you can make one yourself, maybe even stitching in some pieces of a childhood blankie. Not a crafty person? There is no shortage of ultra-plush comforters available to buy online. Try to get one in a deep, rich earth tone to complement your earth sign! Want to kick the comfort up a notch? Try warming your sheets in the dryer right before you get into bed!

Make Your Home Your Haven

Earth signs like to feel protected in their home, almost as if it were a sheltered cave. A feeling of enclosure may seem stifling to other signs, but for earth signs there is a comfort in the closeness and warmth. Emphasize that feeling in your home by decorating with darker colors and with accents such as lamps with shades to give off a soft glow in your rooms. This warm and welcoming shelter will make you feel protected and safe whenever you enter it.

Color Your Home Like the Earth

Earth signs tend to feel most at ease in their homes when they are surrounded by calming earth tones. Greens, browns, and whites are great choices to decorate your home. Of course, given your simple tastes, you'll want to make sure these colors are muted versions, nothing too garish or bright. Loud colors will actually take away from your comfort level at home, something you don't want to do. Also, wood floors, dark finishes, and plain walls will all add to the elegance and polished feeling of your home, while fitting in perfectly with your classic and understated vibe.

Embrace Your Practicality

Sometimes earth signs get a bad reputation for their serious sides, but your practicality is really a positive thing. Earth signs are incredibly sensible and resourceful, and they have a talent for solving problems that others give up on. You come up with real-world solutions that actually work! You love to ponder and thoroughly understand a problem or concept, and you like to make charts, graphs, or diagrams to further explore the topic. You stick with a problem through the long haul and come up with a solution that works—so celebrate the positives of being the perfect problem-solver!

Take One Step at a Time

Some people like to jump headfirst into a problem and work it out while trapped in the midst of it. Well, that may be great for them, but the thought of it gives earth signs nervous feelings. Earth signs approach almost everything they do with a methodical, step-by-step approach. This method allows you to thoroughly understand exactly what you're getting yourself into, come up with a well-thought-out plan to solve it, and then actually resolve the issue. While it may take you a little more prep time than other people when faced with a problem, you often have a higher success rate too. Breaking down obstacles into clear steps makes earth signs the best problem-solvers around.

Make Your Home on the Ground Floor

Earth signs instinctually prefer to keep their feet planted firmly on the ground— so their homes should be, as well! Creating a safe, comfortable home is important to earth signs, since it gives them a place to focus on their creative impulses and build a space that's perfect for feeling stable and reenergized.

Ground-floor apartments have plenty of perks, such as access to outdoor yard spaces and easier move-in days. And better yet, you'll recharge best in a home where you can easily see (and touch!) the ground. Skip the high-rise apartment, and go for something closer to the first floor instead.

Become a Plant Parent

It should come as no surprise that earth signs find it reassuring to include touches of nature in their homes. Keep yourself centered and relaxed by surrounding yourself with plants. If you're not able to live in a place with easy access to the natural world, try bringing nature to you! City dwellers can plant window boxes or fill their apartments with different types of houseplants.

A window herb garden is a great place to start. Try common herbs like basil, chives, cilantro, oregano, or parsley, which can be great additions to any meal and have many other useful qualities. (Did you know basil is a natural mosquito repellent?) Go all-natural and see how many ways your new garden can benefit your daily life!

Save Your Seat

Earth signs are known for seeking stability in their lives—and their work environment is no different. No matter your organizational style or tasks at hand, a sturdy, well-designed office chair is a must-have for any busy earth sign. It isn't easy to get through the workday if you're uncomfortable and distracted. You'll be able to stay focused and work more productively if you're settled at your desk in a chair that's comfortable for you.

Not only will you be better able to concentrate at work, but you'll be taking care of your body too. No more stiff necks or backaches for you!

Send Flowers...to Yourself!

No matter the season, earth signs benefit from having plants around. Just like you need plants in your home, you also need some for your office. Especially during dreary rainy days or cold months, you'll need something to reframe your mind-set and spark a positive attitude throughout the day.

Try a monthly flower or plant subscription service to get your plant pick-me-up. Whatever your preference, treat yourself to the perfect desk accessory, with options ranging from handcrafted bouquets to potted plants...or even a succulent or two! No secret admirer is needed—these services will deliver plants of your choice to your desk all year round.

Choose Only the Softest Fabrics

Earth signs have a highly developed sense of touch, so choose soft materials for your clothes and sheets. Don't spend your day feeling distracted by an itchy wool sweater or spend all night tossing and turning on scratchy sheets. Restore your healthy skin (and cheerful attitude!) by choosing materials like cashmere, silk, organic cotton, and suede.

You'll prefer any materials or fabrics that touch your skin to be soft and comforting, so go ahead and splurge on high thread count sheets, fluffy towels, and warm, downy blankets.

Indulge In Comfort Food

Craving some mac and cheese? A homemade chocolate chip cookie? Maybe even a simple, classic PB&J (peanut butter and jelly)? Reliable earth signs sometimes need to reclaim their roots and find comfort in the well known and well loved.

After a long day, indulge in your love of comfort food, whether that's a cheesy slice of pepperoni pizza or a gooey brownie still warm from the oven. Take an uplifting trip down memory lane with simple foods that remind you of your childhood. Enjoyed in moderation, these treats will keep your stomach full and your heart happy.

Treat Your Sweet Tooth

Earth signs are known for their appreciation for the finer things and may enjoy opportunities to indulge. Some earth signs sometimes instinctually gravitate toward sweet flavors. While it's certainly important to eat a balanced diet and enjoy everything in moderation, a sweet treat or two can be just the pick-me-up you need to improve a grumpy mood or curb an unhealthier craving.

Although you may prefer to stick with your reliable, tried-and-true favorites, prevent yourself from becoming "stuck" by looking for your sweet fix in unexpected places. Expand your cultural palate by trying food from different cuisines.

Find Balance for Your Finances

Self-care isn't always about having fun—sometimes it's simply about that sense of accomplishment you get from checking off a task on your to-do list. Perfect for practical earth signs, prioritize getting through those financial day-to-day activities like reviewing your budget or looking for ways to lower bills.

Earth signs can be cautious and like to have a sense of security, instead of taking unnecessary risks. A balanced earth sign is able to successfully manage their cautious tendencies and their indulgences. That careful decision-making can help you handle your money well; earth signs have a natural awareness that helps them judge their financial situation exactly. Just make sure you're not obsessing over the task!

Give Yourself a Time Limit

Earth signs are known for being hard workers; they're resourceful and know just how to tackle tasks to make them manageable. They're also notoriously persistent when they're working to achieve their goals. Being productive and getting things done feels great to driven earth signs.

Stay on top of your to-do list with this productivity hack! Simply set a time limit with a timer to get your task done. Since you know you only have a limited time frame, you'll stay focused, quicken your pace, and accomplish a lot more than you expected. You'll feel satisfied and proud of all you'll be able to complete.

Reward Your Patience

In today's fast-paced world, it's important to stay patient, even when lines are slow, orders are misplaced, and Mercury in retrograde causes all kinds of confusion with communication. Luckily, earth signs are known for their ability to stay calm and forgiving. That's a great quality to maintain, so make sure you reward yourself on those days when your patience has been truly tested.

Whether it's enjoying a glass of fine wine, listening to some new music, or splurging on something you've had your eye on for a while, make sure to protect yourself from negativity and do something relaxing and restorative for you and you alone.

Try a Dance Workout

You know it's important to take care of your body by exercising. But did you know that earth signs have a good sense of rhythm and may find a new workout routine through dancing? Dancing is also a great way to add fun into an existing exercise schedule or try something new so your usual routine doesn't get boring.

Try a peaceful ballet class for discipline, or experiment with jazz and hip-hop for a fun, high-energy workout. Or look for other dance-inspired classes like barre, which combine dance elements and workout styles for unique and challenging programs.

Put on Your Headphones

Earth signs love music. When you're feeling stressed in work, try using music to relax yourself. If you find yourself in a difficult situation, try to take a break to re-center and calm down. Put on your headphones, and let the sound of the music soothe you and distract you from your worries. Experiment with different genres to see what works best for you. No one needs to know what you are listening to! Even a 10-minute private music break will improve your outlook and reenergize your spirit!

Hum Your Way Through Chores

Sometimes, chores get to be boring and stressful for even the most practical and grounded of earth signs. And whether it's breaking out the vacuum cleaner or dusting every horizontal surface in your home,

everyone has that one task that seems so unpleasant and difficult to finish.

For earth signs, this is the perfect time to turn to your love of music to keep yourself mentally alert and refocus yourself on the task at hand. Humming while completing your everyday tasks will keep you relaxed and help you tackle even your least favorite chores with ease. If there is someone else around, challenge them to name that tune!

Train for a Marathon

Patient earth signs are in it for the long haul; their workout style is more marathon than sprint. These slow and steady athletes are disciplined and committed to achieving their goals.

So what better goal for an earth sign than to train to run a marathon—or participate in a triathlon, which will really test your endurance with a series of swimming, biking, and running challenges. These activities will keep you feeling refreshed and rejuvenated, while helping you develop strength and stamina. Seek out a trainer or training team to help you reach this long-term goal.

Go for the Goal!

If you're looking for a team sport, keep in mind the earth signs' tendencies to look for ways to use their strength and stamina. Try sports like soccer or volleyball that combine those skills. With team sports like these, you'll be able to take care of your body and develop strong, supportive friendships, all while having the added benefit of keeping your feet in your comfort zone...firmly on the ground.

Your endurance will keep you going from the beginning of the game to the very last second. And your goal-oriented nature is sure to keep you on the winning side as you help your team toward victory!

Try a Stress-Free Workout

If the thought of running a marathon has you sweating already, don't worry! There are other workouts perfect for earth signs, like learning to work on a balance beam or taking some beginners' gymnastics skills classes. With your disciplined attitude, you'll be able to focus on improving your strength and stability while mastering these challenging skills.

This type of workout can be a great way to take care of your body and keep it healthy and toned. But it can also be a much-needed opportunity to relax and compose yourself on an otherwise busy day. The focus you'll need to master carefully controlled movements will help take your mind off the stress of your day and give you a chance to recharge.

Change Up Your Workout Routine

Earth signs enjoy having an established routine they can count on, so try developing a well-rounded workout routine that works for you. Consider adding stretching—or visiting the weight section or the machines that you don't normally go to—to change up your routine. Adding new steps to your practice will refresh what you normally do at the gym to help keep you motivated, strong, and healthy. If you find yourself feeling stiff from a long day at the office, even after your normal routines the night prior, it may be a sign that you need to spruce up your routine. Your new, revitalizing additions to your workouts will make your body feel great.

Use Yoga to Recharge

Working out is all about finding the right balance. Try mixing your weights and cardio with yoga stretches to keep muscles limber. Think yoga isn't right for you? Don't worry—there are many different styles and class types, so you'll be able to find the perfect, restorative approach that's right for you and your body's needs.

By adding yoga into your routine, you may find yourself becoming stronger and more flexible. But your brain will also benefit by getting a break from thinking, worrying, and stressing. Since it's important to focus your awareness on your body and concentrate on performing each pose as best you can, you'll find your worries can take a back seat while you recharge.

Look Before You Leap

Earth signs are logical thinkers, who often like to fully evaluate their options before deciding. They're seeking safety and security, so they aren't interested in taking big risks. Taking that essential time to think things through can be a major benefit for their mental health. You certainly don't want to be rushed into making a decision! If you find yourself faced with a problem or challenging situation, think it over privately before confiding in a friend. Give yourself permission to reclaim the time and space you need for yourself. You'll feel more confident sharing your decisions and more comfortable moving forward.

Meditate in Nature

It's important to take a few moments to yourself to relax, refresh, and gather your thoughts. To get some peace of mind, try meditating in nature. Particularly for thoughtful earth signs, this time-out ritual can be helpful to clear your mind.

One option is to find a comfortable seated position, close your eyes, and focus on your breathing and the present moment before allowing yourself to pay attention to the natural world around you. Or try meditating while walking and see how nature interacts with each of your senses. What sounds can you hear? What are you able to touch? How does your body feel? Earth signs may find it particularly helpful to meditate on the flowers and trees around them.

Reduce Stress with Grounding

It's no surprise that earth signs should be in close contact with the earth itself. One way to literally connect with the earth is to try "grounding," or standing or walking barefoot outside on the grass, soil, or sand. Not only does being barefoot outside just feel good, but it may reduce stress and inflammation while improving your circulation and mood. Try to spend 30 minutes a day grounding—either all at once or broken up into smaller chunks of time. Afterward, you'll find yourself relaxed, restored, and recharged.

Go Forest Bathing

Just like regular bathing involves immersing yourself in water, forest bathing is the process of immersing yourself in trees and nature. The Environmental Protection Agency recently found that the average American spends 93 percent of their time indoors, but earth signs especially benefit from more regular contact with Mother Earth.

Forest bathing is an easy, relaxing way to enjoy the outdoors. Silence your devices so you savor your senses—see the various shades of green, smell the different flowers, feel the crisp air, and listen to the crunch of branches under your feet.

Declutter Your Home and Your Mind

Earth signs are known to hang onto too many belongings. While you may enjoy the memories that these items bring, keeping too many of them will eventually clutter your physical and mental space.

Take a day to go through your possessions and decide what's most meaningful to you. If an item has outlasted its usefulness to you, donate it to someone who would enjoy it more. When you've finished, take notice of the physical space you've created and meditate in or near it for a few minutes if possible. You'll likely find that you've also freed up mental space for new ideas.

Detox with a Mud Mask

After a long day, nothing feels better than a relaxing facial mask. And what better type for an earth sign than a mud mask? Clear away the pollutants and bacteria your face is exposed to on a daily basis using an element of the earth itself.

If time and your budget allow, you can visit a spa for a mud mask—but if that's not possible, pick one up at a drugstore or natural foods store and apply it yourself at home, taking slow, deep breaths as you let the mixture sit on your face. You'll find this detox to be especially restorative and cleansing.

Paint a Rock

Earth signs like to be crafty, so let your creativity shine by painting a symbol of the earth—a rock! Head outdoors to find a few suitable rocks—usually, flat, smooth ones are the easiest canvas. You might want to start by painting a base layer of white paint so other colors show up better. Add details or hand lettering with fine-tip permanent markers.

Let the experience be quiet and meditative—listen to ambient music as you paint. When your design is complete, cover it with a clear coat of Mod Podge (following the directions) to seal it in. You can keep the rock for yourself as a reminder of your connection to the earth, or pass along its good energy and give it as a gift to a friend or loved one.

Set a New Goal for Yourself

Many people use the start of a new year to set goals. But there's no need to wait for January 1 to do that. As an earth sign, you'll benefit from setting a practical goal for yourself, and then tracking your progress, no matter what time of year it is. Whether you're trying to get rid of a bad habit or institute a healthy new one, the act of setting a goal and noting checkpoints along the way makes you much more likely to be successful.

When you think of a goal, write it down and post it in a place where you'll see it frequently. Be sure to reward yourself every time you meet one of your checkpoints to keep yourself motivated.

Treat Yourself to New Loungewear

Everyone owns some favorite sweats or comfy shirts. But many of us wear this loungewear until it's ripped, stretched out, and stained. Take stock of what you currently own and see if some of it can be recycled or donated. Then treat yourself to some new items, and enjoy them the next time you're unwinding at home after a long day in less-than-comfortable work clothes.

Earth signs love to be comfortable, so repeat this process once a year. You'll look forward to relaxing and recharging in your new pieces!

Try Aromatherapy

Earth signs are closely in touch with all of their senses. Aromatherapy is a simple and easy way for you to connect with and savor your sense of smell. You can enjoy a citrus bodywash to energize yourself during your morning shower, sip some ginger tea to recharge in a midafternoon slump, read in a room scented by a soothing vanilla candle, or spritz (diluted according to instructions) lavender essential oil on your pillow before bed to relax.

When you begin practicing aromatherapy regularly, you'll find yourself more in tune with your sense of smell all the time.

You'll notice the scent of your neighbor's flowers, the mixture of flavors wafting from your favorite restaurant, and the earthy smells after a spring rain.

Volunteer for an Environmental Cause

Donating your time and effort to a cause you're passionate about is a great way to show you care about the world around you—and yourself. After all, research shows that people who volunteer are less stressed, have more friends, and are more confident! As an earth sign, you can honor your connection to the planet by volunteering for a group that protects the environment, reduces pollution, encourages people to get outside, or safeguards animals.

There are many ways to help, including performing manual labor, organizing fundraising, and offering skills like bookkeeping or web design. You will feel fulfilled and proud—and your work will be making a difference.

Get Outside!

Lying on the couch after work might have become routine for you, but what if you switched your habit? Earth signs are prone to becoming lethargic, so try to get outside for a walk almost every evening after you eat.

Walking will aid digestion, help you stay fit, and encourage you to decompress and unwind in a healthy way. Vary your route periodically to keep the walk from getting boring. An evening stroll is also a great way to engage with your community—say hi to people you walk by, purchase lemonade from a kids' stand, or even join in a pickup basketball game.

Visit a Farmers' Market

Farmers' markets offer an astounding array of local produce and homemade foods. You might be surprised at what's being grown right around you. There's sure to be a market in your area—find out its schedule and pop in regularly. Let your senses savor the offerings—see the brightly colored displays, smell the fresh peaches and herbs, and maybe snag a sample bite that a stall is offering. Look for organic produce, which is good for the environment and your health.

Try to find recipes that use your farmers' market haul for a couple of dinners a week, and grab the whole fruits for easy snacks on the go.

Live It Up on Weekdays!

There's no need to wait for a weekend to go out for dinner or a night on the town! As an earth sign, you probably enjoy structure and routine, but you don't want to fall into ruts either. To avoid that, shake things up and enjoy a concert on a Monday evening, head out to dinner at a new restaurant on a Tuesday night, or go dancing on Wednesday after work. You'll release any stress you've been holding on to and take the pressure off your weekends to supply every bit of fun in your life.

Invest Your Money

Earth signs are conscientious—money matters tend to come easy for you. Still, you want to be sure that your money isn't just sitting in an account somewhere. Put it to work for you by making wise investments.

Do some research with trusted sources to be sure your investments are smart, and work with a broker or on your own to make the actual transactions. Check in periodically to see how your accounts are doing and adjust as needed. Over time, your investments will grow and you'll enjoy even more fortune.

Spring for an Expensive Bottle of Wine

Life is too short to drink inexpensive wine all the time. Every once in a while, treat yourself to an expensive, high-quality bottle of wine. As an earth sign, you can appreciate the finer things in life, and you have a great sense of taste. Ask an employee at your local liquor store for a recommendation based on your preferences, or reach for a longtime favorite of yours.

Take out your nice glassware, let the bottle breathe, and then swirl and sip slowly so you can really taste the subtle notes in the glass as you relax and unwind.

Try to Compromise

Earth signs have so many wonderful qualities, but one characteristic that might trouble you sometimes is your stubbornness. Instead of getting down on yourself, turn that trait around by consciously working to compromise whenever possible.

For example, if a friend wants to go out to one type of restaurant and you want another, talk for a few minutes to determine someplace you'd both like. If your partner prefers one couch but you want to buy another, work out a solution based on what's best for your space. These types of thoughtful, caring conversations go a long way toward ensuring harmony in your relationships.

Create Your Own Pottery

You've probably seen gorgeous pottery in stores, but have you ever tried to make it yourself? For a fun activity, work with some clay to make your own creation, be it a simple bowl, a mug for your morning coffee, or a plate to give as a gift. Earth signs are in touch with their senses, and this hands-on craft allows you to get your hands dirty and really savor your sense of touch.

Take a class at a local art center or craft store where you can make a piece from start to finish. Once you've made your

creation, you can have it fired by the professionals in its natural or painted colors.

Daydream to Calm Your Mind

In today's world it's easy to have your brain running nonstop. Work, family, and other responsibilities are on your mind—you probably jump from one practical thought to the next with no break. It's time to change that and give your head a break!

Allow yourself time to daydream about something positive every day—whether it's while you shower in the morning, during your lunch break, or before you go to bed. Banish thoughts of bills or deadlines and think of something wonderful—a favorite vacation spot, a warm memory with a loved one, or a life goal you're trying to achieve. You'll find this practice leaves you mentally energized, refreshed, and balanced.

Whip Up a Delicious Green Smoothie

Feeling tired, hungry, and de-energized during a late afternoon slump? Instead of overindulging in an unhealthy snack you eat mindlessly, restore yourself with a smoothie made with fresh, leafy greens from the earth. Kale, arugula, and spinach are good sources of folate, fiber, and vitamins A and C, plus they are filled with antioxidants and are known to improve heart health.

Grab one at a juice bar near you, or make your own, adding chunks of pear, honey, or apple to the greens to create a bit of sweetness in your drink. Savor each sip, and notice how it makes you feel restored and rejuvenated with no guilt!

Indulge In a Day Off

Earth signs are very practical and dependable, but they can take that dedication too far and end up overworking themselves. Treat yourself to days off from work or regular life periodically to recharge your batteries. A mental health day can do wonders for your happiness, creativity, and health.

Be sure to take the whole day to relax—don't fill it up with errands and appointments. Go for a long walk outside, enjoy a coffee at a local café, take a warm bath... Spend your time focusing on what your body needs to restore itself—you deserve it!

Talk to a Friend (in Person!)

These days we often rely on texting to keep in touch with friends. While that's a good method a lot of the time, it's also vital to keep friendships strong by talking on the phone or, even better, in person. Earth signs are very loyal, and your friends are important to you. Show them that by prioritizing them in your schedule. Find time to catch up so you can move past emojis and nurture the type of close bond you and your friend deserve.

If finding a mutually agreeable time is proving difficult, get creative—for example, take a walk or jog together so you can exercise *and* catch up.

CHAPTER 5

Essential Elements: Air

The air element is perhaps the most elusive element of the zodiac. Air is everywhere, invisible, and yet completely necessary for life. We are so sensitive to air that we even feel a momentary change in the currents around us or the amount of oxygen in our body.

In astrology, air is the third element of creation, preceded by fire and earth. The air signs (Gemini, Libra, and Aquarius) are the thinkers of the zodiac. Their dominion is mental—the realm of ideas and concepts. For example, you may have heard the saying that a person "has his head in the clouds." For air signs, this expression describes the essence of who they are. Air signs live in a world of both rational and intuitive thought. They are imaginative and dream of new and better ways to be, to think, and to communicate. Any self-care they do must reflect that disposition as well. Let's take a look at the mythological importance of air and its counterparts, the basic characteristics of the three air signs, and the things they all have in common when it comes to self-care.

The Mythology of Air

In Greek mythology, the legend of Icarus has a symbolic connection with the air element. In this myth Icarus and his father, Daedalus, a talented Athenian craftsman responsible for building a labyrinth for King Minos to imprison the Minotaur, were themselves imprisoned in the labyrinth in Crete for crimes against the king. To escape the Minotaur, Daedalus fashioned wings of wax and feathers that he and his son could use to fly over the sea. Daedalus warned his son not to fly too near the sun as the heat would cause his wings to melt. But Icarus became enchanted by his freedom and flew too close to the sun. Soon, the wax melted and Icarus fell into the sea.

The lesson for the air signs in this myth is that going beyond sense and reason usually does not work out. In the case of Icarus, he followed his desire instead of his rational side, and ended up falling to his death. Ideas are wonderful—they are the foundation of many great creations. But for air signs, ideas are followed by the hard work of grounding them in physical reality. Self-care rituals that cater to both mind and heart are key for air signs, but balance and rationale are often paramount.

The Element of Air

Air signs are known for their curiosity, pursuit of knowledge, and keen ability to communicate. They delight in conversation and feel most passionate when they are confronting a dilemma of the mind straight on. But their grand ideas sometimes make them unpredictable. Because of this, they must be challenged in all parts of their lives. Doing the same thing over and over will just leave them bored. This goes for self-care as well. They need variety and different options for wellness activities, or they may not participate at all. Air signs are buoyant, perceptive, and inventive. For example, Gemini is expressive and always ready to entertain. Libra is gentle and will listen to a friend's troubles for hours. And Aquarius is ingenious, helping to solve problems with different approaches.

Astrological Symbols

The astrological symbols (also called the zodiacal symbols) of the air signs also give hints as to how air signs move through the world. Each symbol ties back to the analytical, curious nature associated with air signs:

- Gemini is the Twins
- Libra is the Scales
- Aquarius is the Water Bearer

All these signs show intimate harmony with the cycles of the seasons and a personal connection with air. Gemini represents duality of the mind, and his symbol resembles the Roman numeral two. Libra brings balance with his scales of justice. And Aquarius represents positive movement and nourishment with waves of water or electricity. Each air sign's personality and subsequent approaches to self-care tie back to the qualities of these symbols.

Signs and Seasonal Modes

Each of the elements in astrology has a sign that corresponds to a different part of each season.

- **Cardinal:** Libra, the second air sign, occurs in autumn; he is the cardinal air sign because the autumn equinox occurs at the beginning of Libra's time. The cardinal signs are leaders, and are action-oriented.
- **Fixed:** Aquarius is a fixed air sign. He rules in winter. The fixed signs are definite, principled, and powerfully stubborn.
- **Mutable:** Gemini is the first air sign and marks the end of spring and the beginning of summer. Gemini is called a mutable air sign because he ushers us from one season to the next. Mutable signs are changeable and flexible.

If you know your element and whether you are a cardinal, fixed, or mutable sign, you know a lot about yourself and your loved ones. This is invaluable for self-care and is reflected in the customized air sign self-care rituals found later in this chapter.

Air Signs and Self-Care

When it comes to self-care, air signs must realize that they have a very sensitive nervous system. Not only do they react to changes in the weather and the "vibrations" around them in social situations, but also, they react to the power of words and ideas. Sometimes, they are not aware that their words can wound others, but they are always aware when someone says something hurtful to them. However, air signs are not a feeling sign, they are a thinking sign. They perceive that they are angry or hurt, but their feelings are expressed more in terms of the other person's actions, so they'll respond with "I thought that was rude," or "How unkind and cruel." Self-care must involve tapping into their emotions as well as the logic that precedes them.

Air signs are not always oriented toward the physical. For instance, they know they have to eat and take care of their health, but the action comes second to thinking about it all. They can lose track of time and forget that they only had a croissant for breakfast! The first part of any self-care program for air signs is to understand the concept that self-care is a good thing to do for an easier and more productive life. Long-range thinking is an air sign specialty, so they should ask themselves: Why not apply it to long-range self-care goals? This makes intuitive sense to air signs. In this way, the most successful self-care activities should be interesting and involve an overall concept, such as "If I do this, I will learn some new ways of understanding myself and others," or "This is a new therapy that promises to eliminate my posture problem. I will check it out." Just doing something is not enough—air signs want to be sure of their reasons.

Repeating meaningless habits is a pitfall for air signs. If they get stuck in a rut, they'll ditch their self-care and run off to a party instead. Air signs are creative, and the same effort they exert for a nice dinner, social outing, story, or song should also apply to self-care. On the flip side, any activity or program that is cumbersome won't last long with air signs. If there is too much equipment to deal with or too much effort to get to that particular gym or hiking trail, the air sign just won't do it.

Air signs have an aesthetic sense in all aspects of their lives, which is why any self-care activity has to be pleasing to the eye as well as effective. For example, a diet plan must be tasty and involve food that is beautifully displayed. Those two qualities please air signs and will motivate them.

The plan also has to be simple to follow: no elaborate timetables, just clear directions.

So now that you know what air signs need to practice self-care, let's take a look at the activities that will help those born under this element flourish.

Go Cloud-Watching

Air signs are intellectual thinkers who excel at creative thought and problem-solving. But sometimes that can mean it's hard to turn off your racing mind. If you're having trouble figuring out the answer to a question, take care of yourself by taking a well-deserved break to clear your mind. Need something else to focus on? Look up at the clouds. Take some time to lie back and watch the clouds move through the sky. You're sure to feel refreshed and will be able to look at any challenges with a fresh perspective.

Head to the Swimming Pool

It may come as a surprise, but swimming is actually great for air signs. Air signs are known for loving to think about problems from every angle, but sometimes it's important to have a mental break. With swimming, you'll need to focus on mastering each movement and maintaining fluid motions, so it's a great way to calm your mind. Allow yourself to relax and feel restored as you take a break from your worries.

Swimming is also a great way for air signs to get some exercise. Regular swim sessions will help you build lung power and stamina. So instead of your regular workout, head to your local pool and do some laps.

Use Writing Prompts

Air signs are often creative and great at expression. Why not try channeling those skills into some writing? Some well-known authors such as Shel Silverstein, Oscar Wilde, Charles Dickens, and Judy Blume were able to direct their air sign qualities into incredible literary works—maybe you can too!

Not sure where to start? Writing prompts are a great way to boost your creativity and give you the kind of challenge you love. Look for a writing prompt book at your local library, or check out different social media communities for ideas to help you get started.

Unplug Before Bed

Even the most communicative air sign will sometimes need a break to feel refreshed and reenergized after a long day. Getting a good night's sleep will also help rejuvenate your nervous system, so do whatever you can to ensure pleasant dreams and a restful evening.

A good first step is to unplug from social media before heading to bed, and, if possible, keep technology out of the bedroom entirely. Stop scrolling through social media and give yourself a break from your tablet or computer. Minimize your information input by avoiding TV—especially news programs—before bedtime. If possible, you can even eliminate clocks from your bedroom for a more peaceful sleep.

Whistle Your Way Through Chores

Vacuuming or washing dishes might not be your favorite activities, but sometimes those boring chores simply need to get done. Intellectual air signs need some kind of fun activity to keep the mind otherwise occupied, especially when faced with a few hours of dusting and sweeping. Try whistling while doing chores. It'll help keep your brain focused as you work, and it may be a good creative outlet if you're especially interested in music. You'll also help strengthen your lungs—all that blowing is a mini-breathing exercise for any air sign!

Create the Perfect Work Space

Air signs are intellectual problem-solvers with great critical-thinking skills. Make sure your work space is ready! Whether you work at home or spend your days in a professional office, it's important to make sure you create a productive work space. Start with your chair so you're comfortable and able to focus. Your chair should be lightweight and on rollers so you can move around easily.

Your spontaneous nature will appreciate the ease with which you can shift around and collaborate with any coworkers.

If you work around a lot of computers and technical equipment, ask an expert about setting up a portable ionizer to help neutralize their electromagnetic vibrations. It will help improve the air quality and keep you feeling your best.

Learn about Aikido

Inspired by various martial arts techniques, aikido is more than fighting—it's really about self-development, focus, peace, and balance. Participants can use their practice to find what they need, whether that's a healthy workout or a focus on spirituality. To get started, look for beginners' classes in your area or check on online course offerings for a better idea of what to expect before signing up.

Perfect for air signs, aikido is a powerful and beautiful martial art. Since air signs may enjoy opportunities for self-improvement and collaboration, aikido can be a great way to focus your overactive mind. You'll appreciate the graceful movements that will remind you of your air-like qualities.

Become a Social Butterfly

Connection is your strong suit, so head out to events, get-togethers, and parties to meet new people. Social events bring out the best in air signs, who are in their element when surrounded by engaging conversation and interesting ideas. Try attending a reading at your local bookstore, checking out the speakers at a nearby college, or simply following your friends to a party. Socializing with different types of people comes naturally to air signs, so you may find your friend group growing rapidly in ways you never expected. You'll increase your own knowledge of the world by meeting other people, so don't be afraid to let your natural social butterfly tendencies shine!

Look for Patterns in Your Ideas

Air signs are creative and often have a lot of ideas. Those ideas may be interesting and worth exploring in more detail, but they can sometimes require a little more thought than you're able to give in the moment. So give yourself an outlet to brainstorm and release those ideas in a constructive manner by writing everything down and keeping a record of your ideas—no matter how big or small they seem. You may consider keeping a journal and taking some time every day to record your thoughts, or you may just want to jot down your notes on your smartphone as they come to you.

Then, at the end of each week, study your notes and look for patterns in your thinking—they might help reveal worries or build on broader ideas you didn't even realize you had.

Walk to Work

Here's an easy way for air signs to take care of themselves: Head outside to get some fresh air! Air signs truly value freedom and openness, so make sure to spend some time outside every day. A great way to get your daily fix is to walk to work (or to your public transportation). If your work location doesn't allow for that, choose to walk instead of drive wherever possible in your life—not only will you feel healthier and more refreshed, but the environment will thank you as well!

"Vitamin O"—oxygen—is one of the most important factors to keep an air sign feeling revitalized and healthy.

Support Clean Air

The environment is important to everyone, and air pollution in particular is a cause any air sign can really get behind. It's important to take care of your health, and air signs will instinctually gravitate toward clean air as a way to keep their bodies strong, healthy, and happy.

Get involved in the movement for clean air! Do some research to learn about particular causes you'd like to support, like wind farms or other alternative energies. Donate to major clean air groups to help them fund their important work. Find out what programs exist in your area where you can volunteer your time. Air signs are great communicators, so volunteer your skills to help get the word out on clean air!

Keep In Touch with Friends

Air signs are great at intercommunication, and it's important for their well-being to have that social interaction throughout their lives. Other signs though? Not so much. Before you get upset that you haven't heard from your friends in a while, try making the first move and reaching out. Send a quick text to a friend you haven't heard from in a while. Give your best friend a call, even if you only want to say hello. Reconnect with old friends over social media, or even send an email to let someone know you're thinking of them.

With our busy lives, people sometimes need reminders to keep in touch, and air signs are the perfect ones to take that step!

(Re-)Learn a Foreign Language

Many of us have taken a foreign language at some point, whether in school or in college. But how many of us have maintained those skills? Air signs are all about the exchange of information. It's important to them that they be able to get the word out and share their thoughts with others. Talking with new people helps you feel revitalized, so expand your communication skills by revisiting that foreign language you learned in school. Try taking a course at your local community college or checking out one of the many apps and online programs to help you tap into those lost or rusty skills. You may even consider planning a trip to the country that speaks that language. You'll get firsthand experience practicing your new skills and likely make new friends in the process!

Head Out on an Air Adventure

Air signs have an adventurous side, and you're known among your friends for being fun and spontaneous. If you're feeling a little bored lately, seek out some new experiences to recharge yourself and give you the excitement you need. Go for something a little unexpected with some wild (but still air-themed!) fun. Take a ride in a hot-air balloon to view your home from an entirely new perspective. Take a class to learn how to swing high on a trapeze for a unique workout. Or head out for a weekend away from home to learn kitesurfing from an expert. Give yourself the boost you need to keep your energy up!

Breathe from One to Ten

Air signs have highly tuned nervous systems, so certain breathing exercises can help you stay calm and relaxed. For a simple breathing technique you can employ anywhere, start by counting up from one to ten on an exhale. Then try counting down from ten to one as you inhale. You may find it helpful to close your eyes or

put your hands on your stomach or chest to feel yourself breathing. Check out online resources or apps for alternate techniques. Whenever you're feeling a little stressed, take a moment to focus on yourself and your breathing.

Avoid Negative Conversation Overload

Air signs are social and love to talk with other people. Since words are so important, air signs are also great at listening. But remember this: Don't let yourself get burnt out by tuning into negative conversations that don't involve you. Air signs can pick up other people's vibrations and energies through words, which can sometimes lead to a mental overload. Take a break and step away from the conversation, head outside for some fresh air, or redirect your focus toward something less draining and more relevant for you.

Keep Your Windows Open

Your home should be a place for you to relax, recharge, and reconnect with yourself. So make sure to pay homage to your air sign qualities in your home décor. Whether you live in a house or apartment, you'll be happiest and most comfortable with lots of windows that open. Try to keep your windows open all year long, especially after a cold spell or heat wave. Even if you have central air or heat, it can be helpful to keep just one window open. Changing the air currents changes the energy in your home, so be sure to let fresh air and positive energy flow throughout your living space.

Make Reading a Daily Habit

Air signs love learning, communication, and the written word, so it makes sense that they'd also be interested in reading. Try to spend at least 30 minutes a day reading something unrelated to your job or studies. If there's a book you've been dying to read or a magazine article that has caught your eye, take some time for yourself and spend it reading, even if you only get to finish a few pages.

Not sure what you want to read? Head to your local library to check out some of the selections there. Look for a well-known classic like *Don Quixote* by Cervantes (a fellow air sign!), or try something brand-new and trendy. Still not sure where to start? Ask your librarian for a recommendation and start a conversation about some awesome books!

Enjoy Some Green Tea

Air signs are curious and great at solving problems—but that can also mean that they're chronic overthinkers as well. Give yourself a restorative break to clear your head and reframe your mind-set. Not sure how to begin? Try making it a habit

to drink a peaceful cup of green tea every day; mix it up with some fruit-flavored or jasmine green teas for a little variety. Use your daily cup of tea as a chance to clear your mind and take a break from worrying about anything stressful in your life. (If you have health problems or are on medication, check with your doctor first.)

Afterward, you're sure to find you feel more relaxed and rejuvenated, and ready to take on any challenges that come your way. Bring your tea outside for the added benefit of a little fresh air on your break!

Dine Alfresco

Remember, fresh air is vital for air signs, so it's important to reclaim that outdoor time for yourself. Free-spirited air signs appreciate a little spontaneous fun; try to be creative about how you find that time. For example, why not eat outdoors? Whether you're spending the day at the beach or boardwalk, or going on a picnic in the park, enjoying a healthy meal outdoors can be great for your physical and mental well-being. If you don't have time for an all-day event, you can still head outdoors by asking to be seated outside at a restaurant or even bringing a home-cooked meal out onto your own patio or deck.

Grow Purifying Houseplants

Did you know that plants can help purify the air around you? Try bringing some houseplants into your home to help improve the air quality. English ivy, bamboo palm, and peace lilies are all beautiful houseplants that will help remove airborne toxins from your home. There are plenty of other options, however, so do some research to see what will grow well in your home. Warning, though, some plants are poisonous to house pets, so make sure to take the needs of your furry friends into consideration as well. Choose the plants that work best for you, and, as an air sign, you will feel your best and most balanced around these natural air purifiers.

Host a Word-Based Game Night

Air signs love to be social, and that social interaction is all they need to spark some happiness and excitement into their everyday lives! You're likely well known for being great company, so grab some snacks, pull out your favorite games, and invite some friends over for game night! Some friendly competition and interesting conversations will help you reconnect with friends you haven't seen in a while.

For some added air sign fun, look for word-based games that will play to your language-loving strengths. Scrabble, Boggle, and Bananagrams are all popular options, but there are plenty of lesser known variations that you might enjoy.

Keep Communication Open

Even great communicators like air signs can have disagreements or miscommunication with friends and family members. But you're likely to feel unbalanced when conflict causes the lines of communication to be closed. So clear the air and reopen those lines. It's important to remember not to hold onto grudges, so if you have any negative feelings, try to let them go and approach the conversation with a positive attitude. Do your best to be patient and flexible with the other person—remember, not everyone is as good at expression as you are! Work together to get back in balance and bring your relationships to a happier state.

Take Yourself to the Movies

Air signs love learning about new ideas, and a great way to do so is to head to the movies. Treat yourself to a couple of hours of comfortable seating, buttery popcorn, and an interesting new movie. You might try checking out a documentary or something that's particularly thought-provoking.

Although it's always fun to bring friends to the movie theater, you might consider making the occasional trip alone. Air signs appreciate the opportunity to think deeply about things they've learned. Enjoy the time alone to really analyze and fully process the movie you've just seen.

Hang Out in a Hammock

As an air sign, it's important for you to get outside and get some fresh air. One great way to unwind and recharge outside is to relax in a hammock. Enjoy rocking in the breeze, and give yourself permission to take a quick mental break. You can chat with friends nearby or spend some time by yourself, appreciating the nature around you. You should even feel free to close your eyes and take a little nap—you'll feel incredibly relaxed when you wake up! But if you're still in need of some mental stimulation to distract yourself, bring a book with you and take a little time to read. Your intellectual side will thank you!

Freshen Up Your Space

Air signs may seem like they're in constant motion. And that's certainly true of their minds, which are often off and running to solve whatever problems come their way. Yet sometimes air signs can get thrown off—both physically and mentally—by stagnant air in their home.

If you start feeling stuck or out of balance, get rid of anything old or musty in your home or apartment. Also consider rearranging the furniture, as moving furniture allows the air to circulate more easily through your living spaces. Or paint a room in a light, airy color to freshen up that area. Keep your windows open as much as possible. Your thoughts will mimic the newly refreshed space and be able to flow more freely.

Analyze Your Handwriting

With the air signs' interest in communication, they're likely to appreciate the importance of writing and may be very interested in what they can learn from their own handwriting. Your handwriting could be an important key to revealing some interesting aspects of your personality. Things like the slant, size, and thickness of your letters can be important, so have your handwriting analyzed! For instance, did you know that large letters indicate a big personality? If your handwriting slants to the right, you might like to meet new people. Learn some basic handwriting analysis tricks and practice your new skills with your friends to see if you can get to know them better!

Plan a Trip

Air signs may seem as if they're always on the move, so think about places you might like to visit to actually get yourself moving. Half the fun of travel is the anticipation and planning before you even go! It's always a good idea to have your next trip planned for the near future. You don't have to go far or plan an extensive, expensive vacation, but a nice weekend away or a few nights in a place you've always wanted to visit can give you something to look forward to and keep your energy high. Try visiting someplace peaceful to give yourself a chance to recharge, or research places you could visit to add an intellectual element to your next trip, like cities with interesting museums or historical monuments. Your adventurous free spirit will appreciate the change of scenery. As soon as you get home, start researching and planning your next trip. There is always more to see!

Continue Your Education

Air signs are the intellectuals of the zodiac and are always looking to learn something new. Continue your education by pursuing an advanced degree. By doing so, you'll be practicing good mental self-care through fully engaging in an intellectual pursuit. However, you might also find some practical benefits to continuing your education. By pursuing a degree in your field, you may discover that you're better qualified for a different position in your company. Or, if you choose to expand your horizons and go for a new degree in an entirely different field, you might be able to move into a new dream job.

Stop Gossiping

Because air signs are so great at communication, people really enjoy talking to them. That can be great news—you love speaking to and learning from a lot of people—but you need to be careful with everything you learn. People will often feel comfortable

sharing their personal issues with you, and it's up to you to be respectful of that. Avoid gossiping, and don't share anyone's personal information without their permission. For someone as social as you are, it's important that you keep your friendships in good shape. Your friends trust you, so remember to honor their feelings to keep your relationships going strong.

Decorate with Wind Chimes

Air signs can sometimes have the energy of a powerful wind with their free-spirited natures. Why not bring that inspiration into your home décor? Try putting some wind chimes on your porch, by the entrance to your home, or somewhere else where you'll be able to hear them often. If you live in an apartment, putting your chimes near a window should be enough to get them ringing.

Putting some wind chimes in your home can be a great way to remind yourself of some of your great air sign qualities. Every time you hear them ringing, you'll be reminded of your fun, adventurous side!

Sign Up for a Writing Course

Air signs are known for being great at expression and deep thinking. So why not expand your communication skills by taking a writing course? Although it may seem intimidating to put all your thoughts onto paper, you may be surprised to find you have a hidden writing talent! The good news is, writing classes span a variety of areas from fiction and poetry to screenwriting and presentation development. You're sure to find something that fits your interests!

You may find that you thrive in a social environment, like a class at a local college, where you can share your ideas with your classmates and develop your skills together. But if you're feeling a little shy about sharing your first writing attempts in person, there are plenty of online courses you can explore to get started.

Learn Calligraphy

If you're an air sign, you're all about communication. Get creative with your style of communicating and study calligraphy! Calligraphy is a beautiful writing form that can take a lot of practice to master but can also be a rewarding skill. You may be able to share your abilities for things like wedding invitations, announcements, or memorials.

Calligraphy can also be a meditative practice, giving overthinking air signs a much-needed mental break. Allow yourself time to slow down and focus on each careful, deliberate movement instead of worrying about a problem at hand. Taking a break to focus on your calligraphy will help you redirect your attention and feel refreshed.

Visit Some Butterflies

Air signs can be spontaneous and would love to head out on an airy getaway. Try visiting a butterfly sanctuary! A butterfly sanctuary is an indoor living space or conservatory designed specifically for the breeding, development, and safe display of butterflies. They also offer lots of opportunities to learn about the butterflies and the ways we can conserve and protect them!

This visit can be a great opportunity to take care of yourself physically since you can spend plenty of time walking around the garden areas. This enjoyable activity can also have emotional benefits. Your positive mood is sure to carry through into your day well after you leave the sanctuary.

Feed the Birds

All birds are friends to air signs—they share your free-spirited nature! You may find it soothing and calming to watch birds fly about. Why not encourage them to come to your yard by setting up a bird feeder? Different birds will like different foods, so try putting out a seed mix, suet, or even the popular black oil sunflower seed that attracts many different kinds of birds. Make sure to place your feeder in a safe place away from predators and windows.

Enjoy the Morning Crossword

Sometimes, doing something to keep your mind sharp is an important way to take care of yourself. Successfully completing a challenging task can help you feel stimulated and ready to take on the next project that comes your way. For air signs who love language and are often great problem-solvers, a crossword puzzle is a great way to exercise your mind. A word puzzle also has the added benefit of helping you learn new vocabulary, which air signs will love. Establish a new daily ritual and try doing your crossword puzzle in the morning—your success will help set the positive tone for the rest of the day!

Attend an Interesting Lecture

Air signs are naturally curious and love learning, so try attending a lecture or some other form of presentation. Keep it fun and interesting by attending lectures on subjects that pique your curiosity. You may even be able to find presentations by popular speakers for free through your local library or other organizations in your area. Take some time for yourself to learn something new!

Doing something mentally stimulating will put all air signs in a good mood, but attending a lecture can also have an added social benefit. You may find yourself making friends with your fellow attendees as you discuss your shared interests after the event is over.

Think Through Your Decisions

Air signs are great at critical thinking and like to make logical decisions. They'd rather follow their heads than let their emotions get in the way of their decision-making. Yet, because air signs like to take their time to see *all* sides of a question, making big decisions can prove difficult.

The best advice here is to not let yourself get rushed or pressured into deciding. If you're feeling unbalanced, you can get trapped thinking in and out of hundreds of potential scenarios—many of which will never occur. If this happens, remember to take care of your emotions and your body; try doing some deep breathing and allowing your intuition to help you figure out which solutions are the best for you.

Clear Your Mind with a Meditation App

We've all heard about the many benefits of meditation: It can reduce stress, depression, and anxiety; increase happiness, focus, and self-awareness; and even improve your physical health. Some research has indicated that meditation can be helpful for everything from minor aches and pains and even the simple headache to major illnesses—including asthma and chronic pain. Thankfully, there are now plenty of apps out there (free or with a small subscription fee) to give you access to some of the best meditation teachers in the world, and all the benefits this practice brings.

Reframe Your Alone Time

Air signs are very social and are known for being great company, because they can keep any situation from becoming too boring. However, it's important that you don't let yourself get burned out by spending all your time keeping other people entertained. It's good to take some time for yourself! Everyone needs time to themselves every once in a while. Appreciate the time you have to spend doing something you like, whether that's heading outdoors or learning something new—and don't criticize yourself for it. With the right attitude, taking time to concentrate on yourself will give you a positive outlook and a fresh perspective. So instead of always focusing on others, reframe your mind-set and simply enjoy being alone.

Listen to an Audiobook

There are all kinds of ways to learn new information, and air signs are especially good at learning by listening. A great way for you to gather more information might be through educational audiobooks. Audiobooks are perfect for when you're on the go, since you can listen wherever you are, whether you're driving, grocery shopping, or even working out. There's a lot to learn, so choose a topic that you find interesting and simply search for the right book for you!

Listening to an audiobook can also be a nice mental break. Centering your thoughts on whatever you're listening to can help you relax and redirect your mind away from any problem that's worrying you.

Cleanse Your Home with a Lavender Atomizer

The state of your mind is often reflected in the state of your home. If there's clutter everywhere and dust is starting to gather, there's a good chance you're feeling stuck emotionally and mentally as well. For intellectual air signs, this clutter can make you feel unbalanced and distressed. Smudging is a simple cleansing ritual that many people use to clear out negativity in your home—but as an air sign, you might not enjoy the smoky smell that traditional smudging introduces to your home. Instead, try an atomizer with lavender, a scent known for its cleansing energy. Tidy up any obvious clutter and move the atomizer around your space to clear negativity. Make way for a refreshed, positive attitude!

Perform Random Acts of Kindness

Air signs can be extremely thoughtful; they're great at being objective when they need to be and genuinely want to see positive changes in the world around them. An easy way for air signs to help make a small change every day is to complete a random act of kindness. This can be anything from adding some extra coins to a parking meter that's about to run out to volunteering for a good cause. You could also pay for your coworker's coffee when you see them in the drive-thru line behind you, pack your partner's lunch for the day, or call an elderly relative just to chat about their week.

Making simple acts of kindness a daily ritual can strengthen your relationships by showing others how much you care about them, and can improve your own everyday outlook!

Enjoy a Rainy Day

Air signs are connected to the weather— after all, your mood can change just as quickly and drastically as the winds! Take some time to connect with and appreciate changes in the weather instead of letting them get you down. Don't let yourself get upset by a rainy day. Instead, enjoy a good rainstorm! Sit by your window and simply savor the wind and rain. You may find it helps you relax to bring a cup of tea with you or take a few deep, meditative breaths. By training yourself to look at things in a positive light, you'll take better care of your emotional needs and feel happier every day.

Balance Your Mind and Body with Pilates

Even though air signs are often focused on the mind, it's just as important to take care of the body through exercise. The secret to consistent exercise? Find a workout routine that works for you and that you enjoy! Not only will your body feel healthy and strong, but you'll also head into your workout with a much more positive attitude.

One routine that might work well for air signs is a Pilates class, which focuses on both the mind and the body as you work your way through different moves. You'll learn to strengthen your physique through careful movement, develop your flexibility and balance, and properly manage your breathing for less stress and more control of your body.

Take Care of Yourself

If you're an air sign, you know you can sometimes get trapped in your own head. Air signs are intellectual people, which makes them great problem-solvers and critical thinkers. However, there's always the risk of overthinking and spending too much time living in your mind. Don't let yourself get too detached from daily life!

Completing necessary, practical activities is essential self-care. Things like eating three good meals a day, showering, and brushing your teeth every morning and evening are important for keeping your life in balance. So remember to stay grounded in the real world and do the things you need to do to keep yourself healthy and happy.

Create an Air-Friendly Home

Air signs are always on the move and can seem a little restless. So it's important that you use your home space as a place to restore and refocus. Create a beautiful, air-friendly home where you'll feel comfortable and able to relax.

Your design aesthetic is likely to be light, open, and airy. To start, don't set up your living spaces with so many components that they feel overcomplicated—simple spaces are important to air signs! Also, take some time to think about the lighting for your home. Ideally, your home should have plenty of natural light. All the lights in your home should be full spectrum, which will help imitate the sunny outdoors, even on the rainiest days. And make sure you have some accessories that also speak to your air sign: purifying houseplants, framed pictures of vacation spots, and lots of books!

Have a Group Laugh

Social air signs love to have a good time with their friends and family. Look for ways you can all enjoy a laugh together! While the emotional and social benefits of sharing a laugh are clear, did you know laughter can also help your physical health by decreasing stress, lowering blood pressure, relieving pain, and even boosting your immune system? Taking some time to laugh will have a wide range of restorative benefits for you all.

All you need to do is head to a comedy club or watch a silly movie together. Or keep a book of puns, jokes, and limericks handy to share a giggle with others. Your love of language will make it doubly enjoyable for you!

Invest In an Air Purifier

As an air sign, you know that the quality of the air around you is important for your health and well-being. Clean air is especially important for your physical health if you have asthma or other lung issues, but the truth is that everyone can benefit! Keeping dust, smog, and other tiny particles out of your lungs is an important way to not only keep you feeling your best, but also help prevent other illnesses. Research and invest in a good air purifier to help eliminate things like pollen, smoke, or other pollutants from the air in your home. An air purifier can be especially important if you live in a city where the increased population and traffic can mean more pollution.

Decorate with Clear Quartz

Crystals can be a great way to add some beauty to a space and help rebalance your energy. Air signs will find lots of benefits from clear quartz crystals, which are among the most common and well-known healing stones. Learn about ways quartz may help treat you physically (crystal healing with clear quartz can be useful for the nervous system!) and mentally. Since clear quartz is believed to increase spiritual connections and clear thinking, it can be a useful tool when you need to expand your thoughts and think carefully.

Try decorating your home and office space with clear quartz crystal clusters so there's always one nearby when you start to feel a little off-balance.

Listen to Interesting Conversations Around You

Air signs are the element of communication, so it's only natural for you to pay attention to the conversations around you. You're also always ready to learn new things, so you're likely to be listening for subjects that might pique your interest. Whether you're riding the subway, waiting in line at the supermarket, or mingling at a party, you're sure to catch some snippets of chatter that grab your attention. You might even consider carrying around a notebook and pen to jot down little bits of conversation you hear or interesting topics you'd like to learn more about later.

Choose Light, Fresh Scents

Air signs find it helpful for their living spaces to be well lit and spacious to mimic the natural world. So it makes sense that you'd also prefer lighter, more natural scents for your home. Whether you're looking for candles, room sprays, or other scented products, choose light scents like lemon verbena and rosewater. Even if you typically hate perfumes or colognes, these scents aren't overpowering. Instead, they'll make the air smell fresh and clean, which will help you feel more relaxed and at home in your living space. Certain scents also come with plenty of other benefits—for instance, a citrusy smell can help you feel a bit more energized!

Learn about the Weather

Air signs are sensitive to changes in the weather, so you're already likely to be very aware of the changes in the air around you. You can encourage your intellectual interests and take better care of your physical self by learning a little more about the weather. Purchase an old-fashioned barometer to keep in your home.

A barometer is a scientific instrument that's often used to predict the weather, because it measures changes in the atmospheric pressure. High pressure usually indicates good weather, but watch out if that level starts to drop! Not only will you learn a fun new piece of information to share, but you'll be prepared no matter the weather with just a glance at your barometer.

De-Stress with Kite Flying

Sometimes, acting like a kid is a great way to release stress. And what is a better throwback activity for an air sign than flying a kite! Air signs can easily get wrapped up in their own thoughts, so an activity like flying kites that gets you out into the natural world, and gives you something to take your mind off your worries, can be a big help for your stress level. If you find you really enjoy kite flying, you might consider checking out a kite flying competition to develop your skills even more, and make some new friends. You may even get a little exercise from chasing your kite around!

Join a Hiking Club

Air signs need to spend plenty of time out in the fresh air, so they're likely to feel reenergized after heading out for a hike. Plus, they love to be social. If you join a hiking club, you'll get a chance to enjoy new company *and* revitalizing air—while viewing some beautiful scenery as you walk.

Hiking is a great workout that can improve heart health, strengthen muscles, and increase stability and balance. It's also often recommended as a natural stress-relief activity. Being part of a regular, organized group will motivate you to continue this invigorating act of self-care. And you might meet new friends at the same time!

Try One Dance Class

Fluid, airy movements are aesthetically pleasing to air signs, so you may enjoy watching ballet or modern dance. If you're feeling ready to jump up and start dancing yourself, consider signing up for a class to learn more about those styles. Just one class can let you know if it is the right style for you. If you don't like it, try another! There are so many dance styles to choose from; you might even just enjoy exploring the different varieties. Dance has a lot of benefits for your physical health—you can develop your strength, increase your flexibility, and improve your posture. But it can also be an effective way to relieve stress and build confidence. As you focus on learning specific steps and developing your skills, you'll have the opportunity to clear your mind so you feel refreshed and ready to take on the rest of the day.

Release Sky Lanterns

Create time for yourself to take care of your spiritual needs! If you've recently experienced a loss of someone from your life, it is important to honor both those people and your own feelings. Turn to your air sign–inspired appreciation for nature and call upon the energy in the air around you for some help by releasing a fire-retardant sky lantern. (Just be sure to check regulations in your area, and research the safest method and locations for releasing the lanterns before doing so.) Simply write a message on the lantern to your loved one and then release it into the sky. Allowing the air, your influencing element, to carry your message where it needs to be can give you the closure and release you've been seeking.

Take Up Tennis

Take some inspiration from fellow air sign Serena Williams, and try tennis (or racquetball)! Many air signs experience bursts of energy, which work well for a sport like tennis. It's no surprise that tennis or racquetball can be great workouts that develop muscles, improve hand-eye coordination, and strengthen heart health. But as an intellectual air sign, you might also find you enjoy the tactical nature of these games. Your critical-thinking skills might help you figure out the techniques, moves, and patterns you need to win the game. Clear your mind from other thoughts and focus on keeping your movements strong and fluid.

Find Balance Through Reiki

Sometimes an air sign can become unbalanced, perhaps due to overthinking or an issue with communication. When unbalanced, you may have difficulty being open-minded, and feel unwilling to accept new ideas—or you may feel overwhelmed with options. A Reiki treatment can be useful for reestablishing order in your life.

Reiki is a healing technique that aims to improve the movement of energy throughout the body through gentle touch. A Reiki session can cleanse your energy so it flows through your body smoothly and gets you back into balance. This practice will help you feel revitalized and refreshed, so be sure to consider setting up a session during high-stress times.

Practice Feng Shui

It's important to get enough rest and relaxation in your home so you go about your day feeling enlivened and reinvigorated. For air signs, rest is also an important aspect of keeping their nervous system in balance. Use the power of some basic feng shui to help you get exactly the right setup for better relaxation in your home.

Feng shui is the practice of aligning and arranging elements in your home to create the ideal energy flow for positivity and good luck in various aspects of your life. For example, feng shui does not recommend using metal headboards on your beds and advises against using certain colors in an area based on the energy you might want to emphasize there. Look online or visit an interior designer familiar with feng shui to learn more about this and other principles of this ancient practice that you can apply throughout your living space—and even your garden.

CHAPTER 6

Essential Elements: Water

Water is the fourth and final element of creation. It is essential for the planet and for our physical existence. It is amorphous, meaning it assumes the shape of its container or geographical location and solidifies only when frozen. Those who have water as their governing element—Cancer, Scorpio, and Pisces—all have a special energy signature and a connection with water that guides all aspects of their lives. Water signs are intuitive and tend to live on waves of feeling. They are reflective, responsive, and fertile, and are often more sensitive than other signs.

Their path in life is to quell their overwhelming emotions and use their instincts for love and compassion toward themselves and others. Their approach to self-care must include these goals. Let's take a look at the mythological importance of water and its fluid counterparts, the basic characteristics of the three water signs, and the things they all have in common when it comes to self-care.

The Mythology of Water

In Greek mythology, water is linked to the god of the sea, Poseidon. Poseidon was brother to Zeus and Hades and was one of the six children conceived by Rhea and Cronos. His father, Cronos, ruled the universe, but was eventually overthrown by Zeus. After the collapse of their father's power, Zeus, Hades, and Poseidon decided to divide the earth between the three of them. Poseidon became the lord of the sea, while Zeus became lord of Mount Olympus and the sky, and Hades became the lord of the underworld. The sea god was especially important in the ancient world as sea travel and navigation formed the principle trade and travel routes. Throughout mythology, going to sea was seen as a precarious adventure, and sailors often prayed to Poseidon for safe return and calm waters. Many myths feature Poseidon saving a ship at the last moment. In other myths he is not so merciful.

Like Poseidon, water signs make their decisions based on emotion. Their gut feelings guide them. This makes water signs highly compassionate and understanding, but it can also make them moody at times. Water signs may try to keep their emotions balanced in the hope of staying in control of their feelings, rather than allowing their feelings to control them. This desire drives their likes and dislikes, personality traits, and approaches to self-care.

The Element of Water

In terms of astrology, the water signs are called the feeling signs. They feel first, and think and speak later. They are very familiar with the emotional expression of tears, laughter, anger, joy, and grief. They often wear their heart on their sleeve and are extremely sentimental. Scorpio is somewhat of an exception to this characterization, but, nevertheless, she has a sensitive feeling mechanism. A water sign's energy moves inward, and they draw people and experiences to them rather than overtly seeking out people and experiences. For example, Scorpio's bravery means she is always open to new adventures that come her way. Cancer's loyalty encourages her to stick close to family and friends. And Pisces's creative intuition makes her a wonderful problem-solver when faced with a difficult conundrum.

Astrological Symbols

The astrological symbols (also called the zodiacal symbols) of the water signs also give hints as to how the water signs move through the world. The symbols of all the water signs are creatures connected with the sea, the cradle of life:

- Cancer is the Crab
- Scorpio is the Scorpion (and the Eagle and the Phoenix)
- Pisces is the two Fish tied together

Scorpio has a complex set of symbols because there are varieties of scorpions, both in the sea and on land, but the sea is home to all these sensitive water signs. Scorpio uses her stinger to sting first, rather than take the time to ask questions. Cancer the Crab holds on to her home tenaciously and never approaches anything directly. Instead, she moves from side to side to go forward in zigzag motions. And Pisces's two Fish tied together symbolize duality—one of the fish staying above the water, paying attention to the earth, and the other living in the sea, where dreams and the imagination rule.

Signs and Seasonal Modes

Each of the elements in astrology also has a sign that corresponds to a different part of each season.

- **Cardinal:** Cancer, as the first water sign, comes at the summer solstice, when summer begins. She is a cardinal sign and the leader of the water signs. She may lead indirectly, but she has a powerful desire to be in control.
- **Fixed:** Scorpio, the next water sign, is a fixed water sign, and she rules when autumn is well established. The fixed signs are definite, principled, and powerfully stubborn.
- **Mutable:** Pisces, the last water sign and the last sign of the zodiac, is a mutable

sign. She moves us from winter to the spring equinox in Aries. The major characteristic of mutable, or changeable, signs is flexibility.

If you know your element and whether you are a cardinal, fixed, or mutable sign, you know a lot about yourself and your loved ones. This is invaluable for self-care and is reflected in the customized water sign self-care rituals found later in this chapter.

Water Signs and Self-Care

Self-care comes naturally to water signs. Oftentimes, they find it is essential to take care of themselves because they feel acutely when something is askew inside them. They may complain bitterly about not feeling well, or about their sensitivities or the weather, but they generally know what to do to get back on course. Physical self-care is the hardest area for the water signs to master, because they do not like to do things unless they feel like doing them. Once they have a routine that has proven will make them feel better, they will stick to it, but before they adopt that routine, they are often hit-or-miss when it comes to diet, exercise, and medical checkups. Water signs are also very in tune with alternative cures and the home remedies their ancestors used for self-care.

Another essential factor in water sign self-care is the atmosphere of the gym or exercise location. Generally, water signs do not like crowds. If it is 5 p.m. and people are pounding out their aggressions from work on the treadmill, most water signs will choose to wait for the crowds to thin, or they will go earlier in the day. However, one of the great encouragements for many water signs is the use of a shower or pool—a water source that they can include in their routine is a great enticement for water signs. Water signs may choose to attend classes at the gym, but most of the time they prefer to make sure that they are not overly influenced by other people's vibes.

Water signs are especially drawn to natural surroundings when it comes to self-care. Walking by a pond or lake is perhaps the best exercise for them, as it combines physical, mental, and spiritual practice. In a low-pressure environment, water signs feel that all their activities are worthwhile, both in terms of money and time. They are very aware of the money they spend and tend to be prudent and almost stingy with funds. And there is a direct relationship between their feeling of well-being and the amount of money they have in the bank.

Water signs are nurturers and make it a priority to take care of family and friends. It is always best for water signs to frame their self-care in terms of their familial feelings about something. For example, the statement "If you quit eating all this junk, you will help your family by setting a good example and you will feel better" is a winning one for water signs, marrying their love for their family with their own self-care. Once the water sign gets the feeling that they can extend the love and care of their family to themselves through self-care, they feel more comfortable designating attention to wellness practices.

In terms of emotional self-care, the most important factor for water signs is to avoid exaggerating their reactions to events or people. The more water signs can stay in the here and now, the less they will feel there are imaginary scenarios of people working against them. They are so sensitive that it is very easy for them to lapse into being self-conscious. A very good technique for water signs is to play a game asking themselves the question, "How would I feel if I were that person?" This thinking pattern encourages compassion rather than self-centeredness in water signs.

Water signs have a gift for feeling. In today's society we tend to diminish the importance of being emotional. Water signs may feel they have to do all the heavy lifting in the emotional department, which may make them feel lonely. Water signs are naturally empathetic, so the trick for them is to balance how they feel about other people and extend those good feelings to themselves. Feelings are different from intellectual, inspirational, and practical concerns. The water signs symbolize the potential of members of the human family to share their individual feelings.

So, now that you know what water signs need to practice self-care, let's take a look at the activities that will help those born under this element flourish.

Get Motivated

If you find that you are feeling unmotivated to work out, start by listening to your favorite music to get amped up. Sometimes just feeling the beat can jump-start your energy level and get your blood flowing. If you are working out at home, you may even want to try dancing around as your entire workout. Dancing for 30 minutes is great cardio. Just blast your favorite tunes and let your body move naturally. Mix up the playlist tempo to keep things interesting. No slow songs allowed!

Belly Dance!

As a water sign, you are drawn to fluid movements. When it comes to exercise, look for things that give your body freedom to move in the way it wants to. The last thing you want is to be restrained. Try Tai Chi or an aerobic dance class. Even Pilates can be soothing for water signs, as it helps build muscle and keeps you moving in a natural way. But why not choose something a little different, and try a belly dancing class! You

are sure to enjoy the solo qualities of this ancient dance. Don't forget your hip scarf!

Schedule Your Routine

Routine can be boring for a water sign (until she finds the right one), but it is key to a solid self-care regimen. It may take discipline to stick to a routine, but without a well-constructed plan, apathy will take over and you'll find yourself doing nothing to improve your overall wellness. Make sure you vary your activities to keep things fresh and new. It may help to buy a large desk calendar and mark off when you are doing what activity. This will help keep you on track and will take any indecisiveness off the table.

Make Water a Part of Your Life

You may think that all water signs are naturally drawn to water in every capacity, but this isn't necessarily true. Every water sign is different and has different preferences. While most water signs take comfort in water-based activities, such as swimming, diving, and water aerobics, others prefer to simply be near water, but not in it. Wherever you fall on this spectrum, water is an important grounding mechanism for you. It calms you, makes you feel safe, and helps orient you when you are feeling lost. Make water a part of your life in whatever way you feel most comfortable.

Stretch

The type of exercise you do as a water sign is very important. Many water signs have smooth muscles that do not usually bulk up, so doing exercises that are designed to add heft to your muscle won't be particularly beneficial. Instead, you should look for exercises that stretch your muscles, such as yoga. You don't even have to go to a yoga class to try it out. There are plenty of online videos for beginner yogis to try—just stick to the basics.

If yoga isn't your favorite, you can still make stretching an essential part of your wellness routine by stretching before and after every workout. It may even help to do some gentle stretches before bed to keep your muscles limber and flexible. As you do so, remember to pace your breathing and focus on the stretches, so your mind and body will be totally relaxed and prepared for a productive day, or a restful night.

Choose Sea Salt

You've probably heard that our bodies are made up of up to 60 percent water. Water signs tend to hold on to water more than other signs do, which means they often have a softness to their faces and bodies.

To keep your salt balanced, choose sea salt. Sea salt has natural minerals like potassium, calcium, magnesium, and more. In their natural form in sea salt, these minerals are easier for the body to absorb.

Too much sodium (either in table salt or processed foods and soft drinks) increases your risk of water retention. If you do experience water retention symptoms, visit your doctor for advice.

Turn to Nature

Stress happens to everyone; it's how you handle it that makes a difference. For water signs, the best way to beat stress is to retreat to a safe space: nature. If you have the opportunity to spend time by a body of water, like a creek, river, or, ideally, the beach, do so as often as possible. Just listen to the sound the water makes as it moves, lapping against rocks or sand, and let the stress melt away from your muscles. If you don't have easy access to a body of water, download and listen to some water sounds outside. It's not quite the same, but it will mimic the calming experience of being by the water.

See the Comedy in Things

Laughter can soothe the soul, especially the soul of a weary water sign. You tend to feel deeply, and need a healthy release to let go of those heavy emotions. Laughter can be that release. If you don't laugh, you may start to get bogged down with too many negative feelings. The only way to survive in life is to see the comedy in things. Water signs are especially good at this, but, sometimes, they need a little push to remind themselves. When you are feeling down, try to see the funny side of the situation. A little dark humor might just make you feel better!

Avoid Crowds

You are a sensitive soul, water sign, one who tends to absorb the vibrations and energy coming from other people. Because of this, it's best for you to avoid large crowds, especially if you are feeling vulnerable or sad. Being in a large group of strangers will just exacerbate those negative feelings you are struggling with, and may even make you feel more alone than you already do. Instead, stay home and allow yourself some quality relaxation time. Give yourself permission to lounge around and be lazy. Enjoy your own company!

Wash It Off

As a water sign, you are used to being affected by other people's energy and the energy of the atmosphere around you. It is essential for your emotional health that you wash away any feelings you may have absorbed from others throughout the day. Make a point to take a shower or bath every night to cleanse your emotional aura. You may even find dry brushing before you bathe to be beneficial. Not only does dry brushing help loosen and remove dead skin from your body, but it can be a wonderfully cathartic experience for water

signs, especially if you envision the ritual as also sloughing away any emotional burdens you have picked up over the past few hours.

Keep It (Mostly) Simple

When it comes to fashion, water signs like to keep things simple and classic. Their favorite colors for clothing are muted tones—like navy-blue, black, gray, and white—along with pops of color, like turquoise. Once a water sign finds a style that they are comfortable with, they'll stick to it. Changing their style requires a lot of energy, so it's easier for them to stay with what works.

Don't be surprised if it takes you a little while to get acclimated to a new fashion accessory or style of dressing. If you get the urge, though, do try out something new. You can always go back to your favorite staple items if you are uncomfortable.

Set Good Bathroom Vibes

Make your bathroom into the oasis you deserve! Having the perfect vessel to indulge your watery tendencies is essential for a water sign's self-care. Invest in a deep tub for your bathroom that you can soak in when you are feeling stressed—the deeper and roomier the better. Buy luxurious bubble baths and bath bombs to use when you draw a bath. Additionally, make sure that you have good water pressure for your shower. Lastly, choose bathroom tiles that reflect water themes and colors, such as light blue, white, and green.

Do Nighttime Activities

Some water signs are morning people, but most thrive in the nighttime hours. That's because the night calls to water signs. It is dark and peaceful, and they often feel that they are protected when the sun is down. If you are feeling vulnerable, plan a nighttime activity, such as stargazing, watching fireworks, or going for a simple drive or walk around your neighborhood with a friend. The key is to take some time to appreciate the quiet and calm that come with the evening hours, allowing the shift from chaotic day to tranquil night to ease your mind.

Sail Off to Sleep

Fortunately, water signs tend to fall asleep relatively easily, but they can sometimes become distracted if their environment isn't conducive to sleep. At night it's beneficial to use room-darkening curtains to keep any light from creeping in. Water signs like to sleep in complete darkness, and may even find it difficult to sleep if their room isn't pitch black. Using blackout shades and dark heavy curtains will help make your bedroom cozy and dark, just the way water signs like it. Alternatively, you may consider using a sleeping mask to prevent any light from bothering you while you sleep.

Get Cozy

There's nothing quite like taking a long bath or shower and then snuggling up in a thick bathrobe. For water signs, self-care means pampering yourself with luxury whenever you can. A simple way to do this is to invest in a cozy robe that you can wear after you've washed away any negative emotions from the day. The soft, fluffy material will help you feel safe and protected. If you have the opportunity, consider matching it up with an equally comforting pair of slippers.

Go It Alone

When it comes to sports and leisure, water signs tend to do best with activities that take place outside and don't involve a lot of people. This means that team sports aren't always the best option for you. Water signs should avoid recreational leagues that attract a lot of people. Instead, they do better with low-pressure activities that focus on nature, such as walking, hiking, and climbing. You may find that you, as a water sign, don't really like competition, and there's absolutely nothing wrong with that.

Find an activity out in nature that suits you best. If you feel like you want some company, invite a few trusted friends along to join you.

Buy a Comfort Food Cookbook

Cooking and baking are wonderful outlets for water signs; though when given the choice, they tend to stick to the basics they've already mastered rather than experiment with new recipes. After all, if you have a handful of staple dishes that you know you can create easily and well, why would you want to try something new and risk it tasting terrible? Comfort food in particular appeals to a hungry water sign. Everything from macaroni and cheese to mashed potatoes and pancakes are usually big hits. So, why not keep your experimentation to your preferences, and buy a comfort food cookbook that can help expand your repertoire of recipes a little?

Take an Island Vacation

Indulge the innate connection you have to water by taking a vacation to an island. Being by the water will help recharge your batteries when you are feeling depleted. The warm weather in most tropical locations is perfect for a water sign who is hoping to lounge by the beach or pool and let their worries fade away.

Look for vacation destinations that also include water activities, such as lessons in paddle boarding or snorkeling, to help you connect with your element. If you can swing an all-inclusive resort, you'll get even more bang for your buck, with food, lodging, entertainment, and drinks included.

Find Some Work Privacy

You may have noticed that, as a water sign, you need quiet and privacy to get your work done. When it comes to your job, you will be more productive working in a cubicle or by yourself than in an open-plan office or large group. You tend to get overwhelmed when you have too many people around you, so when you really need to concentrate, try retreating to your own secluded space. This will help keep you away from all the hustle and bustle, and limit your distractions.

When you feel the need to talk to others, a communal kitchen or break room is your ideal space. This is where you can comfortably mingle with coworkers before going back to your cubbyhole to get some work done. If you have a job where a group environment is highly valued, try speaking to your supervisor and letting them know how you work best. You might be surprised by how understanding they will be!

Seek Out a Steam Room

The benefits of a steam room go far beyond simple stress relief. Sitting in a steam room can improve your circulation, ease muscle pain, and help with some skin problems. For water signs, using a steam room is a great way to cleanse the soul and calm the mind. Look to see if a local gym or spa has one you can use. Sit and let the hot steam of the steam room surround you and loosen the stress in your body. If you have any health concerns, check with your doctor first.

Take Ice-Skating Lessons

Even frozen water has a special place in a water sign's heart. Just because you can't see the water moving and hear it lapping doesn't mean it is any less soothing or refreshing! In fact, ice can be invigorating for a water sign. Try embracing your cold side by taking beginners' ice-skating lessons. A number of world-class ice-skaters have been water signs. If you already have had some practice and aren't in the mood for a full lesson, try going to a local skating rink and just skate on your own for a little while. You may find that the smooth cut of the blade over ice soothes you.

Learn a New Concept

Mentally, water signs can understand a whole concept quickly because they intuitively feel it, rather than logically piece it together. The details are not important to them; all they need is to trust their gut and the emotions they are feeling inside. Their empathy is what helps them understand.

Use this superpower by learning something new—topics like philosophy and religion are a great place for water signs to start. These categories often require your ability to grasp a larger concept and understand things at a holistic level, rather than memorize detailed facts and figures. You may even find it beneficial to watch documentaries or listen to lectures in addition to reading a book—whatever sparks your passion!

Try a Boxing Workout

While water signs don't usually respond well to exercises that require a lot of repetition, a boxing workout is definitely an exception. In fact, a few world champion boxers over the years have been water signs. Boxing workouts are a great emotional and physical release if you've been feeling stressed or angry. The power and strength you'll feel when you learn with an expert to kick, punch, and duck properly will keep you coming back to the gym for more. Initially, you may find it difficult to get used to the new motions, but once your body adapts, boxing training is actually a very fluid activity, perfect for water signs! Look into beginners' classes in your local area.

Express Your Feelings

You feel so deeply, water sign, it's only natural that sometimes your emotions spill over and become overwhelming. Water signs are often receptive and inwardly focused. While you are very good at recognizing your feelings, you find it difficult to express them to others. You have trouble articulating what's inside. Instead, you would prefer that your loved ones just understand what you are feeling rather than having to explain it to them.

Practice expressing your emotions by keeping a journal. At night after you've spent the day processing emotions, write down how you feel. If you are struggling with where to begin, start with the words *I feel* and go from there. Once you have got in the habit of describing your emotions on paper, you will find it easier to articulate them in person. Writing your emotions is just the first step; then it is time to express what feels natural.

Take a Walk in the Rain

Some water signs prefer moody, cool, gray weather to bright sunshine. If you have the opportunity, indulge in a rainy day by going for a walk in the rain. Choose a day with a sprinkle of rain, rather than a downpour. Make sure you have the right equipment— every water sign should have a decent raincoat and pair of rain boots. Check the weather forecast often to stay ahead of any potential rainy days.

Keep Photo Memories

Scrapbooks, photo albums, and iPhone picture galleries are all treasures to water signs. They love to flip through their favorite memories and reminisce about old times or relive their happiest moments.

Spend time putting together collections of photos that chronicle each part of your life. You can organize them in whatever way feels right to you. The goal is to make sure you are surrounded by your most cherished memories at all times. You may even consider putting together a photo collage that you can frame and hang on the wall. You can indulge your love of photos even further by creating a scrapbook or online photo book for your loved ones on their birthdays. The personal touch will bring tears and smiles.

Embrace Your Sentimental Side

Whether they are celebrating birthdays, Christmas, or Valentine's Day, water signs love the holidays and any happy occasion. You especially love the sentimentality of tradition. Think about all the ways you can participate in holiday or birthday customs with the people you love. This may mean cooking a special meal for everyone, setting up decorations, or just spending time catching up with family and friends. Use your creative side to start new traditions, and encourage your loved ones to get involved. These rituals will help you feel closer to the people you cherish most.

Make Water a Part of Your Sleep Routine

While many water signs don't have trouble falling asleep, you may find that turning on a sound machine that features the sounds of rain, waves, or running water will make you feel more relaxed when you are drifting off to dreamland. Some water signs find that they are distracted by their emotions when they are trying to go to sleep. They replay things that happened throughout the day and relive how those things made them feel instead of quieting their minds. Sound machines can help focus your mind and ward off any distractions. Simply breathe deeply and listen to the sounds around you, and you'll be asleep in no time.

Stay Grounded

It is important for water signs to live close to water (or visit it as often as possible) as a way of staying grounded. A view of some body of water from your home window will orient you and keep you stable, especially when you are feeling vulnerable or overwhelmed by your emotions. Seeing water can bring balance to your life that you would otherwise miss. The closer you can get to the water, the better. Watch out for high-rise apartments, though, even if they have a great view of water in the distance. Being up high can make water signs feel lost and aimless, as if they had no roots.

Decorate with Ocean Hues

Your home is a reflection of who you are and what you love. Water signs need a calming and soothing environment to thrive in, and the first way to accomplish this is to surround yourself with colors that are reminiscent of water. Look for muted, cool tones like light blue, gray, and deep green, accented with splashes of vibrant, warm colors like red and orange. You may even want to try painting a mural or pattern that makes you think of water on one of your walls. Above all, your home should be comfortable and familiar to you. Use color to make it your own.

Buy an Aquarium

Just because you don't live right next to a body of water doesn't mean you can't make the aquatic a part of your everyday life. One of the easiest ways to bring the ocean home is to invest in an aquarium. As a water sign, you'll find solace in the cool blue ripples of the water and the fluid movement of the fish swimming by. It's true that keeping a healthy aquarium does require research, advice from experts, money, and time, but the cost is well worth the benefits you'll see almost instantly in your mood.

Create Your Own Water Feature

Running water is soothing to water signs at work and at home. Purchase a small water fountain that you can keep near your desk at work to help you through stressful moments. When you are feeling overwhelmed, take a few moments to focus on the sound of the water and nothing else. You can leave the fountain running all day to help keep you feeling balanced and calm. If you have space at home, purchase another water fountain for your living room, or wherever you spend the most time. The trickling water will keep you company whenever you need it. Spending time outdoors is also beneficial for water signs, so look for a water fountain that can be set up on a deck or in your backyard.

Don't Go to the Desert

Dry climates don't suit water signs well. You need to feel moisture in the air in order to breathe easy. While it's not advisable for water signs to live in a dry climate like the desert, if you do, there are certain things you can try to keep the air around you moist. The easiest is to research and purchase a humidifier for your home and run it as needed. This will significantly improve the quality of the air.

You can also look for an essential oil diffuser that uses water, which not only adds a little moisture to the air, but also diffuses essential oils to impact your mood. Experiment with different scents to find the one that is right for you.

Skip the Spicy Foods

Water signs can be picky when it comes to their diet and nutrition. For example, they often don't like spicy food and tend to stick to more muted cuisines, with the exception of salami and cured meats. The salty taste of these treats appeals to them. In fact, you may find you have more cravings for salty foods than sweet foods. That's not to say you don't like something sweet every now and again. A small piece of candy or baked good is all you need. Water signs also love carbs and will never pass up a piece of pizza when offered; though they are partial to pizza with meat toppings instead of vegetable toppings. So listen to your body, consider skipping the spicy, and choose the foods that most appeal to your taste buds and your nutritional needs. Bon appétit!

Stay Away from Strong Scents

Have you ever noticed that you are very sensitive to scents and often get headaches or feel nauseated when you are around heavy perfumes or colognes? Water signs have a very keen sense of smell, which can be a superpower, but also a hindrance at times. To avoid being overloaded with an offending smell, it's best for you to avoid sharing elevators or enclosed spaces with anyone wearing a heavy scent. It will stick to your clothes and linger around you all day. You should especially stay away from the perfume section in any department stores!

Cherish Family Heirlooms

Family is very important to you as a water sign. You take comfort in the familial connections you have, and take pride in your loyalty to family no matter what. Because of this, your bond to your family only grows stronger day by day.

Every family is unique and has their own collection of heirlooms that are passed down from generation to generation. Display your own family heirlooms proudly. They are a special link to your ancestors and show off who you truly are.

Surround Yourself with Succulents

Succulents are some of the easiest plants to care for—some can grow well in indoor environments and require less frequent watering. These are the perfect plants for a busy water sign. A jade succulent is a particularly popular choice—it is known as the lucky tree, or the money tree, and needs very little care to thrive. The color of the flowers that bloom from the plant can be either pink or white. Not only are succulents beautiful to look at, but surrounding yourself with green is a great way to reduce stress and create a calming, nurturing environment. Succulents can also increase productivity and concentration, so consider placing one near your workstation as well.

Meditate Alone

Spiritual practices such as meditation are best done alone for water signs. That's because meditation is a time of emotional vulnerability, and water signs are highly sensitive to other people's energies. If you are meditating with a group, you may inadvertently absorb other people's feelings rather than focus on your own. Instead, find a comfortable, private area where you can let your guard down and feel safe. Make sure your meditation spot is relaxing and inviting, with a soft seat and soothing ambience. It may help to listen to quiet music or put on a sound machine to keep you focused.

Chase Your Wanderlust

Sticking close to home is a comfort for many water signs. It's okay to prefer staying in to going out, but you should try to challenge your homebody habit by booking a trip somewhere far away every now and again. You may initially feel anxious about being away from home, but the excitement of seeing far-off, different lands may outweigh the discomfort. The good news is, as long as the room you stay in while traveling is comfortable, you'll be able to feel safe. Water signs just need a secure place to rest their heads, and they'll be able to enjoy new places without too much worry.

Adopt a Dog or Cat

The world is broken up into dog people and cat people. While there are many people who enjoy both types of domesticated animals, they usually prefer one over the other. Water signs are definitely more cat people, but have been known to fall in love with small dogs as well.

Cats are independent and curious, traits that water signs appreciate. Small dogs can be outgoing and rambunctious (depending on their breed), also characteristics that appeal to a sometimes moody water sign. The key for water signs is finding a small animal to share your space with, one that fits well into the home you've already created for yourself. Just make sure to get expert advice on adopting (and properly caring for) your chosen pet from a local animal shelter before you commit.

Spend Time with a Small Group of Loved Ones

Even though water signs are homebodies, they do like to socialize when the environment is just right. This usually means hanging out with a small group of close family members or friends. Water signs need to be surrounded by people they trust to feel comfortable enough to kick back and relax. There is just a different atmosphere when you all know each other well!

If you aren't in the mood to venture out beyond your front door, consider inviting your friends or family over for a small dinner party where you can all enjoy one another's company and speak candidly about your thoughts and emotions. This is a water sign's dream get-together!

Enjoy an Outdoor Concert

Live music is invigorating for many water signs. While being in crowds can sometimes be overwhelming for them, the positive energy of the music can help them overcome that discomfort. There's nothing quite like singing along to one of your favorite songs live. Surrender to the spirit of the music and let it permeate your being.

If you have the opportunity, look for an outdoor concert where you can combine your love of nature with the power of live music. During the summer months, you'll find outdoor music shows popping up all over the place that attract a variety of fans. Find one that speaks to your unique musical taste!

Attend the Opera

As a water sign, you are driven by emotion and feeling. This is why you may feel such an inherent draw toward the performing arts, like dance and theater. Indulge this love by attending an opera performance in your area. Opera presents a vivid story through the power of song and language, and it can be an opportunity to dress up in your classiest wear and enjoy a night out.

Attending the opera can be a very emotional experience for the audience, so bring your tissues, water sign!

Embrace Your Love of History

Water signs love to travel to different times in their imaginations—that's why historical fiction is the perfect genre for this literary sign. Why not turn that love of different time periods into an excuse to actually visit those historical sites?

Make a list of sites that you have always wanted to see, and start visiting. Studying history requires that you imagine yourself in the same situations as the people of that time. As a water sign, you are incredibly empathetic and understanding, so this skill probably comes easily to you. Use it to your advantage and relive some of the most important moments in history with your own eyes.

Trust Yourself

Do you sometimes find that you intuitively know what time it is without even checking your watch or phone? That's because water signs—when they are at their best—have a great internal sense of time. During those periods, you're probably often early to your appointments, and don't even need to set an alarm to wake up in the morning.

Learn to trust your intuition more in all parts of your life, not just when it comes to being on time. As a water sign, you can usually trust your gut instinct. You have a talent for reading situations and people through how you feel. This is a strength that you can rely on. Don't second-guess yourself so much—learn to listen to that voice in your mind. It's usually right!

Try Cognitive Behavioral Therapy

While water signs have a lot of emotions swirling around inside, classic therapy might not work for them. They don't like to get too stuck living in the past, mulling over things that have already happened. To them, the past is a bottomless well of memory. When it comes to talking about their feelings, they prefer to focus on targeted problems. However, they can certainly benefit from the journey.

If you are considering therapy, ask your doctor for recommendations, and then look around for a therapist who understands exactly what you are looking to get out of your sessions. Cognitive behavioral therapy (CBT) is one approach that works for many people; it can be used to target problem-specific areas in your life. It may take some trial and error, but eventually you'll find the right professional and right approach for you.

Depend On Your Water Friends

Sometimes, in order to really work through a problem, you need to turn to someone who just intuitively understands you. For water signs, this means seeking out other water signs. They are usually just as good at listening as you are, and they can help you work through whatever is going on in your life at the time. Since water signs are so sympathetic, they will always be around to lend an ear when you need it. It is important for water signs to support one another, especially when it comes to their emotional health and balance.

Chant Your Way to Calm

As a water sign, you may become easily overwhelmed by a lot of noise, but chanting may have the reverse effect on you if you are looking to relax and zen out. For centuries Buddhist monks have used chanting as a way to prepare the mind for meditation. You, too, can use this ritual to find peace. Repetitive chanting often mimics the ebb and flow of water, something that innately pleases water signs. Try researching a few chants that you can use in the comfort of your own home. When you are ready to meditate, start chanting, and repeat the words over and over again until a sense of calm sweeps over you.

Meditate with Blue Lace Agate

Employing the help of the right crystal at the right time can do wonders for balancing your energy and emotions. Look for crystals that are reminiscent of the ocean, such as blue lace agate. Blue lace agate can calm anxiety and worry, perfect for when you feel the stresses of daily life overwhelming you. When you are meditating, hold the crystal in your hand or close to your heart. Use its energy and power to achieve your goals and calm your fearful thoughts, no matter what they are.

Explore Your Artistic Side

Water signs are instinctively very artistic. Tap into your creative side by trying a new craft, such as watercolor painting. Watercolors are a more forgiving medium for novice painters than oil paints. Try painting ocean scenes, waterfalls, or lakes. The act of painting can be very soothing for the artist. If you are struggling at first, you may find it helps to look at an image to replicate as you paint, or purchase an acrylic paint-by-numbers kit. Once you've gotten the hang of brushstrokes and color blending, you can create an original piece.

Show Off Another Time Period

If you love a particular historical period, consider decorating part of your home with objects from that era. Because of their empathetic abilities, water signs are able to build worlds in their minds that they can visit every now and again. Bridge the gap between your reality and imagination by surrounding yourself with objects that remind you of another time and place. You could create an American Civil War room, an ancient Egyptian room, or a Viking room.

If you are more in love with a certain place than a time period, apply the same principle. Collect objects from that area and put them on display.

Hone Your Photography Skills

As a water sign, you have incredible observation skills and an eye for beauty. This makes you the ideal photographer. You are able to identify poignancy in any scene, and isolate it with the perfect shot. You also love to keep copies of all the photographs you take so you can revisit these moments whenever you want.

To enhance your photography skills, consider investing in a high-quality camera with digital capabilities. This way you can have a digital record of your work, in addition to prints. Before you purchase, do some research to find out which camera will be best for you and your skill level.

Pamper Yourself with a Hydrating Facial

Pampering yourself is essential for any self-care routine. For water signs, this means spending time focusing on their outer appearance as well as their inner wellness. Dedicate time to indulging yourself with a hydrating facial—perfect for a water sign! These facials are great for increasing circulation in your facial muscles and moisturizing the skin. They can also decrease puffiness and slow the formation of wrinkles.

If you don't have the budget to pay for a spa-level facial, you can always try at-home hydrating masks. Many of these masks are made from ingredients that are already in your pantry or refrigerator, such as cucumber. Research which kind of ingredients will work best for your skin type.

Flavor Your Water

You already know that drinking enough water is one key to good health, but this is especially true for water signs. You need to ingest enough water every day to keep your body strong. Staying hydrated doesn't have to be boring, though. Hydrating with water is by far the best option, but you can spice things up by adding a few ingredients to make your own flavored water. Try stirring in a few strawberries or raspberries, or just add a splash of lemon juice or cucumbers to your water pitcher. Not only do these ingredients brighten the flavor of your water, but many of them have antioxidant properties that can boost your immune system.

Protect Yourself from Energy Vampires

Water signs feel deeply and can easily be drained by emotionally manipulative people. Trust your gut when it comes to those you spend your time with. If you find that someone is particularly toxic to you or you feel that your energy is depleted after seeing them, consider removing them from your life. As a water sign, you need to care for your emotional wellness and protect yourself against energy vampires. If you are feeling particularly vulnerable, try carrying around a piece of rose quartz to buffer against negativity. Wearing the crystal as a necklace near your heart is even better.

Write a Short Story

Your imagination is expansive. As a water sign, you have the gift of creation, seamlessly moving between reality and the made-up worlds in your mind. Some of the best writers working today are water signs, so try putting your visions down on paper and sharing them with the world. Start small by writing a short story, or even just the beginning paragraphs of a larger project. Live inside your own imagination for a while and see what comes forth. Remember that not every sentence you write needs to be perfect. Just focus on expressing your ideas, and you can go back and revise what you've already written later on.

Volunteer Remotely

In nature, inactive water becomes stagnant and attracts bacteria. Water needs to run, gurgle, babble, and sway. Water signs are the same way. Doing nothing can make a water sign feel useless and bored. To quench your desire to be active and helpful, volunteer at an organization that you care about deeply. There are organizations online that will help you pair your skills with an appropriate organization. Some positions might involve you working from home and volunteering remotely. For you, being active doesn't have to always mean moving your body; it also means spending your time meaningfully. These small acts can change the world!

Join a (Small) Club

Water signs love to be included in groups—even though they can sometimes get overwhelmed by too many people. The sense of belonging is important for them to feel appreciated and loved. The key for you as a water sign is to find a small group that focuses on something you really love. This could be a book club that meets once a month, a cooking class, or a wildlife club that goes on adventures in nature. There will be no shortage of interesting conversation; you'll find loads to talk about with people who share your loves.

Re-Create Your Dreams

Water signs have notoriously vivid dreams that stick with them after waking. You may even dream of future events, or have trouble deciphering if what happened was a dream or reality.

Try using your dreams as a creative source, and re-create them in whichever way seems most appropriate. Many song-writers and artists have said their inspiration comes from their dreams. On waking, spend some time focusing on and remembering your dreams. Then, use them as a prompt to write, as a picture to re-create, or as a melody to build upon. Use your vivid dreams to express your artistic side!

Feel the Positive Vibrations from Water

Since water signs feel at home near bodies of water, it makes sense for them to pick up pieces of those water sources with them wherever they go. Start collecting stones, rocks, or shells from every body of water you visit. The energy of the water will stay within these objects and help keep you balanced when you are on dry land. When you are feeling lost, sit quietly and hold each object in your hands. Feel the positive vibrations radiating from them. If you'd like, you can create an altar of your water objects in your bedroom to help attract calm thoughts while you drift off to dreamland. Or, when you need an energy boost, put one in your purse or pocket so you can hold it whenever you want as you go about your day.

PART 3

Self-Care by Sign

* ✳ *

CHAPTER 7

Self-Care for Aries

Dates: March 21–April 19
Element: Fire
Polarity: Yang
Quality: Cardinal
Symbol: Ram
Ruler: Mars

Not only is Aries the first fire sign, but it is the first sign of the zodiac. The astrological calendar begins with the vernal equinox (usually about March 21), and all of the astrological signs are calculated from this date, which is called the Aries Ingress. The vernal equinox also marks the beginning of the renewal holidays of Easter and Passover, which is interesting when you consider that the images of the ram or the Paschal Lamb figure strongly in both the Jewish and Christian traditions. The Ram, with his beautiful curled horns, is also Aries's symbol. The ram was also identified with the Egyptian god Ammon, and in Greek mythology, Phrixus sacrificed a winged golden ram (the bearer of the Golden Fleece) to Zeus. As a reward for this sacrifice, Zeus placed the ram in the heavens as the constellation Aries.

In Greek mythology, the god of war was Ares, and he was known for his hot temper, aggressive fighting, and skills in weaponry. In Roman mythology his name was Mars. Although he had a quieter and more complex reputation than Ares, he was still ruled by the red planet.

Like all fire signs, Aries is an extrovert and delights in expressing his power. All of the four cardinal signs of the zodiac that begin the seasons are very active, but Aries leads the group in terms of the sheer amount of energy he has available. However, Aries's energy is not concentrated, nor can it be easily tamed. He tends to begin many projects but complete few.

As soon as his enthusiasm wanes, he is on to another idea or quest. The challenge for this sign in life and in terms of self-care is containing and channeling his fiery gift. As the first sign, Aries is just beginning to develop his personality and soul qualities. This childlike enthusiasm that Aries has is the source of his energy. He is boundlessly interested in seeing what he can do in the world and thrives on variety and activity. He delights in expressing himself. Aries is self-centered in a charming but sometimes abrasive way. These are not negative soul qualities, just Aries's energy playing with the fire of creation. For others who are not filled with this spirit, Aries can be very irritating. He is impatient and quick to anger, and he has no qualms in walking out of a room when bored or disenchanted with something. Aries, in the main, cannot be directed.

An Aries can become a timid sheep, but the spark of an idea or project that really interests him is enough to fan the flames and get him back to his fire power. A subdued Aries needs to be encouraged. He is trying to balance his native energy with an imposed idea of what would be nice or good. This problem can be especially pronounced with a female Aries, as she feels the yang fire but might be reluctant to express it for fear of not being perceived as "feminine." This dichotomy was more pronounced in other generations, but the split can still exist today. Fortunately, there are now many ways that the Aries girl or woman can assertively express herself.

Self-Care and Aries

Aries rarely thinks about taking care of himself until something sidelines him. Perhaps it is an injury or illness, as Aries can be accident prone. When and if such a bump occurs, the best way for Aries to get back on track is an appeal to his sense of competition and physical fitness. Aries needs a healthy body that can respond to his energy demands—and he needs it right away. Aries usually heals very quickly because he is so impatient. He is also inspired by the spiritual gains of a healthy mind, body, and spirit. His intuition works much better when he is healthy.

The best way to approach self-care for Aries is to make the program quick. Using apps to monitor exercise, calories, and any other measurement of health is a good way to get Aries keen on taking care of himself. If Aries decides to go on a diet, his first step is to find a program with food that tastes flavorful. Tabasco sauce, garlic powder, and horseradish are Aries-ruled and can keep his taste buds engaged while he sheds pounds.

Aries Rules the Head

Each zodiac sign rules a part of the body. Aries rules the head, skull, face, and sinus passages, which relates to his headstrong nature. It is especially important for Aries to protect this vulnerable area of the body. However, it may take a few near collisions or accidents to convince Aries that headgear is important. He prefers to be free, and only experience will encourage him to pursue safety first.

Aries can suffer from headaches, which are usually a sign that he is damming up his vital energy and overthinking what comes naturally. He is also prone to sinus problems, which are partially environmental/seasonal and which can thwart Aries's usual buoyancy. Like all the fire signs, Aries rushes through these problems until they hamper his fun and enthusiasm. Then, the idea of self-care becomes an immediate and necessary requirement. For any physical imbalances Aries may have, acupuncture can be a very good therapy—especially for headaches. The needles could be thought of as a "weapon" to reroute the energy traffic in Aries's system.

Psychological self-care for Aries is a bit more complex. Aries is just developing his personality. His naive and eternally youthful enthusiasm for life can appear abrupt. He doesn't think before he acts and this may make others angry. Aries is always stupefied when this happens because he doesn't really know what he did wrong. Conventional therapy usually is not effective for Aries, because he is too busy getting on with life to contemplate the past or parse out why a relationship or event turned sour. His MO is to move on quickly and try again. Therapy apps may come in handy here, as well as talk therapy conducted over the phone. The exchange between therapist and client is often brief, but can be effective. This can help Aries to sort out his energy and to improve his communication skills.

Aries and Self-Care Success

The pitfall for Aries's self-care program is any time things become too complicated. Aries needs a direct goal and a clear way to achieve it; otherwise, he is likely to say, "I'm out of here!" Additionally, any activity that requires psychological subtlety with complex communication and emotions is a total downer for Aries. This sign is not superficial, but Aries is not interested in exploring shades of meaning. Rather, he operates in a direct line of action: "I want to do this, so I do it." And if someone or something gets in the way, Aries either says that it isn't worth it or that tomorrow is another day.

Aries is at his best when pioneering new projects, and, when executed correctly, a self-care program can be an experience he relishes. His pursuit in taking care of himself is based on development of energy coordination, conservation of energy, and completion. This is his soul mission. When these goals align, he feels all the excitement of a child opening a gift—and there is no better gift than taking a vested interest in lifelong wellness. The best way to ensure wellness is by making self-care a priority in life, so let's take a look at some self-care activities that are tailored specifically for Aries.

Find a Bike Trail

As a fire sign, Aries thrives on heat and energy, so spending active time outside on a warm summer day is an ideal way to practice both physical and emotional self-care at the same time. Look for a bike path in a natural park nearby. Taking a relaxing bike ride is a great way to release the problems on your mind. Use the energy of the sun to recharge and reconnect with yourself. Clear your mind of all of the stress that's been following you and just focus on the road ahead, literally and metaphorically. But be careful! The head is ruled by Aries, so be sure to protect it with a sturdy helmet.

Try a Neti Pot

A stuffed or runny nose is miserable for anyone, but Aries is especially bothered since he is ruled by the head. When you're dealing with a head cold, it's time to slow down, rest, and drink plenty of fluids.

You might also find that a neti pot can help flush out your blocked nasal passages. A neti pot is a small teapot-like vessel that you fill with sterile water to make an irrigation solution. Stand over a sink and pour the solution into one nostril. The liquid should flow through your nasal passages and out the other nostril, clearing out mucus and freeing up the cilia that line your nasal cavities. (Be sure to follow the specific directions and irrigation solution guidelines on your neti pot.) It might be just what you need to restore yourself to good health.

Practice Aerial Yoga for Flexibility

Aries is an intense sign who loves to burn up his excess energy with a heavy workout. But stiff, bulky muscles can lead to injuries, and Aries doesn't want to be slowed down.

Get those muscles loose by practicing some aerial yoga. A relatively new form of yoga, the fluid movements and routines of aerial yoga (yoga practiced in a suspended sling) can stretch your muscles to attain greater flexibility and body control while helping to build core strength.

Find some beginners' classes near you to learn the basic moves and safety considerations before jumping in too far. There are many varieties of practice, so do some research to find the one that is right for you. You'll find yourself getting a great full-body workout that uses your Aries energy to boost your flexibility and balance—while appealing to your sense of adventure.

Punch It Out!

Aries can be a determined sign and, like the Ram that represents it, you may use this trait to push your way to success in pretty much everything you try. However, this level of intensity isn't always a good thing for your health or overall well-being. Take care of yourself by getting all that tension and intensity, and any residual anger, out of your system...by taking some swings at a punching bag!

Get some tips from an expert, and then pretend you're punching that frustrating work project, the coffee shop that never gets your order right, or that computer that crashed right before you were about to send your email. This type of physical self-care will get your heart rate up—perfect for a fire sign!—and you'll be able to clear your head and focus on what's really important: you!

Go for a Fast Run

Aries is fueled by the power of Mars, which means you're an energetic go-getter. If you're feeling overwhelmed or stressed out, try heading out for a run. A slow jog probably won't do much for Aries—you'll want something fast-paced, because the more you sweat, the better you'll feel! To keep your runs from getting boring, create upbeat playlists, buy new workout clothes, and check out new trails periodically. Your Aries determination will love the challenge of a tough run, and you'll end up with a stronger body and a clearer mind.

Running is a great way to re-center yourself after a harried day—think of it as a meditative experience, and focus on your breathing and any beautiful scenery around you.

Throw Darts to Relieve Stress

Darts aren't just for dingy barrooms—they are a perfect game for Aries. Ruled by the war god Mars, Aries presides over sharp objects—and throwing darts is a great way to release any pent-up negative energy you have. Hang a dartboard in your office, in your garage, or in an outside space. You can find a dartboard to fit any aesthetic preference, from the traditional red and green style to a modern version with artwork on its face. As you get ready to play, take several deep breaths and recite a simple mantra like "This too shall pass" several times to quiet your mind. Then point your dart, and see how close you get to the bull's-eye!

Tap Dance

If you're getting bored with your current exercise routine, try tapping! The percussive sounds of tap dancing are well suited to Aries's extroverted yang energy. If you're new to tap, don't worry—Aries's fearlessness and determination will ensure that you're brave enough to join a class and learn in no time. Many dance studios offer beginners' adult classes in the evening, so grab a friend and pop into one. You'll work up a sweat dancing to the cheerful tunes and forget your worries at the same time. This invigorating dance style is also infectious and fun—you'll find your toes tapping even outside the class.

Bang on the Bongos

Aries is represented by the Ram, and rams are known for butting things with their horns to get what they want. You may not have horns, but you do have hands—and you can use them to pound on a drum to change your mood and release stress.

Percussion instruments align well with Aries's outgoing, vibrant nature, and it's easy to get started playing simple drums like the bongos. Look for a class at a local arts center and lose yourself in that irresistible beat. Bongos can create many different types of music—so experiment with both energizing and upbeat options, and steady and relaxing ones.

Stand Up Tall

Even the most confident Aries can have moments of doubt. At those times your body language probably reflects your mood—you might be slouched, slumped, or hunched. Recharge yourself by taking a moment to focus on adjusting your posture. Stand up very straight and put your hands on your hips. Look straight ahead and take three slow, deep breaths. Sometimes acting as if you're confident can get your mind to believe it. This simple yet effective exercise has an amazing ability to reframe your mind-set, restore your self-confidence, and reclaim your leading Ram qualities!

Give Yourself Space to Think

Aries's busy mind and body are always working—but they need emotional and physical space to do their best work. Give yourself the physical freedom to thrive by walking around your home or office while you think. Pacing keeps your body busy, and Aries loves thinking in motion. See if your furniture could be pushed against the wall to open up some space. If your home or office doesn't have the space you need, take a break and move around outside. You will find yourself more relaxed and more productive as a result.

Wear Fun Baseball Caps

Everyone should protect themselves from the sun's rays with hats—but it's especially important for Aries, who rules the head. This self-care act can do wonders for your skin health. Instead of straw hats, try fun baseball hats instead! They're more likely to match your energetic personality. Though red is Aries's signature color, you can experiment with any colors or styles of baseball hat to match your preferences. You can also look for hats with words or phrases that align with your passions and interests. If typical baseball hats tend to make your head too hot, look for breathable, moisture-wicking fabrics.

Clear Out Stale Energy with Sage

Sometimes energy can linger, even after a person or influence has left a space. If someone left positive energy in your home, that's great! But if the energy that remains is negative or stale, it's time to cleanse the space and restore positive energy to your home. Burning sage is a time-honored Native American practice that clears energy—and it's simple and easy to do.

First, purchase some ceremonial sage (not the type found in the spice aisle at grocery stores). Second, tidy up any obvious clutter and open as many doors and windows as possible in your home. Finally, place the sage in a fireproof bowl and light it. Blow it out and use your hands to direct the smoke around your home. Both your body and your home will feel more open, more relaxed, and more balanced.

Rethink Your Bed Placement

According to the Chinese art of feng shui, the placement of your bed can impact your health and well-being. You likely spend a good chunk of your 24-hour day in bed, so you might as well make the most of it.

Set up your bed so that your head faces east and your feet west as you sleep. If it's comfortable for you, sleeping toward the east is the most beneficial direction for Aries. If you have a window in the east, the rays of the rising sun can gently wake you in the morning, ensuring a relaxing and calm start to your day.

Spice It Up!

Aries is passionate, adventurous, and energetic—and your diet should reflect those traits. To make sure that it does, nourish your body and mind with a range of healthy whole foods seasoned with various spices. To avoid falling into a rut, change up your spice choices and combinations frequently. Whether you pair classics like garlic and basil or rosemary and thyme, or branch out and create a new mixture all your own, your taste buds will thank you. Try out various spice combinations on the vegetables and proteins in your diet for meals that will satisfy and energize you.

Use Iron Cookware

Mars, which rules Aries, is aligned with metals like iron, so it makes sense that you would benefit from using iron pans when you cook. Their durability, versatility, and high-quality makeup means that they're a practical choice as well. After you season a cast-iron skillet, it becomes nonstick, and is perfect for sautéing the spicy mixtures that Aries likes. Cast-iron pans also transfer seamlessly from stove top to oven, so they can accommodate a wide range of recipes. Sauté your favorite protein in a fiery spice combination in your cast-iron pan, and you'll be a believer in no time.

Savor Saffron in Your Dishes

Sharp and tangy saffron is a wonderful spice for the fiery Aries. Saffron comes from crocuses, the first flowers of spring, and is therefore associated with Aries's season as well.

This spice pairs well with such varied foods as apples, lamb, seafood, and citrus fruits, and it is known for being a foundational flavor in classic paella (which you can make in an Aries-friendly cast-iron pan!) and risotto dishes. Saffron is expensive, but treating yourself to it once in a while is a worthy indulgence. Slow down and savor the exquisite flavors as you enjoy your meal.

Refresh Yourself with a Watercress Salad

A midday salad can do wonders for your body and mind—it's a light meal that keeps you fueled but doesn't weigh you down. But boring iceberg lettuce can get old quickly for Aries. Instead, try a dark, leafy green watercress salad—its peppery flavors suit Aries's fiery tastes. Plus, it packs a powerful nutritional punch—watercress contains lots of vitamin K (which helps with bone health and blood clotting) and vitamin A (which supports skin health, boosts immunity, and improves vision), and is also a source of calcium, manganese, and potassium. Eat the salad slowly and mindfully so you can relish the intense flavors you're experiencing.

Visit a Thai Restaurant

If your fridge is empty and you've had a busy week, it's time to relax and let someone else do the cooking. Consider heading out to a local Thai place once a month for a fragrant and filling meal.

Thai food in particular is great for Aries's passion for boldness, so grab a friend and indulge in a meal that appeals to all of your senses. You'll find your Aries enthusiasm fired up with the intensely delicious flavors of dried chilies, coriander, ginger, star anise, and even sriracha. Choose your favorite classic dish, or try one of the restaurant's new options for a contemporary twist.

Create a Sanctuary for Sleep

If you often have trouble falling asleep or staying asleep, you might want to examine the mirrors in your bedroom. Feng shui teaches that mirrors can make anxiety worse, and can bounce energy around a room in a frenetic way. Unfortunate mirror placement in a bedroom can therefore lead to an unpleasant sleeping environment.

To be sure your mirrors aren't causing stress or sleeplessness, do not place mirrors so they are facing your bed. You shouldn't be able to see your reflection in a mirror while lying in bed.

Boost Your Immune System with Garlic

Your immune system is responsible for keeping all of your body's systems functioning at their best, so it's important to take good care of it. You can do that by getting plenty of rest, eating a healthy diet of whole foods, and drinking lots of water. You can also turn to an ingredient that has been proven to increase the number of T cells (which fight off disease) in your blood and help you recover from colds faster: garlic. Garlic is also associated with the planet Mars, which rules Aries, so it's an especially good fit for the Ram.

Garlic is a very versatile seasoning—it pairs well with many different foods, and you can make its flavor sharper or more mellow depending on your personal preference. (If you're worried about your breath, just chew a little parsley after you eat!)

Sip Ginger Tea

Even high-energy Aries needs to relax sometimes! Make your moments of relaxation delicious by sipping on some restorative ginger tea as you recharge and reboot. This hot-blooded fire sign typically loves spice, both in his food and in his life, and the subtle heat of the ginger will help keep Aries warm, well-rested, and rejuvenated.

Try making homemade ginger tea: Simply peel and slice a 2-inch section of fresh ginger, and then boil the slices in 1½ to 2 cups (12 to 16 fluid ounces) of water for 10 minutes (for a milder tea) to 20 minutes (for stronger tea). Use the time while the water is boiling to meditate or visualize yourself in a peaceful scene. Remove from heat, strain to remove the ginger, and add honey if desired.

Decorate Your Home with Chinese Ginger Jars

Ginger is a powerful spice that matches Aries's passion for intense flavors. Try storing ginger in a ginger jar, and protect your spice while adding beautiful décor to your home. Chinese ginger jars are painted with elaborate and intricate designs (often in the color blue, but available in other colors too) such as flowers, dragons, and landscapes. The jars vary in size but usually have rounded tops and small openings. They make a visually interesting addition to any kitchen shelf. They're so beautiful that you might find yourself building a small collection!

Relax with Incense

After a long, busy day, it can be hard for the energetic Aries to unwind. If you're feeling restless and your mind is racing, try to quiet it with some deep breathing while you enjoy incense burning. Choose any type of incense you like, but look for an incense burner made of tiger's eye or malachite. Both of these stones are associated with Aries and are very compatible with Aries's personality.

As you breathe in the smell of the incense, gaze at the stone burners and reap the additional self-care benefits: the deep brown and orange tiger's eye is known to help concentration and decrease anxiety, and it's associated with the health of the nose, which is ruled by Aries. Malachite's stunning green swirls help you push out of everyday sadness and find new growth and progress.

Soothe Sore Muscles with Arnica

Aries likes to put his all into everything he does. Whether it's a morning run, a work project, or a volunteer position, Aries gives 100 percent all the time. All that dedication can lead to sore muscles once in a while—legs that burn from a run, tense shoulders and neck from a long day at the office, or a sore back from an afternoon of hard work. That soreness is your body telling you to slow down and heal. Try rubbing arnica cream or gel (which comes from a yellow daisy-like flower) into your muscles and joints; it comes in cream or gel forms. Arnica can stimulate circulation and decrease inflammation, thus relieving your pain.

Treat Yourself to a Cardamom Coffee

A morning cup of coffee is almost a ritual unto itself: a quiet kitchen, a beautiful mug, the mesmerizing swirl of the steam. Kick your morning cup up a notch by adding a small amount of cardamom to your coffee. This spice, used frequently in Middle Eastern cooking, is an Aries favorite because of its bold herbal and piquant flavors. High-quality cardamom is expensive, so only indulge once in a while in small amounts. Savor the unique combination of coffee and cardamom as you contemplate your day.

Host a Henna Party

Perhaps one of the most effective types of self-care is to relax and talk with good friends. There's just no substitute for casual, meandering conversations, abundant laughter, and heartfelt, genuine connections. The next time your group gets together, consider making it a henna party.

Henna is a natural reddish-brown plant dye that you can paint on your skin to create temporary body art (henna should not be black or contain any unsafe added chemicals). In the Middle East (an Aries-ruled area), people often celebrate gatherings by painting amazingly intricate designs on their face and hands with henna. If you've never created henna patterns before, search online for how-to instructions and add a new dimension to your nights in with friends.

Boost Productivity with a Mirror

Aries loves to be in command. Watching himself taking charge is a very effective way to maintain self-confidence and boost productivity. Try hanging a mirror in front of your desk, at home or at work, so you can see your whole face and head. The power of watching yourself thrive while you work does wonders for your emotional health—don't be surprised if you start coming up with even more amazing ideas than before. Plus, no one can sneak up on you!

Decorate Your Desk with a Single Flower

Being stuck inside all day working can wear down the adventurous Aries. Bring a little bit of nature inside by placing a single flower in a vase on your desk. Because red is your natural color, look for a red bird-of-paradise, gerbera daisy, or poppy. Not only are these stunning flower choices visually interesting, but they'll also keep you upbeat and energetic as you go through your workday. When the color or petals begin to fade, replace the flower with a new one.

Rest Easy with Green Malachite

Green malachite is associated with Aries, and it's a gorgeous stone with many amazing properties. While toxic in its unfinished state, when polished and finished, it is commonly used in the creation of figurines or jewelry. Malachite is a protective stone that can cleanse your energy and the energy of the space it's in. It's also a stone that can bring with it good fortune and wealth. Green malachite is especially useful near your bed because it can stimulate positive dreams and bring vivid memories to life. Restful sleep is a vital part of self-care, and sleeping next to green malachite will ensure that you wake up restored and refreshed.

Add a Splash of Color and Sound with a Cinnabar Bracelet

Your signature color of bold red lends itself well to accents in your wardrobe. Try out cinnabar bracelets (for men and women) for a distinctive and multisensory option. Traditional cinnabar bracelets were made with a red mineral that contained mercury. Nowadays, thankfully, they're made with lacquered wood, and are carved with intricate designs. When you wear two or more together, they click and clack against each other, making a light percussive sound that's appealing to Aries. Wearing them will make you feel dynamic, confident, and unique!

Use Bergamot Oil to Fall Asleep Fast

If you tend to toss and turn before you fall asleep, it may be time to reevaluate your bedtime routine. If you are typically looking at a screen right before trying to sleep, you're inadvertently stimulating your mind, not quieting it. Instead, try meditating, reading a book, or writing in a journal for several minutes before you shut off the light. Another tactic that's especially effective for Aries is putting a few drops of bergamot oil on your pillow before you go to bed (diluted according to instructions). Bergamot is the oil in Earl Grey tea and is

aligned with Aries. Its relaxing and calming qualities will help prepare you for a night of peaceful rest.

Re-Center Yourself with Patchouli

Aries's active mind and body can be hard to slow down. But sometimes taking a few quiet moments to recharge will help you be more productive and energetic going forward. Aromatherapy is a great resource for re-centering, because it encourages you to slow down and breathe deeply.

Try applying some patchouli scent to your temples when you need to find balance. The strong, musky scent is a good match for Aries's assertive personality. Take several deep breaths and relax while you massage the oil (diluted according to instructions) into your temples. Then get ready to take on whatever task awaits you.

Escape to the Desert

Some people think of clear waters and white sand when they think of vacations, but Aries might also want to consider another destination. The wide sky and intense heat of the desert is a perfect match for Aries's fiery personality. The expansiveness of the desert is also a reminder of the infinite possibilities of the world—and a motivation for Aries to find his place in it. There are many amazing desert resorts around the world where you can both enjoy the luxuries you expect on a vacation and find the peace of miles of uninterrupted sand.

If you can't get away just yet, instead just visualize a desert scene to relax yourself. Imagine feeling the hot sun on your skin, seeing the beautiful patterns in the sand, and hearing the wind as it whistles over dunes.

Discover Florence

Travel—whether in person or through pictures or videos—is a great way to recharge yourself. The Aries-ruled Italian city of Florence is an especially amazing destination. Its unparalleled architecture, delicious food, and hospitable people are undoubtedly worth a trip overseas. Florence sits in the popular region of Tuscany, which is well known for its gorgeous vistas and incomparable wineries.

If you can't make it in person, instead explore the city via books full of photographs, interactive websites that teach you about its history, or food or travel shows that visit this unique spot. Just looking at images will enable you to relax and imagine that you're sitting at a café in central Florence, watching the bustle of people, listening to the chime of the Duomo's church bells, and sipping a cup of caffè.

Watch a Circus

Circuses aren't just for kids anymore! Modern circus events encompass much more than just clowns—you can find talented acrobats, lively music, and magical stories.

When you need to relax at a fun event, consider getting tickets to a circus. You're sure to see some fire-based tricks—right up Aries's alley—and will be treated to sights and sounds you won't see anywhere else. Whether you opt for a traditional type of circus outside under a tent or see a Cirque du Soleil show in a theater, the unique entertainment will help you laugh and forget all your worries.

Try an Extreme Sport

Aries is an adventurous, daring spirit. Feed your thirst for excitement by trying an extreme sport.

Love the water? Learn scuba diving, wakeboarding, waterskiing, or kitesurfing. Want to see things through a bird's-eye view? Try rock or wall climbing, skydiving, bungee jumping, or parasailing. If you want to stay closer to the ground, try BMX bicycling, trail running, in-line skating, skateboarding, or paintballing. You might even try riding a motorcycle—with training and a helmet, of course.

No matter what you pick, you'll get the adrenaline flowing and get some exercise in!

Add Some Green to Your Wardrobe

Although red is a signature Aries color, green is also in harmony with Aries's season: spring. Shades of green that are in alignment with nature—such as grass green, emerald, and sage—are especially complementary.

Spruce up your spring wardrobe with some of these greens, whether as full pieces or accents like jewelry or pocket squares. The color will remind you of your special season and help motivate you to focus on new beginnings and growth.

Wear Comfortable Shoes

Aries is always on the go—and you're going fast. You don't need fancy, uncomfortable shoes slowing you down, so opt for sneakers whenever you can. You'll be agile, and your feet will be grateful for the support. If you really must wear something dressier, only wear shoes you could run in at a moment's notice. Many shoe brands today offer comfort *and* modern designs—look around for some options that will work for both your fashion sense and lifestyle.

Host an Island Party

When you need to kick back and have some fun, host an island party with your friends! Create a signature drink (with paper umbrellas, of course), and serve themed appetizers like jerk chicken bites, coconut shrimp, or grilled pineapple. For entertainment add some music and dancing. Steel is an Aries metal, so cue up some infectious steel drum band music and lead a conga line. The percussive beat is energizing, and leading a bunch of people will make Aries feel confident and happy.

Lead Others

When you practice regular self-care, you'll likely find that you have more energy that you want to give to others. In fact, one of Aries's missions in life is to inspire others, so look for ways to incorporate leadership into your life.

Whether it's mentoring a colleague at work, encouraging others to join a volunteer effort for a cause you're passionate about, or inviting friends to practice various self-care methods, you can lead others with your Aries sense of adventure. You'll feel rewarded by all the positive outcomes you'll see from your efforts.

Practice the Warrior Pose

Aries is ruled by Mars, the god of war, so it follows that the Warrior Pose would be perfect for his sensibilities. This strong, fierce yoga pose improves balance and strengthens your shoulders, back, and legs.

From a standing position, bend one knee 90 degrees (keep your knee over your ankle) and push the other leg far out behind you, with the sole of your foot on the ground and your back heel placed perpendicular to your front heel. Raise your arms straight up into the air with your palms facing each other, and look up to the sky. Breathe deeply.

Rediscover Your Power with a Bloodstone

Crystals and stones carry amazing powers from the earth. Bloodstone, a green and red gemstone, is known for its ability to restore your body and rebalance your mind. Bloodstone is also connected to Mars, and holding it in your left hand while you meditate will make you especially powerful. (The left side of the body including the left hand receives energy. The right side discharges energy. When you hold a crystal in the left hand, you receive the mineral's benefits.) Take deep breaths for several minutes, or recite a mantra that resonates with you. You can purchase this stone in a raw form, or polished in various types of jewelry or accessories. The raw unpolished form of some crystals and minerals have more energy.

Meditate On the Color Green

An Aries-focused meditation can help bring his seemingly boundless energy and intensity levels down a notch. At least once a week, try spending 15 minutes focusing on the color green, which helps calm any passion or anger you might be holding on to. Green is also associated with spring, which is Aries's season and is connected to rebirth and new beginnings. Whether you think of a wide, green meadow or a grassy hillside, allow yourself to de-stress and unwind with this quiet, relaxing imagery.

Pamper Yourself with a Facial

Since Aries rules the head, be sure to take good care of yours with a relaxing facial once in a while. Slow down after a tough workout or a long week of work by visiting a tranquil spa and let yourself relish the soothing hands of a professional spa technician.

Choose the type of facial that's right for you based on your skin type (consider an organic or natural type if possible)—perhaps one that's moisturizing, deep cleansing, or exfoliating. Then sit back and let it work its magic to improve your skin tone and decrease your stress levels.

Listen to Relaxing Music

When Aries wants to relax with some music, he might not prefer the quiet strums of a harp. Instead, he finds percussive music to be calming and entertaining. Drum solos and spirited classical music like the "William Tell Overture" will help Aries forget his worries and clear his mind. Create a playlist of this type of music that aligns with your preferences and turn to it when you need to re-center yourself. A 15-minute midday music break can be an especially effective way to disconnect from your tasks for a few minutes before you power through the rest of your day.

Expand Your Reading List

Reading is a wonderful way for Aries to relax. It can also be inspiring and meditative. The next time you're looking for something new to read, consider material written by an Aries that will speak to your Aries soul.

The well-known Robert Frost poem "The Road Not Taken" can serve as your motto. Another Aries poet whose works will resonate with your sense of individuality is Maya Angelou.

If you're looking for something to feed your adventurous spirit, James Patterson's mysteries are well written and thrilling. By reading regularly, you can reduce stress and expand your horizon—a win-win.

Keep Your Eye on Mars

Stay in touch with your ruling planet: Mars. Although Mars is exceptionally visible only once or twice every fifteen years or so, it can be spotted from earth up to two hundred times some years since Mars moves very slowly across the sky.

When Mars is close to earth, you'll be able to see a very bright red star. Even when it's farther away, though, you can still see the red star, albeit less easily as it won't appear as bright.

Take a moment to pause and enjoy the beauty of your ruling planet. As you gaze upon it, contemplate its energy and take deep, calming breaths. While Aries can sometimes be aggressive, taking time to reflect and focus can restore you to a more peaceful state of mind.

Decorate with Red Geraniums

You may not think of fast-moving, industrious Aries as much of a gardener, but geraniums are one of the flowers associated with this dynamic sign—and caring for these flowers is a way for you to relax. Don't be afraid to festoon your window boxes and balconies with bright red geraniums to suit your fiery sign. And, if you're worried about getting bored and moving on to another project, don't be too concerned. Geraniums are hardy plants and, while they hate the cold (just like Aries), they are perennials that will come back year after year, especially if they're moved inside during those chilly winter months.

Eat a Balanced Breakfast

Aries is always on the go, which makes sitting down to a healthy breakfast somewhat of a chore for this energetic Ram. However, properly fueling your body for what's bound to be a busy day is something Aries can't afford to skip. Plus, as a cardinal sign, anything Aries can do to get himself off to a good start is sure to make his day go more smoothly. The solution is an easy-to-eat breakfast that you can take on the go. Feed your body, and your spirit, with healthy muffins, spicy everything bagels, or cinnamon oatmeal.

Play a Strategic Game

Aries feels restored and rejuvenated when he lets his competitive side come to the forefront. Use your competitive nature to lead you to victory by playing a friendly board game with your friends or family. Just don't take things too far; it is just a game, after all.

A simple game may not give Aries all that he needs, however. Aries thrives when he's able to use his above-average ability to strategize as a way to achieve his goals. Save the cooperative games for another day and engage in a fast-moving game of Monopoly or Risk or a mock war video game instead.

Sponsor a Lamb

You might not have the space or inclination to own a ram (or lamb) yourself, but you can sponsor someone who does—especially someone in need. Look online for reputable charity groups (such as Heifer International) that help connect farmers with sponsors who can help them expand, feed, and take care of their herd. Honor your Aries animal with this act of kindness and generosity that will do your soul good and help someone live a better life.

Rest Your Head

Even the most on-the-go Aries needs to stop and rest sometimes. Make sure that rest is as high quality as possible by splurging on a therapeutic pillow to add to your bed. These pillows are designed to support the head and neck while you're sleeping, which helps Aries protect the most important part of his body. Not only does this support relieve physical neck strains, but a good night's sleep alleviates stress and helps repair and restore the body.

This type of restful, restorative sleep is a vital part of self-care—yes, even for Aries—so do whatever you can to rest that heavy head and lull yourself off to dreamland as easily as possible.

CHAPTER 8

Self-Care for Taurus

Dates: April 20–May 20
Element: Earth
Polarity: Yin
Quality: Fixed
Symbol: Bull
Ruler: Venus

Taurus is the first earth sign of the zodiac. She is a fixed sign, which means that her season, spring, is in full bloom and well established. The fixed signs are also known as the "serpent signs" of the zodiac. In the Hindu tradition, the serpent power is called kundalini energy ("the juice of life"), and it travels from the root chakra at the base of the spine to the crown chakra at the top of the head. As the first fixed or "serpent" sign, Taurus has this kundalini energy in abundance, but it is not yet fully expressed; it lies latent.

Though she is a powerful and determined force when she sets her mind to something, she cannot be pushed or forced to do what she is not inclined to do. Taurus takes time to adjust to new ideas and situations. Though it is rare, her power can erupt into anger, and much like her symbol, the Bull, she will see red. Patience is key when Taurus is in this mood; it is best to wait until things calm down on their own: The mood will pass.

The Taurus glyph (picture) represents the head and horns of a bull. The bull is a symbol of rich, fertile power. In ancient Greece the beginning of Taurus was celebrated as the feast of Maia (similar to the traditional May Day), with the sun represented by a white bull with a golden disc hanging between its horns, followed by a procession of virgins who exemplified the fertility of nature in the spring.

A Greek myth to consider for Taurus is that of Europa and Zeus. Europa, a beautiful Phoenician princess and mortal, had a dream that two continents were trying to possess her. The first, Asia, was where she was born and where she lived with her family; the other continent was nameless. Awakening, she went out to gather flowers. Looking down from Olympus, the god Zeus desired Europa, and to escape the watchful and jealous eye of his wife, Hera, he turned himself into a beautiful bull, spiriting Europa away to the island of Crete. Zeus went on to other lovers, but Europa remained in Crete and gave birth to three sons. Europe, the other continent Europa had dreamed about, eventually was named after her. This ancient story speaks to Taurus's love of land and nature, as well as her connection to the bull.

Self-Care and Taurus

Taurus's ruler is Venus, the planet of romance, pleasure, and beauty. Taurus loves the way beauty feels. She likes to touch materials, people, trees—anything. The texture of what she touches communicates directly to her senses and impacts how she perceives the material world around her. Taurus's sensuality also extends to food and drink.

The tantalizing powers of Venus can also incline people to be overindulgent, and in terms of self-care, this is where Taurus needs to be mindful. Appreciating the tastes of food and drink, and the feel of bodily pleasure, is a good thing. But if this appreciation becomes unbalanced, there is a tendency to fall into a case of the "too much" syndrome (too much food, too much drink, too much relaxation), which can lead to a decline in energy and mood. If Taurus falls into this rut, it can be hard to break out of, because no matter what Taurus is doing, she likes routine. And if the routine is pleasurable, Taurus will need to tap into her strong bovine willpower to break the cycle.

Taurus Rules the Neck, Ears, and Cerebellum

Taurus rules over the neck, cerebellum, and ears, so self-care related to these parts of the body is especially important. Like her celestial symbol, the Bull, the defining features of Taurus are a thick neck and small ears. Shoulder and neck rolls should be a part of her daily exercise, as tension can often form in these areas. Using yoga foam rollers to massage the spine and neck area will prevent soreness and help move energy through the body.

Perhaps more important than the outer neck muscles, however, is the throat. Taurus is connected to the throat chakra, which controls expression of thought and emotion. Taurus should consider wearing a scarf in both the cold and warm months to protect against cold drafts and sunburn, so she can ensure her voice is always loud and clear. The throat is also key in singing and humming, activities that come naturally to Taurus. Many great singers, pop and opera alike, are Taurean. Bing Crosby may be from a past time, but his rich, crooning style is a hallmark of Taurus's sensual approach to life. Singing in the shower is a primo self-care activity. There should be no room for judgment: Just letting her voice resonate in those great shower acoustics is a perfect activity for Taurus! And while doing chores, Taurus will find that humming is a great way to keep stress levels low. Taurus should also consider singing herself a lullaby before she falls asleep. The soft music will prepare both her mind and body for dreamland.

Just as essential as outward expression is the Taurus ability to listen and reflect inwardly with the information she collects. To keep her ears alert and healthy, she should be mindful of temperature changes and wear earmuffs or warm hats in colder weather. She should also avoid prolonged periods of loud noise that could damage her hearing.

Taurus also rules the cerebellum, which controls movement, coordination, and balance. Exercises that improve and build on good motor function and rhythm are important to the Taurean wellness. Great sports for coordination and motor function include tennis and combat routines. Taurus also has a flair for contact sports that require muscular endurance, such as boxing, and many champion fighters have been Taurean. Coupling exercise with music through dance is the best way for Taurus to keep her rhythm and enjoy exercising.

Once Taurus finds a routine that works, she will keep it. If part of Taurus's routine involves extended periods of joint pressure, such as running on a treadmill, it can cause stress on the body because of the repetitive pounding. Taurus's great asset is continuity and routine, but if this routine locks in tense muscle patterns, it becomes counterproductive.

Taurus and Self-Care Success

The first step in good self-care for Taurus is feeding the senses moderately. Taurus is especially susceptible to every sound, taste, touch, or smell, and this can easily lead to a sense overload that can leave her overwhelmed and unmotivated to do anything—except run from it all. She will be led to successful self-care by the promise of feeling better and the pride in mastering self-control.

If part of Taurus's self-care involves meeting with a personal counselor or other wellness adviser, she must have an emotional bond with that person. Again, Taurus's senses are heightened, so she needs an established connection and foundation of trust to properly interpret and absorb what that person is expressing. A pitfall in counseling for Taurus lies in her resistance to change. If she feels she is being ordered or pushed toward something new, she can become stubborn, either closing herself off to the idea, or doing the exact opposite. Guiding her toward improved self-care in a more indirect way will lead to a successful change.

A key sense that is highly developed in Taurus is the sense of smell, which can be instrumental in her self-care. Many "noses" who work in the perfume industry are Taureans. They can detect notes of different oils and essences, and blend them to create a wonderful perfume. Even if someone is not a professional "nose," the power of scent can relax or invigorate, improve mood, recall happy memories, promote communication, and change the entire atmosphere of a space. Taurus should implement different scents into her self-care routine. For example, if she was a bit indulgent the night before, a whiff of diluted (according to instructions) peppermint or bergamot essential oil will encourage her to practice more self-control the following day.

As in counseling, pitfalls to successful self-care for Taurus are overly disciplined approaches to anything. Taurus needs to feel relaxed about any kind of program.

She wants the good feelings of exercising her body, and the pleasure of knowing that her body and mind are in control. A surefire way for Taurus to stick to a self-care routine is to "pay" herself for every good action she takes toward caring for herself. This can be in the form of a treat, such as buying a new scarf or eating dinner out, or a certain amount of money that she moves into a savings account. For all of Taurus's appreciation for the finer things, she understands the importance of spending her money wisely, and a boost to her savings will be just the motivation she needs to reach her goals.

In terms of her soul development, Taurus shares an intimate relationship with both spirituality and the physical world. She views the two as entwined, each growing and balancing the other. For Taurus, spirituality also goes hand in hand with generosity and kindness, and as a nature lover, Taurus's kindness extends to the earth. Restorative self-care practices for Taurus are those that allow her to balance her spirituality with her love for the natural world. Strong and patient just like her element, earth, Taurus values stability and determination. What she shows is that steady progress can bring about actions that make a difference in both personal well-being and the well-being of the world around her.

Be they physical or mental, self-care practices are vital to a healthy, happy Bull. So let's take a look at the self-care activities tailored specifically to Taurus.

Don a Cashmere Scarf

Taurus rules the neck and throat. It is important for her to keep her throat chakra open, as it promotes self-expression and communication with others. Tying a yellow scarf around your neck will encourage the sharing of your ideas, as well as restore energy to turn those creative thoughts into actions. A light-blue scarf will promote communication and a sense of stability when you may be feeling less steady on your feet in your social or private life. Try cashmere, as it is a stimulating textile for the luxury-loving Bull.

Promote Abundance with Emeralds

Invoking the feelings of nature, rich-in-color emeralds welcome abundance and confidence into your life. Wear an emerald in a ring or bracelet where you can always see it to feel more grounded.

This deep-green gem also has a calming effect on emotions. Ruled by Venus, Taurus often has numerous feelings coursing through her. She is especially sensitive to the actions of those around her, and these interactions can drive her mood. Wearing an emerald (or two or three) can help keep your emotions in check.

Protect Your Ears

The perceptive Taurus's ears are very sensitive to noise and temperature. Promote the health of your ears with proper protection from the elements. Wear earmuffs or a hat in cold weather, and keep the volume at a low to moderate level when using headphones. If you notice a frequent ringing sensation in your ears, make an appointment with your doctor to check for causes and treatment. Taurus is a master of listening and reflection—so keep your ears protected and on alert!

Collect Dolls

Taurus is a collector. Ruled by Venus, she is a sentimental sign who loves keepsakes. She will enjoy collecting dolls or action figures, which can hold memories of her childhood, and can also appreciate in value over time. Antique dolls are also a good choice, as Taurus will admire the beauty and tradition of the dolls, as well as the craftsmanship used in earlier times. She may also consider eventually passing on the toys to a younger loved one, who will cherish them and carry on their tradition.

Take a Woodworking Class

Taurus loves working with her hands, feeling the sensation of tools in her hands as she gets to work. She also loves the sense of accomplishment in creating something useful! Tap into both sensation and utility with a woodworking class. An instructor will show you how to safely use the different tools to shape the wood, and you get to return home with your masterpiece and a sense of accomplishment—plus some wood shavings everywhere. Fortunately, earthy Taurus doesn't mind.

Open Up to Love with Rose Quartz

Pink and sweet, rose quartz is the stone of Taurus's planetary ruler, Venus. The celestial embodiment of love, Venus influences the emotions of Taurus. As a stone of love itself, rose quartz opens you up to love of all kinds, and it helps you to understand the perspective of a romantic partner, close friend, or family member, strengthening your connection. A smooth piece of rose quartz held in your left hand or kept in your left pocket will keep your communication centers open and your emotions calm.

Try a Dessert Wine

Entertaining guests or looking for a sweet host gift? Purchase a dessert wine, or a selection of dessert wines, to have on hand. Ruled by sensual Venus, Taurus loves tantalizing flavors that ignite her sensitive taste buds. And sharing a luxurious treat with her friends or family is the icing on the cake!

Rich and sweet, dessert wines are made by adding in sugar or reducing the amount of water used in the fermentation process. In some cases, the grapes are even dried first to make a raisin wine. As a rule of thumb, the wine should be sweeter than the food it is paired with. It makes a wonderful companion to fresh fruits, custard, or semisweet biscuits.

Embrace the Possibilities

Nod your head frequently to give a positive yes to the day—and also to keep the neck area relaxed and flexible. Taurus knows the importance of stability, but change is just as crucial to personal growth. Say yes to what comes your way! You can also massage your muscles as you nod. One simple technique is pushing your fingers from your shoulders in toward your neck, then lightly pushing down on the muscle connecting your neck and shoulders.

Avoid Neck Pain with Lateral Raises

Weighted lateral raises are a great way to strengthen Taurus's thick muscles and avoid tension buildup in the neck due to inactivity. They may also ease any neck strain you may currently have. Be careful of straining your neck muscles with intense or improper lifting practices.

To do the lateral raise, stand straight with your feet shoulder-width apart and your knees slightly bent. If you are a beginner, you should start with one 4- to 9-pound (approx. 2- to 4-kilogram) weight (based on factors such as your individual weight and fitness) in each hand. Lift your arms up straight at your sides until they are parallel with the floor. Slowly lower your arms, then repeat eight to twelve times per set. Always ask your fitness trainer for weight and technique guidance.

Slip Into a Turtleneck

Stylish and cozy, a turtleneck is the perfect addition to the Taurean closet. The unique design of the turtleneck protects the throat and neck, both ruled by Taurus. It is important for Taurus to be mindful of these areas, which are vital to her self-expression and can be sensitive to cold weather and direct sunlight. Keep a collection of turtlenecks in different Taurean colors, such as green and pink. Be sure to invest in soft fabrics that will soothe your throat and remind you to be gentle with yourself.

Adopt a Bull (Dog)

An ideal pet for Taurus is the English bulldog. Just like Taurus, bulldogs are strong and loyal, and are fond of a lot of relaxation. Owning a dog will also establish a routine of walking and feeding times—stability that Taurus will enjoy bringing into her life.

Not ready to adopt? You can spend quality time with a bulldog through volunteering at a rescue, or by downloading an app that connects pet owners to local people like you who can take their dog for a walk when they get stuck late at the office or are away for a short time.

Find a Chiropractor

Every Taurus knows the healing power of touch, especially as a great way to relieve and release tension in the body. As an earth sign and headstrong Bull, Taurus can often hold on to certain things—physical or emotional—and this weight places stress on her body.

Visiting a trained, recommended chiropractor is a wonderful way to pull this stress out of your joints and muscles. As you relax, a chiropractor manipulates different areas of your body to alleviate stress, and finally crack that hard to reach spot on your back. Afterward, you'll find it easier to balance your energy, and you'll experience relief from joint pain, muscle soreness, and more!

Accent Your Home with Lily of the Valley

Taurus has a keen sense of smell, and the aromas she surrounds herself with play an important role in her mood and her perception of the world around her. Lily of the valley is a simple yet elegant flower that features a sweet, classic floral scent.

Place attractive vases of lily of the valley around your home to evoke the refreshing aura of spring and nature's gorgeous springtime bounty. The flower's scent can draw any points of stress out of the room, opening up the space for your creativity and powerful Taurean spirit to flourish.

Drum It Out

Though Taurus is usually temperate, sometimes the sparks fly and she needs to blow off a bit of steam. Purchase a small drum to take out when you need to release frustration or stress. The vibrating rhythm of the drumming, as well as the sounds, will ease you of negative energy while tapping into your love of music. Taurus enjoys using her hands, so the best drums for her are the conga, bongo, or other traditional hand drums. For a bit of extra flair, a tambourine allows you to drum *and* shake things out.

Indulge In Rich Flavors

Rich, unique flavors, coffee and butterscotch are ruled by Taurus. Combine the deep kick of coffee ice cream with the salty-sweet taste of butterscotch sauce into a special ice cream treat. While a sundae every day isn't the best idea for your health, an occasional indulgence is the perfect thing to help you unwind after a long day or treat yourself for a job well done. Taurus responds well to small rewards for her work, so these types of incentives help establish good routines that will motivate you toward your goals.

Go for a Nature Walk

Taurus's element is earth, which means that her inspiration, drive, and strength come from a deep bond with the great outdoors and all of its beautiful creations. Take a rejuvenating walk through nature—be it on a hiking trail or through a meadow where you can celebrate your connection to Mother Nature with wildflower crowns, observations of various wildlife, and perhaps a few grass stains. When you return to your home and office responsibilities, you'll have the refreshed energy and motivation to tackle any task that comes your way.

Affirm Your Prosperity

A great self-affirmation for Taurus is "This beautiful earth feeds me." Written down and kept where you can easily come back to it as needed, this phrase serves as a reminder that you are provided for. As an earth sign, Taurus seeks stability and a sense of overall security in her life. Sometimes, though she plans things out and has routines in place, the universe has other plans, and she is left feeling overwhelmed and unsteady on her feet. This affirmation is the perfect comfort that although you may feel out of control, you are taken care of. Change can be a little scary, but you are right where you need to be.

Purchase a Mechanical Bank

Taurus may enjoy the finer things, but she also appreciates the importance of good financial habits. Buy a fun mechanical bank to add a little whimsy to your saving rituals. You'll be motivated to put a bit of money into your savings each month—or even each week—when you hear the satisfying musical sound of it entering a slot, or see it sliding through a sorter, into the chamber below. That extra change, whether it is $1 or $20, adds up. You can also celebrate your celestial roots with a miniature mechanical-bull bank.

Soothe Your Throat with Loquat

A small orange fruit grown in Asia, loquat has a number of healing properties, most importantly in soothing the throat. Syrup from the plant is popular in China in cough drops.

Ruler of the throat, Taurus is sensitive to throat-related ailments such as dryness and coughing. Keep loquat cough drops on hand to ward off sore throat during the colder months, so this important channel of Taurean self-expression and communication will remain open and healthy.

Squeeze a Stuffed Cow

Symbolized by the Bull and ruled by the earth element, Taurus has strong connections to the cow. A plush cow reminds Taurus of her astrological symbol and deep ties to nature. The soft material of a stuffed animal is also comforting to Taurus, as she draws understanding of the world around her through her senses—specifically her sense of touch. During times of stress or confusion, giving a cow stuffed animal a squeeze will ground you in the physical world and help you to release those racing thoughts or fears.

Take Your Workout Outdoors

As an earth sign, Taurus receives more satisfaction in doing things outdoors. Sensual like her planetary ruler Venus, she wants to feel the wind and sun on her skin, hear different critters scuttling around in the distance, and see all of the colors of Mother Nature's beauty.

One way to encourage Taurus to stick to an exercise routine is to take that workout into nature. Do you usually exercise on a treadmill or elliptical? Go for a jog on a nature trail or chase your dog around the yard. Do you lift weights? Take them outside! The natural scenery and boost of fresh air may even have you working out longer or more often than before.

Get a Nose Ring

Feeling powerful and a bit adventurous? Get a nose ring. Though the change may seem drastic to steady Taurus, choosing to do something new for herself like getting an eye-catching piercing is the perfect blend of empowerment and control. Choosing a septum nose ring also forges a connection to your symbol, the Bull, which has donned this distinct piercing throughout history. Before you take such a big step, research a good piercer and all the safety guidance on nose rings.

Of course, if you are looking for a less permanent homage to your celestial roots, you can find many rings that do not require piercing, instead using a magnet or a gentle clip to fasten the ring to your nose.

Find Your Footing with Green Moss Agate

As an earth sign, Taurus has a special connection to nature. She derives her confidence from having her feet planted firmly on the ground, where she can experience everything through touch, taste, smell, hearing, and sight. Green moss agate is the perfect crystal to help Taurus find and maintain her footing. Smooth and deep green in color, green moss agate will ground you to the earth and create a nurturing vibration that will give you a sense of calm and security.

Enjoy a Steak

Ruled by Venus, Taurus is a sensual sign who enjoys living the high life and pampering her senses. She will delight in savoring a richly seasoned meat such as beef, especially paired with a lovely red wine.

This simple addition to a weekday (or weekend) night is the perfect act of self-care for Taurus, as a tasty meal can release both body and mind of the chaos of the day. As you let go of all of the thoughts, to-dos, and conversations of the past hours, you will be able to properly unwind and restore your warm, earthy energy.

Clean with Chamois Cloth

Determined and practical, Taurus enjoys checking things off her to-do list left and right. In fact, a burst of productivity can be just as relaxing to her as a bubble bath. As you move into your household chores, use a chamois cloth to clean your counters, tabletops, and other surfaces. Made from a plush material you will enjoy feeling under your palms, this cloth is natural, durable, and absorbent. It's the perfect environment-friendly and efficient helper—and Taurus does love efficiency.

Organize by Color

Ruled by Venus, Taurus is a sensual sign who is deeply affected by the five senses, including sight. Color can have a huge impact on her mood, leading to a day filled with confidence, adaptability, and warmth—or one filled with insecurity, stubbornness, and indifference. Organize your closet by color and season so you are always ready with the best colors for the day—even when you're running a little late for work.

The best colors for Taurus are yellow, pink, and earthy green. Yellow and pink promote creativity, energy, and positive thinking, while green embodies the essence of nature (even when the weather outside is disagreeable). Taurus should avoid red, which signifies anger and obsession. And do not fall into the all-black habit!

Take a Farm Vacation

While some may think Taurus desires only the poshest of posh vacations, her deep connection to the earth and her hardworking nature make a simple farm vacation the perfect rejuvenating experience. Load up your overalls, sunscreen, and a friend or two, and travel to a farm for the weekend.

Between the fresh air, farm animals (say hi to any fellow bulls), and sense of accomplishment if helping out around the property, you'll return home just as satisfied and refreshed as you would after a spa getaway. The opportunity to share your experience with a friend or loved one—and maybe teach them a thing or two along the way—will make the trip even more memorable.

Grow Your Own Produce

If you live in an area with a backyard or communal space—or even if you live in a studio apartment with a kitchen window—try your hand at growing vegetables. In a larger space, you can plant rows of different vegetables, while in a smaller apartment space you can grow a pot of herbs or hang a bucket with tomato plants in direct sunlight.

Seeing Mother Nature's creations flourish firsthand will give you an even deeper appreciation of her power—plus, you will have a healthy, pesticide-free treat to enjoy right from the pot or mixed into a homemade meal.

Decorate with Pink Cyclamen

Add a bit of Mother Earth's bounty to your décor! Sturdy, much like Taurus, pink cyclamen is a lovely pink flower that also serves as a reminder of nature's tough but delicate beauty. Pink is also a Taurus power color, and a vase of pink cyclamen in a living or office space will boost energy and creativity. To care for your plant, ensure that it receives plenty of indirect sunlight. Cyclamen also requires a humid atmosphere, so spray the leaves with water at any sign of dryness.

Balance Your Element

As an earth sign, Taurus enjoys routines and planning. She rarely steps out of the house without a schedule and a clear vision of her goals for the day. While her ambitious, thoughtful nature is one of the things that make her so impressive, sometimes this need for routine can lead her to become stagnant in her progress or resistant to change of any kind.

Balance out your earthy side with an airy dose of spontaneity. This can be as simple as hopping on your bike for a quick ride around the block when you had been planning to just recline in front of the TV. Whatever you do, do it on a whim. This rejuvenating experience is sure to clear out any stagnant energy.

Meditate On Your Security

Taurus is rooted firmly on the ground. As a fixed earth sign, she values stability and careful planning. However, life can have things in store for Taurus that she may not expect. A powerful mantra for Taurus to meditate on during these uncertain times is "I am secure in all parts of my life."

As you come across surprises that may shake your Taurean confidence, reciting this mantra will allow you to ground yourself back in reality and meditate on the stability you do have in both your surroundings and your own character. A good place to begin is to sit in the lotus pose with your eyes closed. Then, quietly chant the mantra out loud. The rhythmic sounds alone will soon draw in a feeling of calm.

Take Time for Self-Reflection

Part of Taurus's ability to express herself lies in her talent for reflection. With her keen senses and an emotional intelligence that derives from her ruler, Venus, Taurus is able to uncover things about herself and the outside world through her observations. A great way to facilitate further reflection is by reading books, especially those written by a fellow Taurus. Taurean authors include Shakespeare, Charlotte Brontë, and Harper Lee.

Other ways to deepen reflection include listening to music, or creating art through drawing or painting. Make yourself comfortable with a soft blanket on the couch and take time to reflect inwardly as you choose an artistic mode—whether it's through written word, music, or artistic expression—so you can recharge and get the "me time" you deserve!

Energize with the "Toreador Song"

A sign that knows just how to stimulate the senses, Taurus is the queen (or king!) of relaxation. Sometimes, however, this leisure can pull her into a place of overstimulation or lethargy. When Taurus has overridden her senses, she becomes overwhelmed and insecure, while a numbing of the senses due to overindulgence leaves her unmotivated.

To kick-start inspiration and provide that much-needed boost of energy, play the "Toreador Song" from Bizet's opera *Carmen*. Not only is this classic aria a wonderful blend of musical talent and enthusiasm, but it is connected to Taurus's astrological symbol, the Bull. It's the perfect Taurus theme song!

Simplify Your Work Wardrobe

Although Taurus can delight in a luxe ensemble, she has many places to be and people to see—and a simple wardrobe is vital. Having a few pieces that you can mix and match makes weekday mornings run much smoother, an efficiency that every Taurus appreciates. Besides, Taurus prefers to channel her creativity into better things like food and the arts. Invest in items that are easy to maintain and go with everything, like wrinkle-free tops, and pants or skirts in neutral and pastel colors.

Keep a Treasure Chest

Reflective Taurus draws wisdom about herself and the world around her by looking back at past experiences. Her planetary ruler, Venus, also governs romantic feelings, making Taurus a sentimental sign. Keep a "treasure chest" of mementos from the past, including photos and other reminders of fond times, to pull out whenever you need a little trip down memory lane.

Has an unexpected change occurred in your life? These keepsakes will lift your spirits and help you feel more grounded. Unsure why your boss chose you for a big project? The mementos of your past accomplishments will serve as a wonderful reminder that you are hardworking and capable—of course the boss picked you!

Slip Into a Silky Secret

Ruled by sensual Venus, Taurus experiences the world around her through heightened senses. One of the most important of her senses is that of touch. Touch is what allows Taurus to truly savor her surroundings, especially as a sign who appreciates the plush side of life. The feel of silk underwear in a Taurus color such as yellow, pink, or green will be a secret delight.

These colors will promote confidence and renewed energy for your day, while the soft fabric will help you to unwind once your work is finished.

Cook with Copperware

Shiny and rich in color, it is no surprise that copper is ruled by Venus, the planet in charge of beauty. Copper cookware is not just beautiful—it is also very useful and efficient. Though she does admire style, Taurus is a down-to-earth sign who chooses utility over physical appeal. With copperware you can have both—and a delicious meal. (Be sure to choose copperware with a nonreactive lining, or follow the manufacturer's instructions for safe use.) A mixture of table salt and white wine vinegar, rinsed off with water, will keep your copperware shining like new; look online for specific cleaning instructions.

Learn a Circle Dance

In many cultures, circle dances are a tradition that celebrates the earth and connects a group of people together through both physical touch and music. With her sensitive ears and appreciation for the arts, Taurus loves both music and dance. She is also an earth sign, drawing energy and confidence from her connection with Mother Nature. It is important, too, for Taurus to exercise her rhythm and coordination regularly, as she rules over the cerebellum—the part of the body that controls motor function.

You can find information online about where to learn a traditional circle dance, or you can use online videos to teach yourself. Share what you've learned at your next friend gathering, and get a circle dance going! All you'll need is a little music to set the mood.

Talk It Out

Taurus is ruled by Venus, the planet of love. Sometimes, Taurus may become overwhelmed by her feelings or view them as a roadblock to getting things done. In these times, her emotions can be pushed to the wayside, where they only grow. Instead of bottling your emotions and wishing they would just disappear, talk to someone.

This person can be a counselor, or even a family member. Whoever you choose, you will find that the people around you are ready and willing to listen and return all of your Taurean compassion and loyalty. As you release your emotions, you will feel any stress or negative thoughts you were carrying lift away, creating the space for your creativity and sense of security to return.

Make Your Own Jewelry

As an earth sign, Taurus loves working with her hands, creating something from start to finish that she can then use in her daily life. One great hobby for Taurus to pursue is jewelry making! You can find aisles of different tools, instructions, and elements to create your own bracelets, earrings, and more at your local craft store. Go for metals, wood beads, and colors of nature that remind you of your celestial element. The sense of satisfaction (and unique new fashion statement) in making your own jewelry will lift your spirits and reconnect you with your earthy roots.

Wrap Yourself in Turkish Cotton

Ruled by sensual Venus and the earth element, Taurus experiences life through her keen senses of sight, hearing, taste, smell, and especially touch. The different textures she encounters impact how she perceives her surroundings, and a pleasurable fabric is the perfect accoutrement for allowing her to relax and recharge. Wrap yourself in a warm Turkish towel after a shower or exercise, and you'll soon find your imagination roaming to a luxurious getaway. Once restored, you will be ready for whatever work project or creative venture you have planned.

Invite Financial Success

Taurus is a hardworking, practical sign who knows the importance of managing finances wisely. Magnetize financial prosperity with a beautiful and useful wallet. This wallet can be compact for your travels—or the latest trend—but make sure it has all of the necessary slots and zippers for securely holding your possessions. Try finding one in one of the Taurus power colors: pink, yellow, or green. Pink and yellow encourage positivity and abundance, while green promotes security.

Savor a Fruity Tea

Taurus is known for having a sensitive palate due to her planetary ruler, Venus. Fruit-flavored teas such as mango, raspberry, and peach delight Taurus's taste buds while promoting calm—and wellness too. The sweet flavors of the tea may have you feeling like you are indulging, but you are actually sipping on quite the healthy treat! Fruity teas boast a number of wonderful health-giving properties, including antioxidants and improved digestion. Tea has also been shown to promote weight loss, prevent cavities, and reduce the risk of heart disease. Drink up!

Do a Waltz

Taurus loves to dance, but it may come as a surprise that it is also important to her well-being. As the ruler of the cerebellum, which controls balance and motor function, it is essential for Taurus to practice moving fluidly and matching a rhythm. The waltz is a soothing rhythm that will allow you to release any tensions from the day and exercise your coordination. Try dancing to the "Blue Danube" waltz, which is sure to leave you feeling confident and upbeat.

Sing a Duet with a Fellow Taurean

Music is for Taurus's ears what food is for her taste buds. Sensitive and expressive like her planetary ruler, Venus, Taurus uses music as an outlet for her creativity and emotions. Connect to your inner performer with a Taurus "duet." True, you may be in the shower with a Bluetooth speaker, or in your living room with a karaoke machine, but singing along with a fellow Taurus is an empowering act of self-care that will leave you feeling inspired and more confident than ever. Talented Taurus singers include Roy Orbison (try his fan favorite "Oh, Pretty Woman") and Kelly Clarkson.

Restore Inner Peace with Coral

Are you at a point in your life where things seem to constantly be shifting? Wear a pink coral necklace (or another piece of jewelry containing pink coral) that you can rub between your fingers when needed. A natural element of the sea, coral encourages balance during times of change. And just as the ocean is full of unpredictable movement, so is life. However, there is calm between the waves, and the ocean is a steady force capable of weathering any storm.

As a fixed sign ruled by the earth element, Taurus values stability, and she can become overwhelmed or headstrong in the face of change. Coral jewelry will serve as a reminder that like the ocean, you are steady, and you have the strength to weather these changes in your life.

Strike a Plow Pose

The Plow Pose is the perfect yoga position for Taurus, as it connects her to her astrological symbol, the Bull. This is not a beginners' pose, so make sure to practice this with your yoga instructor for technique guidance. To do this pose, lie flat on your back with your arms at your sides. Breathe in, and lift your legs and hips up (using your hands to support your lower back) toward the ceiling. Straighten your legs and slowly lower your toes to the floor behind your head. Be sure to keep a space between your chin and chest. Gaze downward and hold for a few seconds. Then gently roll out of the position.

Go for a Picnic

Picnicking wraps nature and your favorite indulgences into one sweet little package of self-care. As an earth sign, Taurus has a special connection to nature, which explains why one of the best ways for her to unwind and renew her creative spirit is through a bit of one-on-one time with Mother Nature. Taurus is also the queen of luxury, as her keen Venusian senses give her one truly refined palate.

Choose a warm afternoon to pack up a basket with your favorite foods and go on a picnic. Be sure to find a location with plenty of trees and wildlife, and you'll soon find yourself released from any stress or worry that may have been weighing you down.

Toast with Planter's Punch

A colorful beach-day favorite, planter's punch is the perfect elixir for Taurus after a long week of hard work. Originating in South Carolina, planter's punch mixes refreshing citrusy flavors with rich dark rum. To create this fruity concoction, simply fill a glass with ice and mix in the following ingredients: 3 tablespoons (1½ fluid ounces) dark rum, 1 tablespoon (½ fluid ounce) lime juice, 2 tablespoons (1 fluid ounce) pineapple juice, 1 tablespoon (½ fluid ounce) orange juice, and ½ tablespoon (¼ fluid ounce) simple syrup. Garnish with an orange slice and a maraschino cherry, and enjoy your ticket to paradise.

Aim for the Bull's-Eye

Ruled by sensual Venus, Taurus is a very tactile sign. Just thinking about her goals and imagining them coming to fruition isn't going to be enough. Taurus needs to see and feel her hard work paying off. Create this motivational visual aid by making your own bull's-eye target. In the center of the target, write down a goal you are working toward. If your progress has stalled, or you need a boost of encouragement in pursuing your dreams, you can take aim and throw beanbags at your target. You can also celebrate an achievement with a satisfying beanbag toss at the bull's-eye. Once you have reached one goal, write in a new one, aim, and fire away!

Ease Into Sleep with Silk

Having trouble falling asleep? Cover your pillow in a peach-colored silk pillowcase. The silk fabric feels sensuous and won't leave wrinkles on your face. Ruled by Venus, Taurus is especially sensitive to texture, so a rough material on her pillowcase will make it more difficult to fall and stay asleep. Silk will feel amazing on your skin, and a restful sleep will make all the difference tomorrow when you are tackling your to-do list.

Taurus is also sensitive to color, so a brightly colored pillowcase will make it hard to wind down for the night. Peach is a soft, welcoming color that promotes calm, so you will feel relaxed and ready for dreamland.

Boost Your Mood with Jasmine

It is no secret that life is full of surprises. Though Taurus would prefer warning of a month—or year—before these changes. Steady and headstrong like a bull, Taurus can lose her footing when the unexpected happens, but don't fear. If you are feeling less than your confident Taurean self, jasmine essential oil is the perfect way to naturally lift your spirits.

Boasting subtly sweet notes, jasmine has an uplifting effect that can help you shake any insecure feelings brought on by change. It also promotes restful sleep and healthy skin! You can diffuse jasmine essential oil in a living or sleeping space or massage it (diluted according to instructions) into your skin.

CHAPTER 9

Self-Care for Gemini

Dates: May 21–June 20
Element: Air
Polarity: Yang
Quality: Mutable
Symbol: Twins
Ruler: Mercury

Gemini is the first air sign of the zodiac. He is yang and a mutable sign, meaning that his sign rules while the season changes from spring to summer. Gemini is a dual sign and symbolizes the duality between the conscious mind and the divine universal mind. The tension between these two forces gives Gemini characteristics that resemble a split personality or, in some cases, a two-faced person.

This is not conscious duplicity on the part of Gemini. It is just Gemini exercising all parts of his mental faculties. In this way Gemini can be exhausting and frustrating to others, but he is usually so charming that his friends feel glad for his company. Gemini's purpose in life is gathering different experiences and knowledge to further his mental and communication abilities.

Gemini's symbol, the Twins, is one of three human signs in the zodiac. It represents the human power of speech, thought, and communication. Using these skills, Gemini is always in the pursuit of his other half. In one legend from Greek mythology, the Twins were represented by the brothers Castor and Pollux. Castor was mortal, while Pollux was immortal. When Castor met an untimely death, Pollux was completely inconsolable. Zeus, ruler of the gods, pitied Pollux's grief and allowed him to live with his brother for six months of the year in the underworld. Another legend asserts that the two brothers never actually meet because when one is in heaven, the other is on earth, never to overlap.

The first legend explains Gemini's desire for unity, while the second explains the divisive impulse that is also native to Gemini. Gemini's quest and lifelong goal is to make peace with these opposing tendencies. Based on these traits, you can understand why Gemini has a reputation for going in two directions and changing his mind frequently. He is hard to pin down, which can be most obvious in intimate relationships.

Gemini is ruled by the planet Mercury, or Hermes in Greek. Statues depicting Mercury always include wings on his feet and a caduceus, a short staff with two entwined serpents and wings at the top, which he carries with him everywhere. Even today the caduceus is a symbol of the medical profession. The serpents represent life's healing energies, and the wings represent the messenger or physician who explains the best way of restoring health. Hermes was Zeus's messenger, or the messenger of the gods. It makes sense that Gemini is always busily gathering knowledge about self-care to give to everyone.

Self-Care and Gemini

Gemini has no problem nurturing and taking care of his intellectual well-being. He is always looking into learning something new, whether that comes in the form of a lecture, a class, or a new book to read. It is in the physical realm where Gemini may need some guidance and help.

Gemini has a very sensitive nervous system that causes him to have a restless mind and body. He has the "monkey mind," as it is called in Eastern traditions, which scatters his thoughts and makes it hard for him to concentrate for long periods of time. His mind is so active that he often neglects his physical well-being. It's not unusual for Gemini to forget to eat or exercise because of his intellectual pursuits. He may not find practical self-care particularly interesting, so the best way to spark his passion is for him to begin researching information on diet, food, exercise, or activities. When he reads that such and such food or vitamin or immune-enhancing practice promotes good health in body, mind, and spirit, then Gemini is on board for self-care and delights in the results (as well as gaining more knowledge).

Gemini Rules the Lungs, Hands, and Shoulders

Gemini rules the lungs, hands, and shoulders. Note that there are two of each of these body parts. The most important of these body parts are the lungs and all parts of the respiratory system. Breathing well is a learned skill, one we have naturally as babies and children, but lose when the tensions of adulthood in life disrupt our well-being. This leads us to hold our breath and then, over time, our natural rhythm of breathing tightens. Mentally and spiritually, finding a breathing practice that calms the mind is essential for Gemini. This requires patience and practice. Gemini's mind is so active that he moves from thought to thought with lightning speed. Meditation, or slowing these thoughts, can be tough to accomplish. Because of this, meditating with sounds or chants is more likely to be successful for Gemini.

Gemini needs to relax his shoulders as much as possible. It may benefit Gemini to keep a yoga roll handy so he can lie on it and rest his neck and shoulders naturally. It may also be helpful for Gemini to do some shrugging exercises and shoulder rotations throughout the day to ensure that these body parts don't get stiff and his breathing doesn't become constricted. It's important for him to avoid propping the phone up with his left or right shoulder. Gemini loves to talk on the phone and be social, but if he props the receiver up against his shoulder, it can form a tension pattern throughout his shoulders and neck.

Turning to therapy or counseling is a great way for Gemini to practice psychological self-care, as it allows him to talk through all of his thoughts and ideas with a willing listener. However, Gemini is a thinking sign, not a feeling sign, and because of this, once Gemini gets his problem clear in his mind, he is not inclined to continue exploring the backstory of his life. He just enjoys the knowledge he's acquired, recognizes the benefits from the experience, and then moves on. Throughout his life he may try different therapies and work with a variety of therapists as the need arises, but it is typically only for a short period of time.

Sports and exercise are usually part of Gemini's self-care program. Gemini enjoys playing both team games and solo sports, depending on his mood. Sports like tennis, basketball, racquetball, badminton, and volleyball all require hand-eye coordination that Gemini excels in. His muscles are usually long and flexible, and he does well in sports that require bursts of energy rather than endurance. Pure cardio is not usually interesting for Gemini unless he has a very jazzy soundtrack he can plug into. The repetitive motion of impact exercise is unpleasant to Gemini. He prefers to keep his eye on the ball and move freely. In addition, sports provide a social outlet for Gemini.

Dancing and singing along to music, or just repeating rhyming lyrics, is fun for Gemini. He is a natural mimic and loves wordplay. Karaoke must have been designed by a Gemini! Whatever Gemini does, he tries to make it amusing for himself and others. He's the member of the friend group that knows all the verses to camp songs. And he may even entertain by performing rap songs. It is the combo of rhythm and words that gets Gemini's system going.

Gemini and Self-Care Success

By nature, Gemini flees from boredom. If any activity or self-care practice is tedious or monotonous, Gemini will not stick to it, even if he knows he is doing something that is good for his overall well-being. He needs constant change to keep his mind stimulated. Because of this, the best approach to exercise for Gemini is to rotate activities so they do not become habitual. Having too many distractions is another pitfall for Gemini when it comes to self-care. If there are too many other interesting things going on in Gemini's life, he'll drop his self-care routine quickly. In addition, the more he speaks about an activity, the less he will do it. It is almost as if using energy to talk about something uses up the energy to do it. For Gemini it's better to just move into action.

Gemini needs socialization to really keep the ball rolling with self-care. For example, if Gemini partakes in a sport, it's a good idea for him to go out after the game for drinks to decompress with his teammates. This is a great opportunity for him to relive the glory of the game he just played, and plan for the next one.

If Gemini needs intellectual self-care, perhaps he can find a group to play chess with, or attend a lecture. Poetry readings, literary clubs, and book groups are also great Gemini self-care activities. All these activities feed Gemini's love of knowledge and words.

Gemini tends to approach self-care with scattered efforts, which can become a hazard for his long-term wellness. Gemini also has wanderlust, and if he is traveling, good health and self-care may fall by the wayside. One way to get around this for Gemini is to locate a gym or spa wherever he goes. That way he can travel and keep his healthy habits intact at the same time. Two really is the magic number for all Gemini activities.

Blogging is a great option for Gemini, especially when he needs to track his health. If he finds he is struggling with keeping up with his self-care routine, maintaining a record of his self-care journey and then sharing tips with an Internet community can reinforce good personal care practices and spread the word to others. Gemini is not really concerned with accomplishing his self-care goals in measurable terms. The pleasure comes from communicating his hard work to others and giving helpful suggestions for their own journey. After all, Gemini is the messenger for us all!

Gemini is one of the most important zodiac signs, as he represents the opposition of the human and divine. Humanity may strive for the divine, but it must confront the narrower human nature first. Gemini doesn't necessarily have "the answer" on how humanity can save itself, but he is a messenger who will always communicate his thoughts and hopes for the holistic development of all people.

Now, let's take a look at some self-care activities especially designed for Gemini.

Add a Little Color

Gemini does not like to be confined. He wants to be free to express himself openly and without judgment. His personality is naturally colorful and buoyant, so he needs space to let those colors shine through. Encourage yourself to be creative and to express what's inside you through color. You can buy a large set of colored pencils and put them in a vase somewhere you can access easily when you feel the desire to draw something or write down your thoughts. Don't be afraid to mix and match the colors based on your mood!

Take a Whiff of Invigorating Scents

Air signs like Gemini can be invigorated by scents that inspire the mind and stimulate the body. If you aren't sure where to begin with aromatherapy, don't worry. Gemini benefits most from two common essences: peppermint and jasmine. Peppermint and jasmine can both help improve memory and raise alertness. Try adding the recommended number of drops of one of these essential oils to an appropriate carrier oil for topical use (diluting according to instructions, and use with caution if you have sensitive skin), or buy an essential oil diffuser that will spread one of these scents all around your home when you need a little brain boost.

Do a Duet

Karaoke, anyone? Gemini loves to do everything in twos, especially when it comes to entertaining and showing off his many talents. When you are feeling the need to let loose and connect with others, try hitting up a local karaoke night with a group of friends. But instead of just getting up on stage alone, test out your vocal prowess by singing a duet with a trusted confidant or even a stranger.

Can't carry a tune, Gemini? Don't worry. Just listening to duets can soothe your soul. The intense creative connection between two people is inspiring and will remind you of how powerful your voice is when it is joined by others.

Embrace Spring

Spring is a time of rebirth and renewal. The flowers are blooming, the bees are buzzing, and the leaves are filling the once barren trees. Gemini thrives on the fresh energy of spring and promise of new beginnings. Hold on to that feeling year-round by surrounding yourself with springtime colors at all times. Everything from pale blue to soft green and light yellow will instantly remind you of that sweet, spring air. These are colors that suggest a spring breeze and will immediately revitalize your heart and soul.

Breathe Deeply

Gemini rules the lungs, so it's important he takes special care with the air he breathes. In winter, that air becomes dry and harsh. It can make your skin scaly and cracked, and cause congestion in your lungs and nose. When the temperature starts to plummet and you start feeling a little tickle in your throat, turn to lemon eucalyptus to keep you breathing easy. You can use a lemon eucalyptus aromatherapy spray mist—or diffuse lemon eucalyptus essential oil in an oil diffuser—to permeate the air with this calming scent, cooling your lungs and acting as an anti-inflammatory agent against viruses. Just a little will do!

Identify Birdcalls

Turn to nature to re-center your spirit, Gemini. Start by waking up early in the morning and going for a short walk, focusing on all the different birds singing in the trees. Each bird has their own special call. Do some research online about what birds are in your area and what their calls sound like. Each time you go out for a walk, try and identify which bird you hear. You may even consider recording their songs on your phone to play back later. As a Gemini, you have a special affinity for birds. A bird's songs can lift your mood and get you ready to take on the day. Embrace your intrinsic connection with these animals.

Take a Historical Trip

Are you in need of a vacation, Gemini? Recharge your battery by indulging in one of history's greatest destinations: Egypt. Located in the northeastern part of Africa, Egypt boasts one of humanity's greatest marvels, the Great Pyramid of Giza, constructed sometime between 2589 and 2566 B.C. The Great Pyramid is the oldest of the Seven Wonders of the Ancient World, with a rich past that you don't need to be a history buff to appreciate.

If you can't make the trip, look for ways to experience history without going too far. Many Geminis have had past lives as scribes. You could have inhabited one of those souls at one point in time. If you can, visit a museum with papyrus scrolls and revel in their fragility and beauty.

Enjoy Some Cotton Candy

No summer is complete without the pink and blue sugar clouds known as cotton candy. Don't be fooled! Cotton candy is not just for kids. It's a fun, airy treat that will bring out your playful side. Plus, it's delicious.

Reconnecting with your inner child is important for air signs. Taking time to do something you haven't done since you were young is a great way to lift your spirit and shuffle off adult responsibilities. This is especially vital for Gemini. You need to feel free. While it may seem basic, a simple bag of cotton candy allows Gemini to reconnect with his most fundamental wants and desires without fear of judgment. So dig in! No regrets...

Keep Your Bedroom Airy

Gemini loves feeling air moving around him. It gives him the impression of being open and unrestrained, like he can take on anything. As an air sign, you need to feel air flow in your home or you might begin to feel claustrophobic. Try adding a few fans to your bedroom to keep the airflow moving freely. You may even consider hanging sheer or gauze curtains that move easily in the breeze. Seeing them sway will make you feel lighter and more hopeful. This is especially important in your bedroom, the last place you see before you sleep and the first you see when you wake.

If you want to lighten the energy in your home, especially your bedroom, consider spritzing a white sage spray. Sage is an ancient herb that can cleanse negative energy from your home and promote positivity.

Listen to Choir Music

Listening to music can be a soothing, relaxing experience for a weary Gemini. That's because when you listen to music, your brain releases dopamine, a "feel-good" neurotransmitter, increasing feelings of happiness. It also decreases the amount of cortisol, a stress hormone, in your body. Gemini is drawn to choir music. In fact, the more voices involved the better! Next time your nerves are frayed and you need to unwind, try listening to a famous choir or orchestra. Allow your mind to wander as you listen to the different voices working together to create beauty and harmony.

Find the Hidden Meaning in Poetry

Poetry is a wonderful way for Gemini to get in touch with his emotional side. As an air sign, you have a strong connection to the mind. You are a wordsmith. You learn quickly and thrive on exchanging ideas with others. Challenge your mind and your creative side by understanding the hidden meaning in poetry. You choose the type—anything from classical to modern. Look for symbolism within the poem. What kinds of poetic devices does the poet use? Maybe they are partial to similes and streams of consciousness. Or maybe they prefer rhyming schemes instead. Appreciate the images each word evokes in your mind, and the feelings that emerge in your heart.

Drink Valerian Tea

After a long day there's nothing quite like settling into bed with a nice warm cup of tea. Every tea has a different effect on the body, though, so make sure you choose the right one for the right moment. For example, if you are looking for one that will calm your nerves and promote sleep, ask your doctor (who is familiar with your health and medications) about valerian tea. Valerian is derived from the valerian plant, native to both Europe and Asia. It is claimed to have a soothing effect on the nervous system, another one of the body systems Gemini rules, so it's a perfect fit for the stressed-out Gemini.

Tell a Story

Gemini is a natural storyteller. You are a gifted communicator who can adapt easily to any situation. This means you can create a story at the drop of a hat without any stress. Use your skills for good and start a storytelling group for children in your local neighborhood. Not only will this give you the chance to flex your creative muscles, but the kids will love every second. It's a low-tech form of entertainment that will never go out of style. If you aren't sure how to get started, check with your local library about putting together a group.

Ride a Tandem Bike

Gemini will forever be looking for his other half. Because of this, he is drawn to activities that are meant specifically for two people, where he can connect and laugh without a lot of distraction. Embrace your carefree side and rent a tandem bike with a family member or trusted friend. You'll need to work together in order to keep the bike in motion. Luckily, Gemini shines in situations that require the exchange of information. Don't be discouraged if you wobble or start to tip over while you get the hang of the bike. Trust your partner and your own abilities, and you'll be peddling like a pro in no time.

Use Traditional Communication

Keeping in touch with friends and family is important for Gemini. Modern forms of communication such as texting and email have their perks, but they lack intimacy and personality. To remedy this, indulge in fine stationery and write notes to friends with a fountain pen. Even just a short note saying hello, and that you are thinking of the person, can have a profound impact on their mood. Your handwriting is unique to you, so it inherently communicates more than computer print. In addition, writing letters by hand can be a therapeutic act for Gemini. He is an expert communicator, after all, and needs the proper outlet to share his talent.

Repeat the Mercury Mantra

Gemini is ruled by the planet Mercury, which, according to mythology, was named for the messenger of the gods. Stories go that Mercury carried information from one level of existence to another, so it's no wonder Gemini is so good at communicating. It's an integral part of your astrological makeup. To capitalize on your strength, repeat the mantra "Words have power." Do this whenever you are feeling lost or overwhelmed. Find power in words and communication. It may help you re-center your mind and stay grounded.

Get a Pet Parakeet

Owning a pet is a rewarding experience, one that can help Gemini become more dependable, vulnerable, and responsible. If you've never had a pet before, it is best to start small. Because of your natural affinity for birds, parakeets are perfect Gemini pets. Not only are they low-maintenance, but they are beautiful, and their chirp is sweet and calming. Just make sure to get

expert advice on adopting (and properly caring for) a parakeet from a local animal shelter before you commit. Also known as a budgie, parakeets are part of the parrot family, and are entertaining and social, and can sometimes be quite talkative. Kind of like you, Gemini.

Visit a Secondhand Bookstore

Books can transport us into other worlds with just the turn of a page. Indulge your innate curiosity, Gemini. Take some time to explore a local secondhand bookstore one afternoon. Walk the aisles and touch each book's spine. Flip through the pages and look for old notes from previous owners. What's the oldest book you can find hidden on the shelves? Buy a book you've never heard of before. Listen to that intuitive voice inside guiding you along to help you find the perfect new addition to your home library.

Pop Some Popcorn!

Popcorn is the perfect snack for hungry Gemini. It's light, fun, and simple to make, so it fits your personality and your schedule. While buying microwaveable bags of popcorn is the quickest way to enjoy your snack, consider buying a hot air popper instead. As an air sign, you'll love how quickly your favorite element can turn those tiny kernels into fluffy popcorn. Try seasoning your popcorn with various unusual ingredients to up the fun factor: anything from garlic salt to caramel drizzle, chocolate sauce, or white cheddar cheese. Your imagination is your only limit.

Practice Origami

Origami is the art of folding paper, which is often associated with ancient Japanese culture. The ultimate objective is to transform a small, flat sheet of paper into a beautiful structure. It is a practice of patience and precision, both perfect goals for Gemini.

Buy a collection of origami paper, and learn how to get started by either researching online or picking up a book at your local bookstore. Don't try to make an origami piece that is too complicated too soon. Start with a simple shape, like a butterfly or fish, and work your way up to more complicated structures, like cranes. Ease into this craft, and enjoy how light, airy, and therapeutic it can be.

Try a Challenging Yoga Pose

Yoga is a wonderful practice for Gemini. It can help you tone your physical muscles as well as your mental muscles. Gemini often needs space to take a break and focus on himself, shutting out the outside world and all the stress that comes with it. Yoga can do just that, while teaching you patience, self-love, and commitment.

If you haven't tried yoga yet, look for local beginners' classes that can help you get started. If you are already a yoga veteran, challenge yourself by trying a Shoulder Stand. Gemini rules the shoulders, so you already have an intrinsic connection to these parts of your body. You'll need expert balance to do this pose, so make sure to practice this with your yoga instructor for technique guidance. They will guide you on where to focus your power and strength during the pose and help keep you upright and safe while you get the hang of it.

Satisfy Your Curiosity

As an air sign, you are always connected to your mind, Gemini. You seek out mental stimulation, looking for your next great challenge. You have endless curiosity to explore different places, ideas, and people. Don't let your curiosity go unsatisfied. Maintain a list of things you want to know more about, and keep adding to it as often as possible. It can include anything that sparks your interest—from history to science or art. Then read about and research these topics. Go to the library, ask questions, and keep exploring!

Become Your Own Writing Prompt

As a Gemini, you love to share your ideas and thoughts with the world. You are articulate and insightful, and never back down when it comes to expressing your opinions—the perfect combination of traits for a master communicator. While you are already good at talking, take your communication skills to the next level by trying out a few personal writing prompts.

Every morning, think of a sentence and write it down in your journal. That evening, read the sentence and just start writing what comes to mind. This approach suits the dual way that Gemini approaches things. Your thoughts in the morning will be different than your thoughts at night. This is a great way to express your creativity privately; though feel free to share your writing with others if you are comfortable.

Find a Double Terminated Crystal

Double terminated crystals are unique stones that allow energy to flow in multiple directions through them. A double terminated crystal has two points, on opposite sides of the crystal. Your crystal may be diamond shaped if it has double termination points. Seek out these rare crystals for their open energy flow. Meditate with them to help clear any negative thoughts and emotions. The two points of a double terminated crystal are perfect for Gemini's dual mind.

Look for double terminated aquamarine crystals and clear quartz in particular. Aquamarine crystals invoke the healing power of the ocean, while clear quartz symbolizes purity. These are beneficial for a calming meditation and continued mental clarity.

Get a Manicure

Gemini rules the hands, so it is important to keep them in good shape. After all, we use them for pretty much everything. If your nails need some TLC, schedule a manicure to restore them to their natural state. While a basic manicure is wonderful, splurging on a more luxurious treatment can really increase your hand health. A long hand massage can improve circulation in your hands and arms, making your skin glow. You may also consider asking about a paraffin wax treatment for your hands. The warm wax coats your hands in hydration, leaving your skin supple and soft.

Try to get a manicure at least once a month for maintenance. Your hands will thank you!

Flavor with Cumin

One of the best spices that an inventive Gemini chef can use in his kitchen is cumin. Cumin is a spice from the parsley family used in many varieties of meals, from soups to meat dishes, and it can give the food you are cooking a warm, peppery taste. Cumin has been used as a healing herb to help boost the immune system, ease indigestion, and fight inflammation. Cumin is also a great source of fiber, iron, potassium, and zinc. It may lower cholesterol, too, so adding just a bit of it to your favorite meals is a wonderful way to support your heart health.

Tap Into Your Inner Child

While Gemini spends a lot of time in his mind, sometimes he needs to break free and do something completely unexpected. One of the best ways to let loose is to channel your childhood by revisiting some of your favorite playground pastimes. Think of activities such as skipping rope and going on a swing. These actions get you moving and your body into the air. You may even remember some of your favorite jump rope rhymes you can test out, which stimulates your mind as well. Don't be afraid to let your inner child have some fun! It's a great way for a run-down Gemini to refuel when adult responsibilities become a bit too much.

Listen to Wind Instruments

When it comes to music, wind instruments get a bad rap. They aren't as cool as the big string and percussion instruments like the guitar, piano, and drums, but the music they create is just as compelling. Wind is especially important to Gemini, as an air sign, so it is only natural you would have a positive response to instruments like flutes, clarinets, and saxophones. Try listening to chamber music with a special focus on wind instruments. Chamber music is composed using only a few instruments, so it is not as robust as orchestral music, making it more intimate and calming.

Record Your Thoughts

Do you ever feel like you have so many thoughts running through your mind at one time that you can't keep everything straight? Don't worry; this is typical for Gemini. Your mind is often very active, jumping from one idea to the next. Try to ease the chaos by recording your thoughts as voice memos. You can just say what's on your mind, or even record inspiring thoughts for yourself to listen to at a later time. Try reciting encouraging quotes that you've always loved, or giving yourself a little pep talk. You may feel silly talking to yourself at first, but you are your own best advocate and cheerleader!

Start a Book Club

Because Gemini rules over the mind, you hold a special love for words and knowledge. You also love sharing your ideas with others. Try putting both of these passions together by joining or starting a book club. Start by seeing if any of your friends are already part of a book club, and, if they aren't, whether they'd like to start one with you. A book club is a great outlet for curious Gemini. Not only will being part of a book club give you a chance to be social, but you'll exchange ideas and learn something new.

Listen to a TED Talk

There's always something new to learn, as long as you are open to it. Gemini knows this better than anyone else. His eagerness to acquire new knowledge is one of his most defining characteristics. But it's not easy satisfying this drive in new and exciting ways. There are only so many books you can read, movies you can watch, and websites you can frequent. To satiate your cravings for knowledge, try listening to a TED Talk. TED Talks are lectures, given by experts in their field, recorded, and streamed online. There are thousands of topics to choose from, and you may even pick up some public-speaking tips!

Think First, Speak Second

Your verbal dexterity as an air sign can sometimes get you into hot water if you aren't careful, Gemini. You are so adept with words and thought, you may not filter what's in your head before it comes out of your mouth. This can lead to insensitive and harsh speech. You may not mean to cause harm or to hurt someone with your words, but if you don't stop and think about what you are going to say before you say it, you run the risk of doing serious damage. Before you say something, pause for 1–2 seconds, and think about the impact your statement may make. If you have any doubt that it may hurt someone, rephrase it or keep it in your mind.

Write a Blog

You've accumulated a lot of knowledge over the years, Gemini. It's time to share what you've learned with others. Starting a blog is the perfect way for you to pinpoint a topic you are drawn to and share that love with the world. Start by picking a topic you are knowledgeable and passionate about. Don't worry if it seems too niche—the Internet is a wide expanse; someone will want to learn what you know. Once you have an idea in mind, just start writing! Try to keep your blog up-to-date and offer your readers new content as often as possible.

Plan a Trip with Friends

Being social is important to Gemini. He often feels most comfortable and relaxed when he is in a group setting, as long as the group is made up of trusted friends and family. Soothe your soul by taking a vacation with a group of friends. Being in a new place with valued friends can nurture Gemini's curious side. Go somewhere warm so you can all be outside together in nature, enjoying the fresh air. Plan group outings that challenge you physically and mentally. Most of all, laugh together and share your thoughts and emotions.

Join a Softball Team

Being a part of a team can build trust for Gemini. He is always on the lookout for relationships that can grow and deepen over time. Team sports like softball provide Gemini with the opportunity to develop a comradery with his teammates based on a common goal: to win! Not only will joining a softball team offer Gemini a social outlet, but also it will spark his competitive side. Look for a softball league in your area.

Embrace Your Twin Mind

When it comes to activities and outings, Gemini, you should likely plan to do two things at a time to fend off boredom and keep yourself entertained. This doubling up feeds your twin mind and keeps you interested. For example, if you go to the movies during the day, go to the ballet at night. If you spend the day playing or exercising outside, go to a museum exhibit or reading in the evening. Balance your activities and give yourself variety. Gemini loves to try new things and learn new information, so always be on the lookout for fun new dual adventures you can try.

Multitask When You Can

Not everyone has the ability to multitask as easily as Gemini does. Because of his twin spirit, he has the power to do more than one thing at the same time without compromising the quality of either action. Use your twin spirit to your advantage and multitask whenever possible. This will actually help keep you focused rather than split

your attention. You do best when your mind is constantly stimulated. You may find that you can often move seamlessly back and forth between different projects without missing a beat. Embrace your superpower, but always keep tabs on your stress level. If you find that you are becoming overwhelmed, scale back and focus on one task for a period of time.

Try a New Restaurant with Friends

In many cultures, dinner time is a social experience as much as a nutritional one. In fact, in some European countries dinner can last for hours with multiple courses. Embrace the celebratory nature of dinner and try a new restaurant with friends. Mix things up, try a new cuisine, and indulge in a food you've never tried before. Gemini loves being social, and there's no better way to keep the conversation between friends going than around a large table with delicious food and drink. Follow your curiosity and maybe you'll discover your next great culinary love.

Slow Down

Sometimes Gemini's energy can get the best of him, and he ends up blowing through social interactions and relationships rather than really participating and engaging. That's because Gemini is so used to multitasking and jumping from one thing to the next that he is always looking to the future.

Don't let your drive keep you from being present. Find a deeper meaning in your interactions. This may entail listening more to your friends, allotting more time for a social engagement so you can really enjoy yourself, or spending some time alone to re-center yourself.

Try Online Gaming

Combine your love of being social with your love for using your mind by joining an online gaming community. There are many different options that you can try, from multiplayer action games to card games and more. For Gemini, the speed of the game is often key. Look for fast-paced games that keep you stimulated. And if you aren't in the mood to engage with others socially, you can always look to Solitaire to keep your mind sharp. No matter what you play, your Gemini skills will help you win. After all, Gemini's planet, Mercury, rules the mind, so he is a natural when it comes to strategy, and his social prowess will help him appreciate connecting with other people from all around the world.

Go Orange

It's hard to get enough of the right nutrients in our diet in such a fast-paced world. With everything we need to accomplish in a day, we tend to just reach for the easiest and nearest food to keep our stomachs from growling. Try to be conscious of what you put into your body. Since Gemini rules over the lungs, start eating more orange fruits and vegetables. Foods like carrots, apricots, and pumpkins contain beta-carotene, which is thought to be helpful in maintaining lung health. Make these nutrient-dense foods a part of your daily diet and you'll start feeling stronger and healthier in no time.

Go Into Savasana

Usually done at the end of a yoga practice, Savasana is a yoga pose that asks you to lie flat on your back with your arms a few inches from your side and your heels spread slightly apart. This pose is a wonderful way to rest and restore after a vigorous yoga class. Savasana is especially helpful for Gemini for two reasons: First, it helps ease tension in the shoulders and arms, and second, it allows Gemini time to focus on his thoughts and feelings. This pose can be a beneficial challenge to Gemini as you need to be fully awake yet fully relaxed at the same time.

Moisturize Your Hands

While you may think that your face ages first, your hands are often the first area where you can see signs of aging. Gemini rules over the hands, so make it a priority to pamper your hands as often as possible.

Start by buying a good-quality moisturizer and use it at least daily, or whenever your hands feel parched. You can also do deep moisturizing treatments at home for your hands, such as exfoliating the skin with a sugar scrub and rinsing, and then covering with a rich moisturizing lotion and moisturizing gloves overnight. When you wake up in the morning, your hands will be soft and silky.

Meditate On Yellow and Blue

Color meditation is a wonderful way to calm your mind and draw on the energies associated with different colors. Keep in mind that as a Gemini, to get the most out of your meditation, you should also add sound to your practice.

Focus on two colors when you practice color meditation: yellow and blue. Yellow speaks to the brightness of your soul and will help energize your spirit. Blue ties into the fact that you are an air sign and symbolizes the openness and freedom of the sky.

Whether it's a morning meditation to greet the day, or a restorative 15 minutes in the afternoon, find some time and a quiet place to meditate. Close your eyes, clear your mind, and focus on the two colors. Picture the bright yellow of the sun washing over your body. Feel it warm your skin and recharge your soul. Then envision the bluest of blue skies and allow that color to refresh your perspective, and imagine a life without boundaries.

Keep Your Hands Busy

In order to be productive, Gemini needs to stay focused. It's often hard to concentrate on a single task when your mind is going in a million different directions. One way to calm your mind and remain focused is by keeping your hands busy. Since Gemini rules the hands, it's best to keep them engaged while you're trying to concentrate. Play with a paper clip, keep some Silly Putty in a desk drawer, or doodle on your notepad. It may seem counterproductive, but by giving your hands something to do while you're working, you'll find it easier to stay on task. Your increased productivity will give you more time to do the things you actually enjoy!

Put Eucalyptus in Your Shower

A nice, hot shower can be therapeutic on its own. With the warm water relaxing your muscles and refreshing your skin, a shower is the perfect way to start your day or a great idea if you are looking to unwind after a stressful one. What can make it even better for you, Gemini, is hanging a bundle of eucalyptus behind your showerhead.

The steam activates the plant's natural healing properties, which work wonders on your respiratory system. Tie a few branches together with some string or twine, and then let the bundle hang against the shower wall (out of the direct water stream). The heat from the water will release the eucalyptus oils into the air, turning your already relaxing hot shower into a full aromatic experience with revitalizing steam.

Upgrade Your Technology

Can you even imagine a time before cell phones, Gemini? Technology has come on in leaps and bounds over the past few years, and, luckily, you are a forward thinker who is always ready to embrace the next wave of technological advancement.

If you haven't already, you should now upgrade your technology, Gemini, especially if you haven't experienced the wonder and innovation of voice-activated devices. Typing is *so* yesterday. Now all it takes is a simple voice command followed by a question and your device will do the work for you. This is very helpful for Gemini since you are always multitasking, looking for a way to streamline how you live and work. You are also a fantastic orator, so using your voice will feel natural compared to typing on tiny screens.

Have a One-on-One with a Friend

Your propensity for being a social butterfly often makes you the life of the party, but it can also keep you from connecting with people on a deeper level. Take time to check in with your close friends by inviting them out for a one-on-one catch-up date. This may mean meeting up at a local coffee spot to chat, or it may mean inviting them to your place for a cocktail and appetizers. Make sure to keep it low key and focused. Your goal is to really connect with someone who means a lot to you, without a lot of distraction. Not only will your soul thank you later, but your friends will feel especially loved and cared for.

Research a New Health Trend

Get your brain involved in your self-care, Gemini. Start by researching the hottest new health trends to see if there is something you'd like to try. Look for current studies and statistics about how well it works and if there are any concerns about its impact on well-being. If you read that a food, vitamin, or immune-enhancing practice is good for your mind, body, or spirit, you are more likely to add it to your self-care routine. There's nothing wrong with needing evidence that something will help before you make it a habit. Next, check with your doctor for their advice. Do your diligence and see what you can find!

Try Qigong

Qigong is a form of gentle exercise where participants do a series of repetitive motions, stretching the body and increasing fluid movement in the joints and muscles.

It is also a form of meditation that can promote stress relief through controlled breathing and spatial awareness. It is an ancient Chinese tradition that has been used for thousands of years to help prevent chronic pain, ease depression and anxiety, and build muscle strength. Try a beginners' class and incorporate this tranquil practice into your self-care routine, Gemini. Its soothing nature will help quiet your mind and give you a chance to zen out, while your body will adapt to each movement and release tension at the same time.

Find an Online Community

As a Gemini, you have a lot of thoughts and interests, so why not share them? Thanks to social media, we live in a highly connected world. People from across the globe can converse daily as if they were sitting right next to one another. Use this technology to your advantage, Gemini. Find a subreddit on *Reddit*, a *Facebook* group, or some other positive online community that shares your interests and passions. Engage in conversation with its members, and see what you can learn from them. You never know what kind of connections you can make until you try!

Hang Double Mirrors

Gemini has dual sides working together to make up a whole, hence, the zodiac symbol of the Twins. To tap into your own duality, try hanging double mirrors around your home so you can see yourself from multiple angles. This may help you discover different parts of yourself and who you really are. But be careful! Whatever you do, do not hang two mirrors in your bedroom. It is bad for feng shui and may disrupt positive energy flow. You only want good energy where you begin and end your day.

CHAPTER 10

Self-Care for Cancer

Dates: June 21–July 22
Element: Water
Polarity: Yin
Quality: Cardinal
Symbol: Crab
Ruler: The Moon

Cancer is the first water sign of the zodiac. She is yin and a cardinal sign, reigning at the time of the summer solstice, when the sun is at its height and daylight abounds. But the light that influences Cancer the most is the reflected light of the moon at night. Holding these polarities (day and night) together are the many feelings and moods that Cancer passes through each day. She is hard to pin down, as she is always feeling out a situation before making any decisions—with no rules, just a sense.

The sign of Cancer is sometimes not easy for males. It contradicts the stereotypical ideal of masculinity, as Cancer is sensitive and desires emotional expression. One way a Cancer man may successfully balance his Cancerian nature and traditional masculinity is by channeling his feelings into his home life rather than pushing them aside.

Cancerian moodiness may suggest a shy and retiring personality; however, Cancer is a leadership sign. She leads indirectly, through encouragement and support, rather than through direct instruction and authority. Cancer's hand-wringing, tears, anxiety, and back-and-forth feelings can try the patience of everyone around her. Some may be convinced that Cancer will never accomplish what she sets out to do, but time proves that she achieves her goals at her own pace.

The Crab, Cancer's symbol, is a half-land and half-water creature. Symbolically, Cancer will make a move on dry land (logic and physical life), and then dip back into the water (feelings and spiritual life) to renew herself. The water allows her to tap into her intuition in order to feel out whether it is safe to proceed.

The Crab symbol comes from a Greek myth. In the myth, Cancer—originally known as Karkinos—was a giant crab who was ordered by the goddess Hera to bite the hero Herakles (popularly known as Hercules) on the foot during battle. Karkinos disabled Herakles for a time, but Herakles subsequently crushed Karkinos. For his valor, Hera rewarded the crab by placing him in the constellation now known as Cancer. Cancer should take this myth to heart as a reminder of her courage.

The other ancient foundation for Cancer is the Great Mother. In astrology, the Moon represents women and all motherly instincts. Ruled by the Moon, Cancer has a natural affinity for babies and anyone who needs to be taken care of. A Cancerian parent fiercely protects her kids. She is wary of anything that could harm her family in any way.

Self-Care and Cancer

In terms of self-care, the two primary motivations for Cancer are family and the lunar cycle. Cancer works hard to see her family grow and prosper. She accumulates money to make this happen, and watches her saving and spending carefully. If a self-care program can prove to Cancer that it will save money in the long run, she will be motivated to stick with it.

Cancer is also driven by the desire to set a healthy example for her children and other family members. If Cancer does not have any kids or close family members, she will develop strong familial bonds with people and groups she encounters. This is a key for her success in exercise and diet plans. She wants to feel affection for a group effort, and feel cheered on by the instructor's and members' approval. Many gym and diet programs foster a camaraderie that creates a family feeling, and this dynamic will encourage watery Cancer to achieve her goals.

The lunar cycle is important to keep in mind with Cancerian wellness, as it can have a direct effect on her mood, thus steering her motivation toward or away from a self-care activity. To keep up with any self-care program, watery Cancer should understand that even if she doesn't feel like doing something one day, she may feel like doing it the next. She should avoid making hard-and-fast decisions, because moods will change.

Every month there is a new moon and a full moon. Cancer will feel energized and inspired during the new moon. She should begin all new projects during this time, from work to self-care. The full moon, which takes place about two weeks after the new moon, represents the culmination of energy. Cancer may feel the need to howl a little during this phase.

After the full moon begins the waning lunar phase. This is when Cancer should ground her plans for self-care, relationships, and anything else, by reviewing the feelings that began during the new moon. Last comes the period of the lunar cycle traditionally called the dark of the moon because Luna, the Roman goddess of the moon, is not visible. This is a time of rest for Cancer. She may sleep more and have very illuminating dreams. This lunar cycle affects all signs, but is strongest with Cancer because the Moon is her planetary ruler.

Cancer Rules the Breasts and Stomach

Cancer rules the breasts and stomach, so self-care related to these areas is especially important. For women, breasts can be a source of nourishment and a symbol of sexuality. For men, strong pectoral muscles may be a hard-won goal. Cancerian self-care for both men and women is very simple: Get regular checkups. The Cancer woman should also take extra care in breast health through performing self-checks at least once a month. These checks can be done in the shower and are a good way to get to know what is normal for her breasts and to monitor for any changes.

The stomach is a more complicated part of the body, as it is linked directly to Cancer's many changing emotions. Depending on the situation, Cancer may have butterflies in her stomach or feel unable to eat anything. Apart from enhancing emotions, the stomach can also tell Cancer whether or not something is right. The saying "trust your gut" is advice Cancer should follow. If she pays attention to how her stomach reacts to a person, project, or environment, she can automatically know whether it is right for her.

If Cancer is not feeling well, she should have a doctor check her digestive system, as it holds the answers to many health problems. Asking her doctor (who is familiar with her health and medications) about using a probiotic or digestive enzyme is an excellent self-care practice for Cancer. If all is well with the stomach, Cancer will be balanced and content.

Eating in crowded, bustling restaurants is not conducive to a happy meal for Cancer. To enjoy and fully digest her meal, she needs to feel that things around her are calm. She also loves sitting in booths, rather than at tables, where she will be in closer proximity to other people. Although there are some very well-known Cancerian chefs, Cancer typically prefers uncomplicated food. She also delights in dishes that remind her of fond memories. Fusion foods with elaborate garnishes won't appeal.

Cancer also enjoys feeding the stomachs of friends and family members. Cooking for a gathering or family dinner and providing nourishment for others is an essential part of Cancer self-care.

Cancer and Self-Care Success

A pitfall to success in Cancer self-care is her slow-moving energy. The water always appeals to Cancer but, oftentimes, she does not like to swim. She may be afraid of the water in these instances, or may just not be interested. However, if she incorporates the lunar cycle into her schedule, she will have a better chance of sticking to a self-care routine even on days when she may not feel like it.

Exercise with music, such as ballroom dancing or rocking out solo at home, provides enough movement for Cancer while appealing to her need for self-expression.

As a water sign, she will also enjoy a walk by a pond, river, or ocean. No matter what mood she is in, these exercises will provide a release that also keeps her active.

Another pitfall for Cancer's self-care program is her overindulgence in sentiment that impedes action. As an emotional sign, she can spend more time fretting over what she has done, or might do, rather than taking action. Learning to negotiate this tendency is an important life skill that Cancer will continually need to work at.

Perhaps the most important pathway for Cancer's self-care success, however, is through her incredible connection to the subconscious. And her feeling memory extends far beyond her own past—into the sentiments of different time periods. She is acutely aware of mass consciousness and trends in the wider society. Her quest is to learn from the past and share her unique perspective with the world. So let's take a look at some self-care activities especially designed for Cancer.

Strike a Half-Moon Pose

Celebrate your Moon mother with the perfect Cancerian pose! This yoga position promotes balance between Cancer's light (summer season) and dark (ruling planet) halves. This is not a beginners' pose, so make sure to practice this with your yoga instructor for technique guidance.

Yoga teachers have tips on performing this tricky pose, including using various transition poses (such as Triangle Pose), blocks, or even the support of the wall. Work with them to find the perfect Half-Moon Pose method for you!

Affirm Your Abilities

With Cancer's care for others, her own needs can fall to the wayside. She freely gives, asking for nothing in return. Thus, people forget that, though she does not ask, Cancer also needs a little encouragement. When you feel self-doubt creeping in, you can give yourself that much-needed confidence boost through the use of an affirmation. An affirmation will serve as a reminder of your abilities.

The perfect affirmation for Cancer is "I build a lighted house and therein dwell." There is a reason people come to you in their time of need. Just as a lighthouse is the illuminating siren for ships caught in a storm, you are a beacon of knowledge and insight. It's no wonder people trust your thoughts—now it's time for you to trust them.

Promote Emotional Balance with Pearls

Just like watery Cancer, the pearl has a special connection to the ocean—in fact, it was born from it. The pearl is also linked to Cancer's ruler, the Moon. This captivating milky-white treasure doesn't just resemble the moon—it also balances your body's hormones with it. In matching your emotions with the moon's lunar cycles, the pearl helps to ease negative feelings while encouraging love, as well as an appreciation for the here and now. Wear pearls on a bracelet, cuff links, or a necklace, where they will be at your fingertips. They will ensure your connection to what is important.

Ground Yourself in the Present

Insightful Cancer is deeply connected to the subconscious. So many thoughts and emotions are constantly coursing through you—and not just your own, but everyone else's as well. Fortunately, you can quiet all of this mental noise and refocus your energy by reciting a special mantra out loud.

When you need to center yourself and tune out unhelpful thoughts, focus on the phrase "The past is rich, but the here and now is better." Use this mantra to ground yourself in the present when you feel your mind becoming tangled in outside stress and past events—especially when those thoughts and memories will only lead to worry and self-doubt.

Sip a Blue Moon Cocktail

What better drink for Moon-ruled Cancer than the blue moon cocktail? This striking purple libation invokes the deep, reflective vibes of the moon wrapped in a dark night.

Romantic Cancer will also love the history of this cocktail, which was created in the 1940s to embody the passion of New York City in that era, when flashy dresses and an appreciation for abstract expressionist art took hold.

To mix up a blue moon, simply add 4 tablespoons (2 fluid ounces) dry gin, 1 tablespoon (½ fluid ounce) Crème Yvette, and 1 tablespoon (½ fluid ounce) fresh lemon juice to a shaker filled with ice. Shake, and then strain into a chilled cocktail glass and garnish with a lemon twist.

Magnetize Abundance with Lucky Bamboo

The lucky bamboo plant is renowned as a good luck charm that symbolizes prosperity. Intuitive Cancer understands the importance of saving wisely.

This plant is also a key element in feng shui, which uses nature to maximize a person's positive energy, or chi. When the full moon has your emotions running high, a lucky bamboo plant placed near the front entrance of your home will help you restore inner balance and displace negativity.

Create an Empowering Cancerian Playlist

Cancer, as an emotional sign, is highly sensitive to her surroundings, including sounds. The right tune can uplift her mood and leave her energized, while the wrong one can lead to feelings of melancholy or irritation. So what songs will Cancer enjoy?

Music that blends energy with emotion is perfect for lifting Cancer's spirits when she may be feeling down or uninspired. Fellow Cancerians know better than anyone how to amplify your unique celestial energy, so be sure to include them in your playlist. The talents of Cyndi Lauper, Huey Lewis, Carly Simon, and Carlos Santana are guaranteed to get you moving to the rhythm.

Make Your Own Holiday Cards

Cancer is a sentimental sign, which is why holidays are her favorite times of the year. What better way to spread your love this season than with homemade cards? Yes, a commercial card is easy to add to your shopping list, but a card that you have created on your own expresses your feelings more than any mass-marketed poem ever could. You can also tailor your cards to each person, depending on the colors or objects they like. If you have a talent for drawing, this is the perfect way to showcase it. Although your loved ones will appreciate the effort and humor of a stick figure too!

Get Lost in a Cancerian Book

A good book not only provides the perfect escape from everyday life, but also allows you to expand your knowledge, and view a topic from different perspectives. As a nurturing sign, Cancer often gives all of her time and energy away to others, leaving her exhausted and overwhelmed. Reading is a great way to recharge your batteries and enjoy some much-needed alone time. But what does Cancer enjoy reading?

You love books that make you reflect on your own experiences, as well as the unique experiences of others. It is through this kind of deep, introspective thought that you draw wisdom. A work by a kindred Cancerian spirit, such as Ernest Hemingway, Octavia E. Butler, Markus Zusak, or Dan Brown, may also top your reading list.

Snack On Cucumber and Watercress Sandwiches

Perfect little triangles with simple, refreshing colors, cucumber and watercress sandwiches are an ideal treat for Cancer. Prone to indulging in not-so-healthy foods, Cancer will love how light, nutritious, and yet scrumptious these sandwiches are. Additionally, they are sliced small, so she can enjoy more than one! Cucumber and watercress are also Cancer-ruled, as they contain quite a bit of her watery element. Bring these sandwiches to your next party with friends or family, or prepare them for a sophisticated touch to a quiet afternoon at home.

Enjoy a Meal at a Diner

Sentimental Cancer enjoys anything that offers a homey feel and delicious comfort food. With down-home meals at a reasonable price, and large booths to seat all of your friends or family members, a classic diner is the perfect choice for your next dinner out. The retro décor and crooning jukebox will have you feeling blissfully nostalgic (even if it's for a decade that was before your time). Invite someone from an older generation to come along and share their stories from the "good ol' days."

Enjoy a Cheesy Indulgence

Dairy is Cancer-ruled, so take full advantage with a cheesy treat! Beyond the typical cheese platter, you can celebrate your love of this dairy delight with a slice of cheesecake, some oh-so-classy caprese, or a bowl of baked mac and cheese. The possibilities are endless.

Still not cheesy enough? Take a cheese-making class! After all, sharing her love for something with others is a dream come true for Cancer. You may even develop a friendship or two along the way.

Treat Yourself to Ice Cream

Watery Cancer isn't just sensitive to emotions—she is also uniquely tuned in to the five senses, especially taste. Ice cream, especially blends with rich flavors such as caramel and dark chocolate, is the perfect pairing of sweet and salty. In need of a pick-me-up? Take yourself out for an ice cream cone, or better yet, invest in a home ice cream maker so you can enjoy this treat year-round. The cold weather blues will be no match for you this year!

Take a Cruise

From sailing across the Pacific to snorkeling in the tropics, there is no doubt that a cruise is the ultimate vacation. This is especially true for watery Cancer. Symbolized by the Crab, Cancer often can't get enough of water—specifically oceans. She doesn't need to be swimming to feel the soothing effects of the salt water: Just relaxing beside it or sailing over it is enough. A small ship is preferable to a huge ocean liner, as Cancer desires intimate settings and personal space to get her daily dose of "me time."

Drink Natural Alkaline Water

Ruled by the water element and symbolized by the Crab, Cancer requires a lot of water in her self-care routine. And this doesn't end with the water outside of her body. Cancer should be especially mindful of the water she puts into her body as well. Slightly alkaline natural spring or mineral water may be a good option for occasionally mixing up your water intake for Cancerian health.

The term *alkaline* refers to the pH level of the water. The lower the pH level, the more acidic a substance is; the higher the pH level, the less acidic it is. Drinking water with a slightly higher pH level may help neutralize the acid in your body, restoring balance. This is especially helpful if you suffer from acid reflux. Some studies have shown alkaline water is also better at regulating blood flow than more acidic water is, and may help reduce high blood pressure. So drink up!

Visualize a Sailing Adventure

As an emotional sign, Cancer is often full of racing thoughts—some not so helpful. A quick meditation break can be just the thing to relax your nerves and refocus your attention. Take 5–10 minutes to sit in a quiet place. Close your eyes and picture a sailboat on the horizon. As you visualize this image, take deep breaths in and out, feeling any pent-up tension or worry release with each breath. You can also add calm waves to your mental picture, and match your breathing to the rise and fall of these waves.

Create a Cancerian "Cocoon"

Cancer is deeply connected to the home. As a deep-feeling sign, she readily gives her all to helping others, but it is important for her to also nurture her own needs. This means plenty of space to be alone. At home, Cancer can truly relax and focus on herself, without the worry of hurting anyone's feelings. Create privacy in your home (a personal "cocoon" from external elements) that lets you fully disconnect from the outside world. Use curtains in deep shades to keep out prying eyes and invoke an aura of moonlight. If you have a yard, consider planting trees or adding a simple fence around the perimeter.

Watch a Cereus Bloom

The beautiful cereus flower is not just special due to its appearance. It also boasts a unique quality: It only blooms at night. Just like Cancer, cereus flowers draw power from the moon, opening up in its light, while other blossoms (and signs) shine brightest in the sun. Some varieties of the cereus, such as *Selenicereus grandiflorus*, only bloom once each year for a single night! You can purchase your own cereus flower and watch it bloom at night, or take a trip to witness the *Selenicereus* bloom in the wild. The *Selenicereus* can be found in parts of Florida, Mexico, and a number of islands in the Caribbean.

Enjoy Refreshing Melon

Summery, sweet, and watery, melons represent Cancer perfectly. Symbolized by the Crab, Cancer lives for days at the beach, and melons such as cantaloupe and honeydew should be her go-to refreshment to keep cool in the hot months. Share your summer vibes with friends and family by serving melon with smoked salmon as an appetizer or side to dinner. If you are attending an outdoor gathering, consider slicing up a bunch of different melons for a delicious fruit salad everyone will enjoy.

Bake a Loaf of Bread

Cancer knows that home is truly where the heart lies. And is there anything homier than a warm loaf of bread fresh out of the oven? As a nurturing sign, Cancer values family, and the home that brings them all together.

If you are missing loved ones, or simply in need of a little extra comfort, bake some bread. The aroma and steam will fill your kitchen—and your heart—with wholesome, happy feelings. Plus, you'll have a tasty treat to enjoy for the whole week.

Decorate Your Home with Seashells

As one of the three water signs, and symbolized by the Crab, Cancer has a deep connection to the sea. Even if you live miles and miles away from a body of water, seashells can bring the water to you. Incorporate seashells into your home with a set of shell wind chimes placed near a window, or individual shells arranged along a fireplace mantel or on shelves in your living room.

Seashells also magnetize love. In Greek mythology, the goddess of love, Aphrodite, rose from the sea in a large shell. Placing seashells in your home will invoke the goddess's power to draw new love to you, or keep a current relationship strong.

Cuddle

Cuddling isn't just fun—it's also good for your health! Experts say that cuddling (whether with a friend, partner, or family member) releases the feel-good hormone oxytocin. Oxytocin boosts mood levels and also helps to ease physical pain.

As an affectionate sign, Cancer is quite the cuddle pro. If you are feeling a little down in the dumps, or have a muscle or joint ache, put your talent to the test. Additionally, if you sleep alone, consider keeping a body pillow on the bed to stimulate that cozy feeling as you drift off to dreamland.

Buy a Comfy Chair

Home is a safe haven for sensitive Cancer. It is where she goes to refocus and shut off all of the noise of the outside world. Because she spends a lot of time at home, Cancer needs accents that make her space as cozy as possible. These allow her to fully relax and restore her Cancerian energy.

A large circular armchair is the perfect addition to your home sanctuary. As you embrace the comfort of your chair, the rounded arms will make you feel as though you are being hugged back.

Invest In Efficient Household Items

Home is Cancer's domain. Here, you have the space and privacy to enjoy all of your favorite activities, such as reading and crafting. It is important that the Cancerian home operates smoothly so you don't need to waste hours on small to-do items that leave you more exhausted than before. Home gadgets such as herb cutters, automatic floor vacuums, and programmable thermostats will save you time, energy, and sometimes money. If there are household tasks getting in the way of your much-needed personal time, you can find dozens of solutions online at affordable prices.

Treat a Friend

As a compassionate sign, Cancer needs to have a self-care routine that balances out her giving nature. Sometimes, though, the best way to restore your own energy is through making someone else happy. Delight a friend with a simple, humorous present that reminds them of you: crab apple jelly. With dozens of online recipes, you can make your own jelly in just a few easy steps. Divide the jelly into clear jars, add a ribbon, and surprise your friend!

Go to a Classical Concert

Cancer loves period music with original instruments. The moving sounds and sophisticated atmosphere of a classical performance delight her keen senses. Bring a loved one along to share the experience with, or go alone to fully immerse yourself and focus on the sights and sounds of the performance. You can also use a pair of opera glasses for a classic touch. For a truly stunning performance, visit a major concert hall, such as Carnegie Hall in New York; Symphony Hall in Boston; or the Sydney Opera House.

Embrace Your "Crabby" Side

Cancer is symbolized by the Crab. With its hard outer shell and soft interior, the Crab is the perfect representation of this tough yet sensitive water sign. Display your astrological connection with a crab totem. A totem is an object that serves as an emblem for a person or group. This figurine will be a proud symbol of your celestial roots, as well as a reminder to remain strong but never lose your sensitive side. Be sure to place your totem on a mantel or table where you will see it daily.

Visit the Past in Style

Cancer is a sign deeply rooted in the romance of the past. In fact, many Cancerians can be found working as historians. Whether it's vintage cars, music, or fashion, you take a special interest in the nostalgia, style, and magic of generations past. Spend an afternoon (or full day if you like!) visiting the past in an aesthetically pleasing way by antique shopping or enjoying a vintage car or fashion show. This quick and sophisticated trip into the past will boost your mood—and maybe teach you something new in the process.

Decorate with Matching Sets

As an emotional and nurturing sign, Cancer delights in both giving and receiving love. Home accents in doubles and matching pairs attract love to you, while encouraging affection and strong bonds among your current relationships. Matching décor will also maintain balance in your home.

Try pairs or sets of three in deep colors reminiscent of the ocean. Shades such as navy blue and teal have a calming effect that will promote relaxation in your home. Great accents to purchase in doubles include candlesticks for your dining room table, lounge chairs for your living room, and nightstands for your bedroom.

Boost Confidence with Narcissus Flowers

Humble and compassionate Cancer is eager to raise others up. Sometimes in this process, however, she may look down to realize that she herself has been sinking.

While care for others is important, it is also crucial that Cancer recognize and celebrate her own triumphs and abilities. A great way to give yourself a little confidence boost is with narcissus flowers.

In Greek mythology, Narcissus was a man so self-absorbed that he fell in love with his own reflection. To teach the importance of striking a balance between humility and self-assurance, the gods turned him into the narcissus flower. Next time you're feeling down on yourself, buy a bouquet of narcissus flowers as a reminder of how special you are.

Go Scuba Diving

In need of a little rejuvenation? Tap into your natural Cancerian element with a scuba diving adventure. Scuba diving blends Cancer's love of water with her deep sense of curiosity. This revitalizing dip in the water is the perfect way to get your blood flowing if you have felt a bit sluggish recently—or recharge your batteries if you are feeling burnt out. Start a recommended scuba diving course, and get your scuba diving certificate. You may even spot a few of your astrological kin (the crab) during the dive!

Draw

Sensitive Cancer is a visual sign. She often needs to see a picture laid out in front of her to understand the full idea, but once she does, she can spot details no one else

noticed. Imagery can also enable her to express and reflect on her thoughts and feelings far better than words ever could.

Embrace your inner artist and release your emotions by drawing. Don't think; just let your pencil or pen guide you. Consider bringing a small sketchbook wherever you go so you can draw whenever the urge strikes.

Visit the Galápagos Islands

Beautiful views, seclusion from the rest of the world, and the perfect blend of adventure and relaxation—is there any location more perfect for Cancer? Probably not. But this isn't your typical tropical vacation: The Galápagos Islands are a special destination every Cancer should journey to at least once.

The historical roots of these islands will especially delight Cancer. From the inspiration for Charles Darwin's theories on evolution to the adventures of sea pirates, the Galápagos hold countless stories of the world. The Galápagos also have a feature that Cancer will have a special connection to: the Sally Lightfoot crab. Common in the Galápagos, this crustacean (and astrological symbol for Cancer) has a beautiful orange and red shell with striking blue accents.

Add a Little Heat

Feeling a bit lethargic? No worries! You can jump-start your motivation with a bit of heat. Inserting just a short burst of controlled heat to your day will balance out your water element without overpowering it. Heat and movement stimulate blood flow, which increases the release of feel-good hormones, such as endorphins, dopamine, and serotonin. Doing a vigorous exercise or diffusing a stronger scent like cinnamon essential oil (just be sure to dilute it in a lot of water to keep the "heat" at a manageable level!) are great ways to clear out stagnant energy. Try attending a hot yoga class, adding a little ground cinnamon spice to your morning tea or coffee, or diffusing a diluted ginger essential oil.

Find Balance with Selenite

Connect with your celestial ruler, the Moon, with the powers of selenite. Long, slender, and semitranslucent white in color, this crystal is named after Selene, the Greek goddess of the moon. Like its namesake, selenite represents fertility and nurturing, which are also qualities of Cancer.

Selenite also regulates the flow of both mental and physical energy. As a neutral stone, it does not hold negative energy, nor does it stimulate enthusiasm or movement. Because of this, selenite is the perfect crystal for promoting balance of the mind, body, and spirit. Place this crystal in a central location in your home, or use it in meditation to draw both balance and lunar abundance to you.

Adorn Yourself with Silver

Silver is reminiscent of the Moon, Cancer's ruling body. Like the moon, silver is a reflective material, but its connection to Cancer's celestial ruler extends far beyond outward appearance. Silver is a healing element that is believed to enhance the powers of the lunar cycle, particularly the full and new moon. Wearing silver will help Cancer sync her emotions to the moon's phases, and manage the thoughts and feelings that are most prominent during the full and new moon. Additionally, just as the moon reflects light, silver reflects negativity away from you.

As a sensitive sign, you can easily feel overwhelmed by the noisy world around you, as well as your own overactive mind. Wearing a silver necklace or earrings will help you redirect negative energy away from your life.

Show Yourself

Let out the real you. Cancer has strong bonds and relationships with her friends and family members. However, she can also hide behind a tough outer shell, refusing to let others see her vulnerable side for fear of getting hurt. Practice letting people in and showing them the real, wonderful you. If it helps, you can come up with a question or empowering statement to ask or say to yourself in times when you feel yourself retreating into your shell. Try asking yourself, "How would I react in this situation if I were not afraid?"

Just admitting that you have certain fears can be enough motivation to face them head-on. Remember this: True friends and family members love you for who you really are.

Ask for Help

Cancer is the most nurturing of the zodiac signs. She gives and gives, and asks for nothing in return. Over time, friends and family members come to expect that she is never in need of assistance. This isn't because they are selfish or uncaring—they just can't remember the last time they heard Cancer ask for help. Practice asking for that assistance when you need it. It is not a sign of weakness, and you are not putting people out when you ask them to help you. For all of the support you give them, they are more than happy to reciprocate. So let them!

Host a House "Warming"

Home is Cancer's sanctuary, and her loved ones are her lifeblood. If you have been feeling a little down in the dumps lately, warm up your home with the love and laughter of friends and family by hosting a house "warming" party.

As a nurturing sign, Cancer is also the perfect host or hostess, and she delights in zipping around her kitchen and living spaces with plates of food, napkins for spills, and great story anecdotes. The fun and love you share will be the perfect reward for your preparation.

Hire a Cleaning Service

Cancer spends much of her time at home, enjoying solitary activities and a lot of rest to keep her batteries fully charged. As a sensitive sign, she is also keenly aware of messy spaces, and this disorder in her home can leave her feeling overwhelmed or unmotivated. Invest in a service that does a complete deep clean of your home once a week, or once every few weeks, to avoid unnecessary stress. Just like you, your home deserves to be well taken care of.

Explore Your Ancestry

Cancer is a sign deeply rooted to the past. A highly intuitive, and many would say psychic, zodiac sign, she has a connection to the subconscious of all things. Explore the history of your family and the past people who helped shape you by digging into your ancestry. Ask family members about their own childhoods, and the relatives who came before them. What were these distant relatives like? What did they do for a living? And how did they impact the lives and values of your current family?

There are also many ancestry websites and digitalized records available to fill in gaps that living relatives cannot. What you learn can help you better understand not only your roots, but also yourself and your place in the world.

Sort Through Your Mementos

As a nostalgic sign, Cancer likes to keep mementos and souvenirs, which can pile up over time. Take a few hours, or a day, to go through your collection. Sort out what matters most and is worth keeping, versus what is taking up space and can be let go. Things that once had sentimental value may no longer have the same meaning. The trip down memory lane will lift your spirits, while the act of moving on and cleansing your space of clutter will free up room for things that are more important—both emotionally and physically.

Get a Worry Doll

Ruled by the Moon, Cancer is a nurturing sign who tries her best to help everyone and maintain peace. But, sometimes, this urge to fix everyone's troubles can lead to a buildup of anxious thoughts. Use a worry doll to soothe your worries.

A tradition of the Mayan civilization, worry dolls originated as dolls that children kept under their pillows to protect against nightmares. These dolls absorb the concerns of the user, so they can sleep (or go about their day) worry-free. Keep a worry doll under your pillow, or carry it in your pocket to ease stressful thoughts.

Buy a Poetry Book

Poetry has a unique way of capturing and channeling emotions. As a sensitive water sign, Cancer has a lot of emotions moving through her at all times, and taking some time to read poetry is a therapeutic act of self-care. The best poems for Cancer are those written from the raw emotion and honest experiences of the author. Talented writers who are particularly well known for their passionate, uncompromising poems include Sylvia Plath, E.E. Cummings, and Emily Dickinson. Consider buying a poetry anthology so you can spend some time appreciating the beauty of the written word—from the classical greats, to the modern up-and-coming poets.

Celebrate the Summer Solstice

The sun enters Cancer on the summer solstice, the longest day of the year. Have a celebration in honor of your birth season by throwing a summer solstice party. Cancer knows how to host a memorable affair, and friends and family members alike will delight in your knack for good food, inviting décor, and thoughtful conversation. You can bring elements of both the sun and your astrological sign into play with sun-shaped cookies, beachy accents, and tasty crab cake appetizers.

Send a Thank-You Note to a Mother

Cancer is ruled by the Moon, which represents motherhood and nurturing instincts. Because of this, Cancer has a strong connection with her mom or other motherly figures. Show your appreciation for a mother figure in your life by writing a thank-you note. Whether she is your own mother, a friend who has a child, or a woman who showed you motherly care and guidance, she will be moved by your simple message. It may be just the inspiration she needs to get through a tough time or remember that she is doing a wonderful job.

Take a Milk Bath

Given Cancer's connection to nurturance and motherhood, it is no surprise that the perfect self-care routine for her involves milk. Channel your inner Cleopatra and indulge in a luxurious ritual she was infamous for: the milk bath.

Many spas allow you to soak in milk- and floral-infused water, or relax as milk is used in massage or other body treatments for your skin. You can also perform this self-care ritual at home by adding one of the many bath products that contain milk (such as bath bombs or soaks) to your bath water.

Try Hydrotherapy

As the first water sign of the zodiac, Cancer needs plenty of H_2O in her self-care regimen.

Ease into your natural element with hydrotherapy. This soothing practice can involve a number of treatments, from underwater massages to soaking tubs full of minerals. Hydrotherapy is also a great tool for exercising your body following an operation or injury. Ask your doctor and research the best practices for you and your health needs. You can find a spa near you that offers the many healing effects of hydrotherapy, or create your own therapeutic oasis with a relaxing bath or foot soak.

Catch Frogs

Water, a bit of whimsy... What more could Cancer ask for? As the astrological caretaker, this sign needs self-care practices that allow her to let loose once in a while and invite her inner child out to play. Catching frogs (or attempting to) is the perfect afternoon activity for Cancer to unwind with. Do some research before you go to make sure you know all you need to about safety, endangered varieties, handling, and hygiene. Try picking a rainy day to go frog-catching (the rain will draw them out and also appeal to your natural element) at a local pond or marsh. You can also bring along a friend for even more fun and fond memories to look back on.

Up Your Omega-3s

As a sensitive sign, Cancer is prone to having dozens of different thoughts and feelings running through her at once. This can lead to periods of anxiety or low spirits. Omega-3s can combat these emotions, and they are also good for your overall health. Fatty acids like omega-3s serve as energy for your muscles, heart, and other organs, and also as the building blocks for your cells. Ask your doctor (who is familiar with your health and medications) about supplements. You can also find omega-3s in certain foods, such as fatty fish (try mackerel or salmon) and walnuts.

Add Some Anchovies

While some may turn away from this ingredient, Cancer loves the salt and texture anchovies add to a dish. Found at most grocery stores, these small fish resonate with Cancer's natural element, connecting her to her love of the sea and everything in it. Add a few anchovies to your slice of pizza! The flavors of the fish are a perfect complement to the cheese and crust.

But why stop there? You can toss anchovies into a salad, mix them into spaghetti, or serve them over garlic and cheese toast. However you enjoy them, be sure to savor every bite as a reminder of your ocean ties.

Practice a Moonlight Meditation

As a sensitive and reflective sign of the zodiac, Cancer often has dozens of thoughts racing through her mind at once. This can sometimes make winding down for sleep at the end of the day a bit of a challenge. One simple way to get your mind ready for bed is with a bedtime meditation. A bedtime meditation is an easy way to channel the stress you've built up from the day and ease your mind into sleep so you are recharged and ready for whatever tomorrow brings.

To do a moon-inspired meditation before bed, simply sit in the lotus position on or beside your bed and close your eyes. Now, picture the calming image of the moon (or look out the window and see it for yourself!). Focus on channeling that sense of peace from the moonlight from your mind down to your arms, fingers, legs, and feet. Take note of how your body loosens with each passing moment. Once you feel fully relaxed, you're ready for sleep.

CHAPTER 11

Self-Care for Leo

Dates: July 23–August 22
Element: Fire
Polarity: Yang
Quality: Fixed
Symbol: Lion
Ruler: The Sun

Leo is the second fire sign and the most vital sign in the zodiac. He reigns in summer when the sun is at its warmest. He is yang and a fixed sign, and his preferred self-care rituals line up with the traits associated with these cosmic designations. Leo's fire power is coiled and ready for action, and he has tremendous amounts of focused energy. These traits are also associated with the Lion, the unrivaled king of the jungle and Leo's impressive symbol. Like a lion, at his best Leo is the generous king sharing his warmth and magnanimity with all who come across his path. At his worst he is an attention seeker who has difficulty sharing the spotlight.

The Greek myth of Phaeton is one to consider for Leo. Phaeton, who was mortal on his mother's side, came to the Palace of the Sun to find out if the Sun God (the Sun is Leo's ruling planet) was indeed his father. The Sun God was touched by the boy's sincerity and told him that, yes, he was his father. To prove his love, he offered the boy anything he wanted, and Phaeton asked to drive his father's chariot of the sun. The Sun God recognized that he had to fulfill his promise, but realizing that doing so would probably destroy the boy, he tried to dissuade him.

Phaeton would not listen. He began his journey but lost control of the reins, causing the chariot of the sun to dip so near the earth that it threatened to burn everything in sight. The god Zeus intervened by throwing a thunderbolt at the chariot, striking Phaeton dead. The story's parallel with Leo's cosmic astrological personality traits is clear: If Leo lets his immature ego take the reins, there can be pain and meltdown. But if he is able to practice self-control, Leo can cooperate and share his enthusiasm and fiery, fun personality with others. The course of any Leo's life will be determined by the extent to which he can shine with other people.

Self-Care and Leo

Leo is a fire sign who is ruled by the Sun; therefore, he's active and adventurous and can be recharged by the sun, so he should look for lots of warm weather, outdoor self-care rituals. This sign is dramatic, confident, showy, and outgoing. Remember that Leo is symbolized by the Lion, so like a lion he is fierce and prideful, and he loves taking care of his glorious mane. Hair care is seemingly a small part of life, but not for Leo. Leo's mane is his pride and joy. It is usually thick and wavy. He loves hair products, and any evidence that his hair is looking lackluster or falling out can propel him into examining how to take care of himself better. As the king of the jungle, Leo is also often enamored with royalty. All of these things combine to make engaging in self-care enjoyable, necessary, and desirable for this fire sign.

That said, Leo is the sign of the father—the leader of the pride—and, in traditional societies, the father as head of the household prayed for guidance to lead his family well. Both Leo men and women feel this responsibility for their family, friends, and circle of acquaintances, and use their ability to inspire others to take care of their own. This pride in responsibility can weigh on those born under this sign, and it can make it difficult for Leo to really take the time to engage in a self-care routine, even though his excellent sense of intuition may tell him that he needs to. However, Leo loves to look good and enjoys indulging himself—no one is going to tell Leo that he doesn't deserve something—so while getting Leo to practice self-care can be difficult, once he's started, it's tough to get Leo to stop.

Leo Rules the Heart and Spine

Leo rules over the spine and heart; self-care related to the spine, back, and heart is especially important. For Leo the bones of the spine aren't as important as the spinal cord, the pathway of energy in the body from bottom to top. This pathway in the Hindu tradition is called *kundalini*, or "vital energy," which travels from the base of the spine to the top of the head. Leo has a natural intuition of what is good for him when all his energy is flowing up and down this light-filled pathway in the body, and (if he's paying attention) he can use this intuition to choose self-care rituals that speak clearly to his sign and fire element. The best self-care practices for maintaining free energy flow for Leo are gentle stretches and yoga. Certain martial arts like Tai Chi are also beneficial; they are both graceful and powerful. Leo doesn't need an aggressive sport; he needs an elegant one such as aikido, fencing, or tennis. Leo lights up with any sport or exercise where he can shine individually and make use of his steady energy. Additionally, if Leo has aches and pains in any part of the back, it means there is a tension buildup that should be released. Self-care such as gentle chiropractic adjustments or cranial sacral massage can easily help Leo keep in balance.

Leo also rules the heart. Phrases such as *brave heart*, *courageous heart*, or *he has a good heart* are frequently used to describe the Lion. He is king not only because of his power but also because of his care and warmth toward others. Eating a heart-healthy diet is an important self-care practice for Leo, and in later years, those born under this sign should make time for annual checkups and stress tests to make sure the heart muscle is strong and steady.

That said, perhaps the more important part of heart care for Leo is emotional. Leo's heart expands with love the more he shares his fire power. His sign is synonymous with heart fire. He can give himself wholeheartedly to projects, to romance, and to his children—and this is the true meaning of Leo's gift to himself and others. Doing whatever he needs to do to keep this most important soul quality front and center is the most vital type of self-care Leo can practice.

Leo and Self-Care Success

One pitfall for Leo's self-care program is that Leo does not enjoy programs that are rigid and mass produced. If he decides to meditate, for example, he will want to find the best teacher or group possible. And if the teacher is a little famous, it wouldn't hurt. Likewise, if there is prestige included in a particular group, it will please Leo's sense of entitlement and self-worth.

Another pitfall for a self-care program is lack of rewards. Leo needs to see progress as quickly as possible. The progress does not have to be measurable like so many pounds lost or reps performed, but Leo does like to see that something he wants to do or have is getting closer. For example, those pants that were too tight and now fit well and look great will encourage Leo to keep to an eating or fitness plan. If he feels discouraged, he can summon his willpower and try another approach. Leo can be very disciplined when pursuing a goal.

The best way for Leo to seek advice and to learn about self-care is to find a common bond with a knowledgeable equal who will help Leo shine more brilliantly. Leo can recognize his faults but does not take well to criticism. Leo does not like to be in a subservient or underling position to a doctor or professional. He is happy to learn and benefit from wisdom and guidance, especially if he is in the middle of stress or difficulties, but not at the expense of his own confidence and pride. Any whiff of competition and the Lion will stalk out of the room very quickly. Praise is the best approach. Leo doesn't need flattery, but a sincere recognition of Leo's very good qualities will help keep the Lion engaged and interested in any of his self-care rituals.

In terms of soul development, Leo is the sign of awareness of self. He always realizes and understands exactly how he's feeling, and his charisma and sense of self-confidence are palpable. Inside, however, those born under this fire sign can feel insecure, seek constant attention, and search for approval. This part of Leo's personality is sometimes hidden, though, as his pride keeps him from showing insecurity to those around him. The ability to balance these two parts of his personality throughout his life traces the soul growth of the Lion.

To keep developing his native soul qualities of generosity and leadership in his self-care program, Leo must feel that his efforts are appreciated. Leo needs a support group or a cheering section to boost and applaud his progress in developing body, mind, and spirit. This could literally be a gang of exercise buddies, a circle of meditation friends, or an intellectual group such as a book group. The essential part of self-care for Leo is that it involves other people who notice him, and any group like this has social possibilities, such as going to the juice bar or out to eat after exercising. This reinforces Leo's warmth and sparkle. He is not a loner.

Self-praise is another restorative way for Leo to encourage good self-care. He could give himself a round of applause for every healthful choice of food, for every good exercise session, or for every generous action toward others. Self-care for Leo can be a natural outgrowth of the sign's pride in his appearance and making a good impression. He could imagine that every day is opening night for the Leo show and his self-care program is the main attraction. This will motivate him to find self-care actions that are effective, fun, and workable. If all of this self-care prompts compliments and good attention, Leo will purr contentedly and maintain the habits of self-care forever.

Perhaps the most important pathway for self-care success, however, is when Leo can be the instructor. Leo is a natural-born teacher. He wants to share his wisdom and knowledge with others—and as he teaches others, he also inspires himself to make self-care a priority in his life. So let's now take a look at some self-care activities that are tailored specifically for Leo.

Enjoy a Tequila Sunrise

Need to unwind, Leo? Sit back with a tequila sunrise. The tequila kick appeals to the adventurous side of Leo, and orange juice represents elements of the Sun, Leo's ruling planet.

To enjoy, combine 3 tablespoons (1½ fluid ounces) of tequila and ¾ cup (6 fluid ounces) of freshly squeezed orange juice in a jigger. Pour mixture over a glass of ice, and slowly add 1 tablespoon (½ fluid ounce) of grenadine syrup. Allow the grenadine to

settle, giving your finished cocktail a dramatic aesthetic that appeals to Leo's showy nature. Enjoy this drink fit for a king!

Salute the Sun

Leo's confidence comes from his core, and yoga is an ideal way to manifest and strengthen Leo's most positive qualities. The best yoga posture for Leo as a fire sign? Naturally, a Sun Salutation. Greet the day with this practice.

There are many variations of this sequence, and you can modify the poses to suit your energy level on any given day. The more quickly you move through the sequence, the more stimulating it is. If you move through the poses more slowly, they can have a more calming effect. Look online or on your favorite yoga app for the Sun Salutation sequence to best suit your ability level and desire.

Decorate with Peacock Feathers

Your home should be a reflection of yourself. Why not make it a regal retreat by working peacock feathers into your décor?

The peacock is a royal, beautiful bird that has become synonymous with the spotlight. Its aesthetic speaks to Leo's regal nature, so consider arranging a collection of cruelty-free peacock feathers in your entryway. When you come home at the end of a challenging day and you feel your crown slipping, you'll be greeted by a colorful display that will remind you of your innate Leo power.

Meditate with Jacinth

This crystal, also known as zircon, occurs in a sunburst range of colors—orange-yellow, orange-red, or yellow-brown. The colors resonate well with Leo's fiery nature, but the affinity doesn't end there.

One way that naturally energetic Leo can benefit from jacinth is through the crystal's unique ability to prevent nightmares and ensure a deep and tranquil sleep.

Prepare yourself for rest. Wearing loose, comfortable nighttime clothing, sit or lie in a dimly lit room and hold the crystal in your left hand. Complete a series of ten cleansing breaths, focusing on releasing any pent-up energy through your exhalations. Keep your jacinth on your bedside table for restorative, restful sleep.

Focus On the Heart Chakra

While Leo is very passionate, his heart is his most vulnerable area. You can protect your heart and strengthen your emotions through meditation, an important aspect of self-care no matter what your sign. Green is the heart chakra color, and it plays an important part in your meditation.

In a dimly lit room, try to clear your mind as you focus on your breath. Each time you inhale, think of taking in the color green and directing its energy to your heart space. As you quiet your thoughts and focus on your energy, you'll be able to hear and feel your heartbeat as you draw healing energy toward your heart.

Repeat this practice any time you feel particularly vulnerable, or need to balance your innate boldness with compassion and love.

Lead with Generosity

Leo leads with his heart, and this translates to a very generous nature. But in times of stress it is easy to abandon our natural gifts in favor of fight or flight. Shift your focus by making "I lead with generosity" your personal mantra, and repeat it often.

During difficult or stressful times (or any time you need to re-center), close your eyes and repeat "I lead with generosity" until you can feel your energy change. If you're in a setting where speaking aloud isn't possible, repeat the phrase in your head. You'll find that by reminding yourself of your innate gift, it will be easier to share it with the world.

Embrace the Drama

Leo has a flair for the dramatic—put it to good use! While chores like cleaning the house or making dinner may not feel like self-care, they are essential to your health and well-being. Turn mundane chores into an event by adding a soundtrack.

Instead of just turning on the radio, seek out music with a dramatic feel to get you in the mood. Show tunes are perfect! Turn the music up loud, and allow the strong voices and soaring strains to turn the ordinary into the extraordinary. Your chores will go more quickly, and the emotion the music evokes will stay with you throughout your day.

Channel a Fellow Leo

Feeling down? Doubting yourself? Channel the energy of a fellow Leo to turn your mood around. Perhaps a dear Leo friend or family member has a swagger you've always admired—ask yourself what they would do in your shoes. By trying to adopt the headspace of someone else, you may see things through a different perspective.

If that doesn't work, look to the stars... as in celebrities! Barack Obama, Tom Brady, Madonna, and Mick Jagger are all Leos. Read some of their inspirational quotes; watch an inspiring game or concert footage; or put on some of their music and let the rhythm inspire you to relax and recharge. Spread that Leo energy!

Experiment with Rosemary Essential Oil

While Leo's confidence and extroverted nature serve him well, it can also lead to stress. Combat burnout and practice self-care for your mind and body by embracing the power of rosemary essential oil.

This luxurious aroma appeals to Leo's zest for life, and it also nurtures your body as you fight feelings of pressure. Try rubbing a few drops into your hands and feet when you need to reset your energy (be sure to always dilute rosemary according to instructions, and use with caution if you have sensitive skin). If constant multitasking is leaving your brain spinning, massage your temples with a few drops of rosemary to improve your memory. Make it a ritual by dimming the lights and putting on some soft music—you'll soon find yourself ready for your next challenge.

Embrace Cooling Citrus in the Hot Weather

When the temperature rises, Leo's already fiery nature can hit a boiling point! But you can cool your jets and freshen your skin in one act! Try freshening up with orange blossom spray or lemon verbena body splash. Leo is drawn to bold, luxurious fragrances, and the strong, sunny colors appeal to Leo's affinity with the sun. Try keeping a bottle in the refrigerator, and misting your body when the heat gets too much. It will hydrate your skin, clear your mind, and reinvigorate you on a steamy day.

Bring the Sun Indoors with a Fruit Tree

While Leo would like to, basking in the sun isn't always an option! Harness the energy of your ruling planet by growing an orange or lemon tree indoors.

Caring for your tree can also be an act of self-care. After selecting the tree most appropriate for your living space, make its care a part of your daily routine—keep it watered and well lit, and keep an eye out for pests or brown/dead leaves.

Not only will you enjoy the vibrant energy of the tree as it grows, but also, you'll have a healthy, flavorful snack at your fingertips!

Add Glamour to Any Day

Even confident Leo can lose a bit of sparkle in the day-to-day grind. When you're feeling particularly un-fierce, take small steps to add a bit of glamour back into your day.

Why not throw on your favorite pair of heels or your favorite item of clothing when you're watching Netflix on the couch? Wear your most luxurious robe while folding laundry. Or use the holiday china to serve your Tuesday-night pizza delivery. Even when the workweek zaps your lust for life, put some celebration back in your self-care and make any day one to remember!

Build a Sacred Space

Leo benefits from any time spent basking in the glow of his ruling heavenly body, the Sun. Find the sunniest spot in your home and create a sanctuary of your very own—a place where you can practice self-care every day.

The time you spend in your sun sanctuary should empower you to lead with your natural generosity and warmth of spirit. If you find yourself veering toward brashness or arrogance, use your space as a place to re-center yourself. Harness the spirit of the sun, allowing you to maximize your potential, and go about your day with a clear, focused mind.

Sit Like a Royal

Leo's home is his castle. Reign comfortably and confidently, in a large, comfy chair.

Every king needs a throne! Visit thrift stores and discount sites for a chair that resembles one fit for royalty. When you need to make important decisions or phone calls, sit upon your throne and be inspired by its power—and yours!

By adapting a king- or queen-like state of mind, you'll channel regal confidence and authority. When you need solace or rest, your throne can be a place for comfort and respite. While it may feel like an extravagance, the benefits of your special chair will far outweigh the cost.

Embrace the Power of Mirrors

Leo is the most aware-of-his-image sign of the zodiac, and often needs to see random glimpses of himself. Feed your desire for attention by placing mirrors in a variety of prominent places in your home. Hang a sunburst mirror center stage in the living room over the sofa. Decorate with mirrors of all sizes—maybe even a collage of mirrors on one wall?

Once you are happy with the arrangement, be sure to keep your mirrors clean. It will make your self-image sparkle.

Make Your Home a Castle

Although Louis XIV was a Virgo, he was known as the Sun King. He was into fashion, décor, and culture. If you're looking to inject some drama and fashion into your home, look to Versailles for inspiration.

Choose a canopy bed for the bedroom. Celebrate your regal nature by introducing royal accents into your home décor. Drape lush, velvety fabrics over your furniture and window treatments. While the exterior world can make all of us feel like lowly servants, Leo can feel like royalty in his home fit for a king.

Take Care of Your Mane

A lion's mane is a point of pride—and the same should be true for Leo. An important part of self-care is feeling good about yourself, so if you need a boost, indulge yourself by cleaning out your old, expired, and no-good hair products in your cabinets, and make room for the new and improved!

New shampoo, conditioners, and vitamin-enriched hair products will keep Leo's mane shining. When you have time, treat yourself to a hair mask, a Moroccan oil product, or a hot oil treatment. Grooming shouldn't be tiresome—it can be an indulgent, spa-like experience. So light a candle, put on your favorite robe, and fluff some towels in the dryer so you have a warm towel after you get out of the bath or shower to create your own at-home spa.

Try Cat Pose

In addition to the heart and back, Leo's ruler, the Sun, has always been associated with the spine. Keep your spine flexible with yoga—particularly Cat Pose, which is an effective, gentle way to warm up your spine.

The next time you feel a bit stiff, take a moment at work or home to take care of your spinal column. Using your favorite yoga app, book, or website, follow the simple instructions for Cat Pose, being sure to keep your knees directly below your hips and wrists. You may also want to complement Cat Pose on your exhales with Cow Pose on your inhales for a gentle vinyasa.

Give Fencing a Try

Feed Leo's desire for competition and drama with fencing! Known as the fashionable sport of the aristocracy throughout the ages, fencing is one of the original Olympic sports. Today, it is recognized as an invigo-rating combination of physical and mental exercise. You can serve your need for both these types of self-care by trying it out.

It can be an incredibly social sport as well. Look for local fencing clubs who wel-come new and learning members, and ask how you might get involved. Pay particu-lar attention to protecting your heart dur-ing this stimulating and challenging sport.

Stay Active in the Winter Months

Leo's affinity for the sun can make it tempt-ing to hibernate in the colder months. Fight the urge and get outside, even when the mercury drops! Doing so will get you some much-needed sun during the winter period.

Braving the cold can also feed your sense of adventure. Why not try figure skat-ing, snowboarding, skiing, or even sled-ding? Honor your childlike side by building a snowman or having a snowball fight with friends. You can get exercise, relieve stress, and enjoy the fresh air—a well-rounded act of self-care.

Accessorize

Your Leo nature means you favor bold col-ors and outfits that command attention. Sometimes, though, professional obliga-tions or other circumstances require more formal or staid looks. In these circum-stances, maintain formality but add a touch of drama with colorful scarves, jewelry, gloves, ties, or handbags.

Keep an eye out for inexpensive, one-of-a-kind accessories in thrift shops and on vintage-clothing websites. Whether multicolored or sparkly, the more eye-catching, the better!

These fun accessories allow you to make a statement and express yourself no matter what the occasion. Let your lion roar, Leo!

Wear Your Heart on Your Wrist

Leading with your heart, Leo, create a piece of jewelry that combines history and beauty.

Beautiful and full of love, a charm bracelet (or leather cuff) is the perfect bau-ble for Leo. Find charms (or other symbolic embellishments) that represent your inter-ests and memories. Gold and rubies are favorites for Leo, with the gold represent-ing bold beauty and the ruby being Leo's birthstone.

This wearable memento can be eye-catching and sentimental at once, inviting questions from curious friends and family that lead to walks down memory lane. Spend time to make your wrist accessory both attractive and meaningful, as Leo prefers.

Expand Your Jewelry Collection

Need a recharge? Look to your jewelry box! Amber jewelry, cat's eye, and tiger's eye are all sun-kissed stones ruled by Leo. Incorporate them into your collection, and wear them when you are looking for a quick hit of sun, or just a way to make a bold fashion statement!

Leo enjoys attention, and these conversation pieces are sure to attract the eye of friends and family. This small action will keep you feeling confident, looking your best, and feeding your desire for the sun—it's an indulgent yet doable act of self-care!

Give Yourself a Hand

What to do when you're craving some attention and praise, but aren't around other people? Give yourself a hand with an applause box!

Congratulate yourself frequently with this round of applause you control. Simply lift the lid and you'll be greeted with warm applause. While it may seem silly, this simple act of self-care can boost your self-esteem and feed your confident nature. Use it to pump yourself up before a work presentation or first date—or to reward yourself for tackling a long-delayed chore around the house. No occasion is too small to celebrate. Take a bow, Leo!

Indulge In the Theater

Leo loves drama and spectacle. There is a perfect place to celebrate this love—the theater! Become a seasonal supporter of a local theater and go frequently. The music,

costumes, and dramatic dialogue combine for an experience sure to feed your creative soul.

If your craving for attention extends to the spotlight, you might even consider auditioning for a part! If you'd rather, you could volunteer to help out backstage, or with costume and scenery prep. Whether in the audience, on the stage, or behind the curtains, the theater is a wonderful place to indulge in the creative aspect of self-care. Bravo, Leo!

Crown Yourself King!

Indulge your inner king or queen—with a crown! While it may feel silly, a crown represents royalty. What better way to honor Leo's symbol, the Lion? Leo enjoys attention, and you're sure to spark conversation when wearing a crown or tiara. After all, royalty needs to be recognized.

Or perhaps you don your crown when you're feeling not-so-fabulous. While the lion is the well-known regal king of the jungle, you can use your crown to boost confidence and to lift yourself up—a true act of self-care.

Test Your Luck

Looking to enjoy an unusual night out? Try a casino! Leo is typically lucky with card games of chance, and the casino setting can be both social and dramatic.

Make the evening more special by adding some Leo flair to your outfit that night—a flashy evening gown or a sharp suit will make you the center of attention at the tables or slots.

Once you've gained some confidence, work your way over to the blackjack or poker tables—there you can show off your excellence at card games!

Embrace Your Childlike Nature

One of the greatest acts of emotional self-care is spending time with children: others' or your own. Leo has a natural affinity with the enthusiasm and charm of kids, and time spent with them can be a wonderful way to de-stress and have fun.

Both Leo and children alike enjoy being outside in the sun, so play a simple game of tag, go to a playground, or just go for a walk. Allow the kids to take the lead, and your eyes will be opened to their joy and appreciation for the simplest things life has to offer.

Celebrate Anything with Champagne

Leo loves adding a pop of drama and excitement to any old day. What better way to do so than to pop a bottle of champagne?

Don't just reserve the bubbly for special occasions—add some excitement to brunch, a touch of class to happy hour, and some fizzy fun to a girls' (or boys') night out. By making these small moments occasions to remember, you're taking care to mark life's small joys and to be more present in the moment—a great way to focus on your emotional self-care.

Visualize the Sun

When you need a mental break but can't get away, try using visualization exercises. Since Leo thrives on the sun's energy, it can provide a great focus point for your practice.

Whether you're working or not, take a moment to clear your head. Then, if you're able, close your eyes and picture the golden warmth of the sun. Imagine the feel of its comforting heat on your skin, and picture the glow of the sun's light reflecting off water. Taking deep, calming breaths during your visualization, continue your exercise until you feel ready to return to your day. It's a small yet effective practice for spiritual self-care.

Let the Beat Move You

Nothing gets Leo moving like music with a beat. When you're looking for some tunes to perk up your day or get the evening started, try samba, merengue, or Latin ballroom—all are sure to get the Lion's toes tapping.

Since Leo is the "look at me" sign, he particularly enjoys music he can be a part of, even in subtle ways. Music that is easy to sing along to or fun to dance to is at the top of Leo's playlist. If you're not familiar with samba, merengue, or Latin ballroom, look online for suggestions for artists and songs to listen to. Or take it one step further and consider signing up for a dance class in these styles, or research places to go out dancing for the evening. You'll feel like you're part of the show!

Add Drama to Your Dining

Just as he enjoys drama in every other aspect of his life, Leo likes cuisine with dramatic tastes. While you may not have the time to make intricately prepared meals every day, there are some easy ways to add some drama to your meals!

In the morning, try making your scrambled eggs with plain yogurt instead of milk—it will give them a tangy flavor. If you like heat, add a dash of hot sauce. For lunch, add dried fruit and seeds to your salad, or fresh herbs and exotic cheeses to liven up your sandwich. For dinner, use cinnamon to flavor meat dishes—this spice will add a rich, bold taste to your meals.

And what's drama without an audience? Try out your new meals for some friends, and get their input on how you're doing and what to change for next time. Eat up, Leo!

Turn to Turmeric

Take a moment for health—and flavor—by incorporating turmeric into your diet.

Turmeric has wonderful anti-inflammatory properties, and its golden, sun-like color particularly appeals to Leo. Work it into your diet for an easy yet effective act of self-care.

Try sprinkling turmeric on rice or vegetables. Rub it into poultry and meat before cooking, or, if you really love the flavor, make yourself a turmeric smoothie. Preparing and drinking this healthy, flavorful beverage can easily become part of your morning routine, a self-care ritual that will start your day off on the healthy foot.

Make It Extra-Virgin

Since Leo rules the heart, it is extra important that he takes care of his ticker. An easy way to take care of your heart? Cook with extra-virgin olive oil!

Olive oil is an effective way to maintain a healthy heart, thanks to its superpowered monounsaturated fat content. It also contains powerful antioxidants.

While it can be hard to find time to exercise, odds are, you cook or eat a meal every day that, with simple adjustments, can be given a heart-healthy makeover with the addition of extra-virgin olive oil. To your health, Leo!

Have a Cup of Chamomile

Soothe your system in the evening by sipping tea made from Leo's herb: chamomile. Medicinally, chamomile can have anti-inflammatory properties and aid in digestion. On an astrological and spiritual level, chamomile is ruled by the Sun, the governing celestial body for Leo. Its flowers are solar yellow, and it can have a wonderful calming effect for Leo.

Rather than buying your tea in a store, consider making your own with fresh chamomile flowers (often found at health food stores or farmers' markets; if you suffer from plant allergies or are on medication, check with your doctor before taking chamomile).

Heat 1 cup (8 fluid ounces) of water in your teakettle or pot. Rinse the flowers and pat dry. Remove the stems from the flowers, until you have 3–4 tablespoons of chamomile. If you like mint, you may add a fresh sprig. When the water has boiled, pour over the flowers and mint. Steep for 5 minutes (or more, if you like a stronger flavor). Pour the liquid through a fine strainer into a teacup, and enjoy.

Treat Yourself to a Head Massage

If a professional masseuse is out of your budget, instead get a haircut (complete with wash and, most importantly, with a scalp massage) or ask a loved one to brush your hair.

Just as his mane is the lion's source of pride and joy, so too is Leo's hair. Anything that stimulates the hair follicles makes Leo happy, because it contributes to healthy, luxurious hair. While your scalp and hair follicles are stimulated, you can relax and enjoy the feeling of someone massaging your head. De-stressing and beautifying—a true dual act of self-care!

Let the Sunshine In

Even the king has to work every once in a while. When you're stuck indoors working, you don't have to miss the light of the sun. Try replacing the light bulbs in your work space with full-spectrum light bulbs. These bulbs cover all wavelengths that are useful to plant or animal life. In short, they imitate Leo's ruler, the Sun.

While nothing can replicate the feeling of being outside in the warming sunshine, full-spectrum light bulbs are the next best thing. While these bulbs are slightly more expensive than their standard counterparts, your self-care is worth every penny.

Keep Your Pride in Check

Self-confidence is a wonderful trait of Leo's. However, pride can easily turn into arrogance, which can be one of Leo's less-attractive qualities.

If a friend or family member has injured your pride, consider forgiveness. Leo's great lesson in life is to overcome inflexible pride. Forgiving someone who has done you wrong, or who you have perceived as doing you wrong, will lift an emotional weight. Consider this an act of emotional self-care, as holding a grudge is unhealthy for you and serves no purpose.

After you have cleared the air, take care not to end up in the same situation in the future. Remember that self-confidence is very good; cocky pride will only get you in trouble.

Re-Examine Yourself

At times Leo can be devoted to the image of himself rather than the substance. Could you be overlooking your genuine qualities? Look within and see.

Choose a quiet moment when you have time to focus. Write down what you believe to be your best qualities. Do not focus on superficial qualities, such as your physical appearance, strength at a particular sport, or role as the life of the party. Rather, think about the qualities you have that can be used for good. Do you have a generous spirit? Are you a wonderful listener? Can you make other people comfortable in otherwise awkward situations? Consider if you are using your genuine qualities to the best of your ability. By focusing on them, you are more likely to do so. Not only will you be taking care of yourself, but you will be taking care of others as well.

Pick Up a New Hobby

With such a strong personality, Leo's interests vary greatly. One thing is for sure, though—Leo does best when he keeps his mental and physical acuity sharp, so if you're lacking in hobbies at the moment, seek out a new one, or revisit an old one.

Since Leo loves being the center of attention, you may want to consider the dramatic or other creative arts. Audition with a local theater group, join a choir, or enter a piece in an art competition. Your creative juices will flow, and you'll be able to indulge your love of the limelight.

At the other end of the spectrum, Leo's abundance of energy makes physical-based hobbies a nice fit. Consider adventure sports, or physical activities that combine your love of attention and exercise, such as ice skating or ballroom dancing.

Go Out Dancing

If you want drama, rhythm, and physical release, a night out dancing is the perfect way for Leo to let off some steam.

Be the star of the dance floor and let loose with friends or family. Whether you're a trained dancer or just want to have fun, an evening spent dancing is a perfect activity for Leo. Consider dressing the part by picking an outfit that gives a nod to the type of music you'll be dancing to. If you're in the mood, sip some bubbly before hitting the floor to add a celebratory feel.

No matter the occasion, a night out dancing is always time well spent!

Try Open Mic Night

Leo loves to be a star—taking part in an open mic night is a great way to express creativity! Get a few friends and head out to a local coffee shop or bar to take the stage. If you can't find an open mic night near you, create your own!

Invite friends and family over for a night to enjoy your talents. In addition to basking in the limelight, you can socialize and, as a natural leader, encourage your more timid friends to show off their talents. It's a time to have fun, feed your creative side, and support your loved ones.

Splurge on the Royal Treatment

Stressed out and need some royal pampering? Head to the spa, Leo!

A luxurious spa day may be the closest we can get to being treated like kings and queens. Whether you decide to get a manicure and pedicure, facial, or hot stone massage, treat yourself by going to a spa where you feel comfortable and pampered.

Perhaps the most indulgent of treatments? The full-body massage. Ask your masseuse to let you pick out a scented oil, and give feedback early on so that they apply the level of pressure you're most comfortable with.

If a spa day isn't in the cards, have a friend over so you can give each other scalp and hand massages, pedicures, and facials (or just treat yourself to an at-home treatment). The point is to indulge your inner royal lion!

Lie Out in the Sun

Any time you're craving an indulgent, relaxing, and inexpensive act of self-care, look no farther than your own backyard.

Break out the sunscreen and towel, and lie out in the sun for a safe period of time. The Sun is Leo's ruling heavenly body, and it reflects the core of Leo's being. Leo's passion for life and confidence comes from the sun, and he craves and draws power from it.

While lying in the sun can be emotionally fortifying, it can also be incredibly physically relaxing. So unwind and soak up the energizing rays!

Adopt a Lion

Perhaps the most iconic astrological symbol, the Lion is the embodiment of all things Leo. And while this regal animal is the king of the jungle, the species is considered vulnerable to the possibility of extinction, and its population continues to decline. Lend a hand to your astrological brother and think about adopting a lion.

Through organizations such as the World Wildlife Fund, you can contribute to the care of lions by symbolically adopting a lion in the wild. You'll help to support those people committed to protecting the species, and make a positive contribution to global conservation efforts. If you have a loved one who is also a Leo, consider gifting them the adoption of a lion—a thoughtful and particularly meaningful gift for a fellow member of your astrological pride.

Make Sunday *Your* Day

While Leo often feels most comfortable in the limelight, being the center of attention can be draining. When you're beginning to feel stressed or drained, be sure to take some time for yourself.

As Sunday is Leo's day, why not make that a day just for you? It could be every Sunday, or a once-a-month treat. The important thing is to schedule some solo time on your special day. Whether it's a day without leaving the house or one spent reading a book in the park, solo time is important when Leo needs to recharge. Afterward, you can rejoin your routine with a renewed sense of energy.

Additionally, you may want to take some time to reflect on what preceded you feeling such a way so that you can avoid feeling emotionally, mentally, and physically drained in the future.

Enjoy Some Retail Therapy

Leo loves luxurious fashions and home decorations. The next time you need a pick-me-up, why not hit the stores and look for your next great find?

Leo enjoys showing off, so be sure to punctuate your wardrobe with glitzy pieces that can dress up your style and reflect your personality. When you're shopping for your home, look for unique pieces that reflect your sense of self and align with the environment you want to create. Your home should be an extension of yourself so that you can truly relax and rejuvenate when you return there at the end of the day.

Not only should you see the act of shopping as an act of self-care, but you should keep in mind how your purchases will contribute to your life.

Repeat the Mantra "I Will"

At his best, Leo is passionate and caring, with a flair for the dramatic. At his worst, Leo can be self-centered and aggressive. If you feel yourself drifting toward selfish behavior, keep yourself in check by repeating the mantra "I will."

When you focus on this phrase, think about what you can and will do to turn your thinking and behavior from self-centered to self-confident. Remind yourself of how you can share your gifts with your loved ones, and how you benefit from the love of others.

Volunteer Locally

Leo is a generous soul. Seek out a charity aligned with the causes you are most passionate about. While national charities do a lot of good work, in your own town you'll find local charities looking for helpful hands. Animal shelters, hospital and hospice services, and organizations serving children or the environment are great places to start.

Additionally, keep an eye out for neighbors who could use a helping hand. Offer to take a senior citizen's trash cans back up the driveway after garbage day. Shovel snow from the walk of a home where you know young children live. No act is too small—it will make a difference to both your day and the day of the recipient.

Try Skydiving

Leo loves seeking adventure and pumping up the adrenaline. Knock off the ultimate bucket-list challenge by trying skydiving. You may find you'll become addicted to the exhilaration of plunging through the sky before releasing your parachute. Your first skydive is truly a once-in-a-lifetime experience and the mental pictures of those gorgeous vistas as you safely glide toward the ground will stay with you forever.

First-timers will be attached with an expert who pulls the parachute at just the right moment, so you don't have to worry about anything. And if skydiving is not for you, Leo, there's always waterfall dives (with experienced guides) or bungee jumping to get your adrenaline pumping.

Run for Local Government

At his best, Leo is confident and assertive; he thrives in the spotlight and leads with generosity. He is a powerful speaker. Why not put these qualities to good use by running for a position in local government?

While you may not consider yourself a political mind, think about your strengths and areas of interest. Are you passionate about animals? Do you love working on behalf of children? Are you an avid reader? Are you dedicated to fighting for the environment? There are positions in animal control, libraries, schools, and preservation that could be a good fit for your Leo passion and confidence.

While it may not be a role you envisioned for yourself, you never know where your talents could take you—and how they might positively contribute to the world around you.

Go to a Music Festival

Leo will fit in well in this eclectic scene—it's an opportunity to spend time in the sunshine, socialize, and appreciate music. While Leo may be most comfortable on stage, dancing with friends in your favorite concert-wear is a close second. Music festivals are a wonderful place to express yourself freely, and flamboyancy is welcome in this "anything goes" environment.

CHAPTER 12

Self-Care for Virgo

Dates: August 23–September 22
Element: Earth
Polarity: Yin
Quality: Mutable
Symbol: Maiden
Ruler: Mercury

Virgo is the second earth sign, and her ruler is the planet Mercury. She is mutable, or changeable, and ushers us from summer to autumn. The mutable signs come at the end of a season and move us into the next season. Virgo is also the last of the personality signs of the zodiac.

Virgo represents the seed planted in the earth that must take root and grow toward the light. Beginning with Aries and ending with Virgo, the soul's journey is to develop internal personality characteristics. After Virgo, the remaining signs of the zodiac evolve from the personality to soul growth through relationships.

Virgo is also the sign of service to others. She gathers information and analyzes what she needs to know for herself and others. The essential nature of Virgo is to search for synthesis and wholeness, and the most valuable quality in this search is Virgo's capacity for analysis. When she uses her analyzing skills in service to herself or others in work, Virgo is balanced. When she criticizes herself and others, she becomes nervously irritable and impossible to please. This critical faculty also cuts off her creativity and leaves a fussy agitation that does not serve her well. Additionally, if Virgo relies exclusively on her critical and analytical abilities, she can become so bogged down in details that she misses the forest for the trees.

Virgo's mission in terms of personality development is the quest for perfection. Virgo wants to get everything just right. But the important word is *quest*, not perfection. In the Middle East a handwoven carpet always contains a flaw, because the weavers believe that only God can create something perfect. Virgo's quest carries her through her life, minding details and working hard. After all, if she achieves perfection, she will have nothing left to do!

The symbol for Virgo is the Maiden holding sheaves of wheat from the harvest. The symbol harkens back to the Babylonian goddess of fertility, Ishtar. In Greek mythology, the harvest maiden was associated with Persephone, the daughter of the earth goddess Demeter. Hades abducted Persephone and took her to the underworld. In despair, her mother forbade the earth to be fruitful during the six months of her daughter's captivity; these were the winter months. When Persephone emerged from the underworld, the next months were bountiful and fruitful. Hence, Virgo's association with the harvest.

Self-Care and Virgo

Self-care comes naturally for Virgo. She has jittery nerves and is very sensitive, and oftentimes these nerves create health concerns, so she makes sure that she takes care of herself in every way possible. She usually follows conventional medicine but also has a talent for exploring alternative medical methods. Like her mythical ancestor Demeter, she has an intuitive understanding of herbs and is familiar with the subtle effects of essential oils. When Virgo is in balance, her body serves her and her work; when she is not, she can be a hypochondriac and run from doctor to doctor seeking cures. The best self-care program for Virgo is to follow regular checkups and then let health concerns go. If Virgo tunes in to her body, she will know what to do. If she is in a mental whirl, then no cure or medicine can calm her.

Mercury, Virgo's ruling planet, rules the mind and communication. This association serves Virgo when she is gathering information, because her mind is quick to make connections. When Mercury spins his whirl of mental preoccupations, however, Virgo can get lost in the details and her mind cannot relax. Every bit of information becomes the thing that will cure, or the therapy that is necessary, or the medicine that will help. Usually this is a panicky reaction and nothing resolves itself until the mind calms down.

Virgo Rules the Intestines

The area of the body ruled by Virgo is the intestines. Physically, these are the organs of the body responsible for digestion and assimilation of food, and, metaphysically, for processing experiences and emotions. The intestines are highly sensitive in Virgo, and the first place for her to attend to for self-care is digestive health.

Virgo can have allergies that come and go, as well as food sensitivities. A Virgo child may be a picky eater from a young age, and parents may need to introduce a variety of foods early so that the child learns that there are many eating possibilities. Also, Virgos of any age may eat the same food for weeks or months and then tire of it. This is a natural rhythm to give the body what it needs. Junk food is never a good idea for Virgo; however, as an earth sign, she may indulge in comfort food every so often. She usually does not like spicy food

or exotic dishes. The more Virgo follows her own senses toward what she eats and doesn't eat, the better she will feel.

Self-care in exercise for Virgo is relatively simple. She likes sports that don't involve a lot of equipment or fuss: going for a jog, playing a game of tennis, swimming laps, and dancing. Some Virgos love the elegance of ballroom dancing and the tango. Running track and graceful martial arts are also great sports for Virgo.

Competition with others is not usually Virgo's style. She is content to play and feel good in her physical self. The primary goal in sports for Virgo is getting away from mental preoccupations. Usually, Virgo's muscles are not physically dense, so stretching and easy warm-ups are essential to staying injury-free.

Psychologically, Virgo needs a counselor to speak to, if only to sort out all the thoughts in her mind. She has no problem exploring her motivations and is eager to gain knowledge about why she may think the way she does—however, Virgo is not an emotional sign. Therapy is for the purpose of gaining insight and knowledge. This process may not unleash emotional clarity, but it will settle her very active brain and give her tools to help in life. Cognitive therapy or hypnotherapy can be very effective for Virgo. Hypnotherapy speaks to the unconscious and can help Virgo relax. Also, hypnotherapy is useful if Virgo has a problem or phobia—it will help clear out the mental debris that might be getting in the way of moving past the issue. It may take practice, but Virgo likes working toward a goal.

One of Virgo's finest qualities is the desire to help and serve others. Virgo wants to keep helping, but if her helpfulness is not balanced with self-care, she can tire herself out quickly. The first rule of serving and helping others for everyone—no matter your sign—is to keep renewing your own energy.

Underlying all the digging for information and efforts that Virgo extends toward her self-care is a desire to be of service to others. This is the part of the personality that Virgo is developing. A prime example was fellow Virgo Mother Teresa. She served with no thought of her own well-being. Of course, she was a saint, but every Virgo has a kernel of this quest to help and comfort others. A motivating factor for Virgo in all self-care is to be well and comfortable in mind and body so that she can serve through work, and through her relationships with family, friends, and neighbors.

When working to serve, Virgo is blessed with an easy optimism and a formidable ability to organize anything. She rarely has enemies and her fastidiousness can be a model for "how to get things done." We all can benefit from Virgo's desire to help and serve.

Virgo and Self-Care Success

Since Virgo is "preprogrammed" to be sensitive to her body and mind's needs, success in self-care is a matter of following the rules. She loves to check things off the list. Physical, done; eating plan, done; massage, done. All these activities help Virgo achieve her goals and improve her well-being. She likes to have fun, but taking care of the details of self-care is more important. Counting is the best approach for success. Virgo wants to know her statistics exactly: What is her blood pressure, how many steps, how many pounds, and what exactly is the problem? She loves to plan exactly how she will go about implementing and improving her self-care actions.

Some pitfalls to success for Virgo are frustration and fear that her plan is not working. She is not impatient per se, but she needs to feel assured that her health and life efforts are working. If the problem is illness, she needs to have confidence that the medical professionals are on her side and doing their best. She measures her success and when she sees progress, her mind relaxes and healing can happen.

With the rulership of quick-thinking Mercury, boredom can be another pitfall for Virgo. If an activity becomes routine and Virgo is just going through the motions, she will feel stiff and stuck and will not feel comforted by the regular rhythm of her plan. That is the time to change things up.

As a mutable sign, Virgo is not usually rigid, but if her to-do list takes over and she loses confidence in her activities, then she needs a new plan.

Virgo can become overworked and overdo anything. If she gathers too much information or has too many "must-dos," paralysis sets in and she won't be able to see a clear way to proceed. Internet research fosters this overwhelming feeling. It is best for Virgo to speak to professionals rather than dive into chat groups on the Internet.

With Virgo's essential nature in mind, let's take a look at some rituals that will help her in her self-care quest.

Concentrate on the Exhale

As a hardworking Virgo, your mind is always busy thinking about your next task. Your dedication is admirable, but you should also work in several breaks throughout your day to quiet and clear your mind. Slow the racing thoughts with a meditation during which you focus on exhaling.

Exhaling is actually a key part of reducing stress and promoting relaxation. Many of us can master the art of breathing in slowly, but then we tend to force air out in a hurry. In your daily breaks, breathe in slowly, counting the seconds, and then try to exhale for the same amount of time. If your exhale is shorter, try with each breath to extend it a bit longer. As you breathe,

imagine yourself in your favorite relaxation spot. Take these breaks at least three times during your workday (set a timer on your phone to remind yourself), and then once again before bedtime.

Don't Worry Too Much about Your Health

It's a great goal to want to be healthy. But Virgo can sometimes take that goal to an extreme and stress far too much about her health, fretting about every ache and pain and committing to adopt every new health food fad.

You'd be much better served by simply eating well, visiting your doctor for regular checkups, and getting quality sleep—then letting go so the universe can take care of the rest. Remind yourself how hard you work on your health, and when you feel particularly worried, practice some deep breathing as you visualize yourself in a healthy, strong, happy state. You can also repeat a mantra like "I am well" to yourself to reinforce the feeling and dispel the fear.

Work Through Tummy Troubles

Virgo rules the intestines, which means that you might experience digestive issues more frequently than other signs do. Luckily, these issues are often just the result of excessive worry and not a serious medical problem.

If your digestive system isn't cooperating, visit the doctor to rule out an infection, and then try to pinpoint what concern might be causing the discomfort. Are you worried about a big work project, an upcoming move, or a particularly large credit card bill? If so, try to break the problem down into small parts and tackle it bit by bit. Addressing the root cause of your stress may well alleviate your tummy troubles as well.

Go for a Jog

Exercise is essential for Virgo, both for its many physical benefits and for its ability to clear her busy mind. While there are countless exercise options out there, sometimes a simple jog is the best idea for you.

Jogging is both inexpensive and easy to do anywhere, inside on a treadmill or outside on trails or sidewalks. And you can make each jog different by trying these ideas: Vary your route so you see different areas of your neighborhood or town, create several playlists so you can listen to music that matches your mood, and revamp your workout wardrobe so that you look and feel your best every time.

Record Your Self-Care

Virgo has excellent attention to detail and is a wonderful record keeper. You might employ those skills at work or with your financial business, but why not apply it to something fun too—like your self-care?

As you know, the benefits of self-care are more strongly felt if you make them a habit. So keep track of your self-care by noting what you've done on your smartphone or tablet, or through another type of online app. You can even go back to basics and jot everything down in a notebook or dedicated self-care journal. Chart your progress, your highs and lows, and make note of any upcoming goals you'd like to achieve. Review your progress periodically and adjust as needed. Keeping track of your self-care will help keep you motivated and engaged.

Play Individual Sports

Virgo loves to be active, and while earth signs find team sports like volleyball and soccer appealing, Virgo's standards for excellence are high, and she might not enjoy having her fate in others' hands some of the time.

This makes individual sports like tennis, golf, and skiing a great fit. You'll get a great workout (especially if you skip the golf cart!), but can play at your pace, and in your own style. You can also use your time spent on the links, hills, or court to clear worries out of your busy mind. These individual sports require intense focus; you can't perfect your serve while practicing next week's board presentation or hit a putt while mentally assessing your bank account.

Use a Scent Diffuser

Savoring calming scents is a great way to engage your sense of smell during the relaxation process. When you need to unwind after a busy day, turn to a scent diffuser to help.

There are many types of scent diffusers, such as reed diffusers or candles, so choose one that you prefer. Then find a scent that meets your needs. Virgo rules all scents, but some fragrances that are particularly good matches are lemon verbena, jasmine, and lavender. Lemon verbena is a strong, invigorating scent that might help get you moving in the morning, while jasmine and lavender are more soothing and relaxing and better for bedtime.

Ask about Royal Jelly

Ever heard of royal jelly? It's a milky secretion produced by worker honeybees to help keep the queen healthy. Turns out, it also might help humans stay healthy as well, as it has the potential to alleviate issues related to menstruation and menopause, boost the immune system, stimulate fertility, and help heal bone fractures.

Assuming you do not have asthma and you're not allergic to bees or bee products, ask your doctor about taking a royal jelly supplement in winter to improve your health. You can find over-the-counter capsules at your local health food store.

Organize Your Closets

Virgo is practical, logical, and neat—so organizing your closets isn't a chore for you; instead, it's a fun activity! Even though you try to keep things tidy, every once in a while it's a good idea to look through your closets and get them organized.

To start, sort through your belongings and get rid of anything that's not useful. Next, assess the items you're keeping and figure out what the best storage method is for them—hangers, open baskets, closed bins? If the process seems overwhelming, call in a professional organizer to lend a hand. When you're done, you'll feel productive and grateful that you have more space and a new system that works for you.

Carry Pink Jasper with You

Because they come from the earth, crystals can connect you to the planet's energy. Whether you wear them in forms of jewelry, place them around your house as décor, or meditate while holding them, gemstones have the power to improve your happiness and well-being. Each crystal has its own unique capabilities.

For Virgo, the pink jasper stone is an especially powerful ally. Ranging in shades from a soft, pale pink to a rich fuchsia, pink jasper encourages grounding. Look for an unpolished stone, which has more intrinsic energy. Carry a piece of it in your left pocket every day (because the left side of your body absorbs energy) to bring you comfort and peace.

Try Bach's Crab Apple Remedy

If you're feeling out of sorts and unsure how to right yourself, you might want to consider turning to a natural remedy. One such option is the original Bach Flower Remedies, which are made from wildflowers and, according to the company, "gently restore the balance between mind and body by casting out negative emotions such as fear, worry, hatred and indecision which interfere with the equilibrium of the being as a whole."

In particular, Virgo can benefit from using the crab apple remedy, which claims to help you overcome any negative self-image issues you might have. If you find yourself critiquing your body or feeling unhappy with many things when you look in the mirror, try adding a couple of drops of crab apple remedy to a glass of water (follow the directions on the bottle) and drinking slowly throughout the day. You might just find that you then see yourself with much kinder eyes. (The Bach Flower Remedies are available online.)

Take a Library-Focused Vacation

Sure, beaches, snowy mountains, and ancient cities are interesting vacation spots...but so are libraries!

Why not create a trip where you visit beautiful libraries in the US and abroad? After all, since she is ruled by Mercury, the planet of communication, Virgo loves books and the written word.

You could head to the University of Oxford's stunning Bodleian reading rooms, with their rich wood finishes and leather-bound books, and view a copy of the Gutenberg Bible. Or visit the library hall in the Clementinum in Prague, with its gilded accents and frescoed ceiling. Vancouver's Central Library is reminiscent of the Roman Colosseum and has an open-air concourse. The Musashino Art University Museum and Library in Tokyo is actually built out of thousands of bookshelves, and simply walled in with glass. Egypt's Bibliotheca Alexandrina is an enormous circular building that also features a planetarium and museums. With options like these, you might need to plan more than one vacation!

Try Licorice to Calm Your Stomach

Since Virgo rules the digestive system, you might find that your stomach acts up every once in a while. Instead of reaching for your usual over-the-counter medication, ask your doctor if you can try an herb supplement that could help your gastrointestinal problems—licorice!

In its natural state (meaning, not the sugar-laden candied form you might be familiar with), licorice is packed with antioxidants that can fight infection, ease heartburn, calm ulcers, and relieve constipation. Because licorice contains a substance called glycyrrhizin, which can cause side effects, make sure to look for DGL, or deglycyrrhizinated, licorice. DGL licorice is available in a capsule supplement.

Enjoy Arugula Salads

Boring iceberg lettuce salads can make anyone reluctant to reach for greens. But there's a whole world of salad greens beyond iceberg.

With Virgo's potential digestive issues, arugula is an especially good choice. Its bright, peppery flavor is anything but boring! Plus, arugula is a nutritional powerhouse—it contains fiber, potassium, calcium, magnesium, iron, folate, vitamins A, C, and K, and even protein! To complete an arugula salad, add a lemony dressing, something sweet like raisins or berries, and a freshly shredded sharp cheese. You'll find yourself looking forward to salads again!

Look Into Beekeeping

Local honey has astounding health-promoting properties—it can soothe sore throats, potentially minimize the effects of pollen and allergies, and boost your immune system. Beekeeping is also a fascinating hobby that you might want to consider.

These days it's more important than ever to promote bee health. Bees are essential to the pollination process for our natural food sources, yet recently bee populations have been sharply declining thanks to industrialized agriculture, climate change, and pesticide use. If you have the space, why not do your part for the earth and your own health and keep a beehive in your own yard? Visit a site like https://beebuilt.com, and contact a local beekeeping organization for information on buying equipment and protective clothing, educating yourself, and starting a hive.

Keep Some Toys on Your Desk

Virgo is a hard worker, which is great for your productivity levels and career success. But, sometimes, you need to take a break and lower your intensity a bit so you don't burn out.

In the middle of a busy workday, it can be difficult to remember to relax—so put some toys or interactive elements on your desk to remind yourself. Whether it's an old-fashioned Slinky, a soothing Zen sand and rock garden, or a place to doodle (like an Etch A Sketch or a whiteboard with colored pens), these items can invite you and your colleagues to clear your minds while keeping your hands busy. Plus, they're just plain fun!

Hold High Tea

Virgo appreciates the proper ritual of high tea: the crisp linen tablecloth, the perfectly folded napkins, the spotless bone china cups, the polished silver spoons, the tasteful floral centerpiece, and the perfectly arranged tiny sandwiches and cakes.

Invite some friends or loved ones over to your place to enjoy this ritual with you. (If you don't own some of these items, borrow them or search local rummage sales or antique stores for inexpensive options.) Create and mail lovely paper invitations complete with your best sophisticated hand-lettering. Brainstorm a menu that matches the tastes of the people coming or the season of the event, and offer two or three types of high-quality tea that you brew yourself. And be sure to hold out your pinkies, of course.

Enjoy the Nutty Taste of Barley

Barley is an ancient whole grain full of fiber, protein, and vitamin B, and featuring an earthy, nutty taste. It offers an impressive array of health benefits: It can lower blood pressure, boost heart health, minimize inflammation, improve digestion, and control weight since it keeps you feeling full. Beyond this plethora of good reasons to eat it, barley is a perfect match for Virgo—after all, the Greeks represented Virgo as Persephone, goddess of the grain harvest!

Perhaps best of all, barley is easy to cook and incorporate into many meals. Add it to soups in place of rice or pasta. Toss it into green salads for a chewy boost in flavor and protein. You can even cook it on the stove top to eat for breakfast like oatmeal. Search your favorite recipe websites or cookbooks for enticing barley recipes.

Finish a Meal with Peppermint Tea

Virgo often needs a little extra help ensuring smooth digestion. One easy idea is to drink a cup of bright peppermint tea after your meal.

Peppermint tea is known to help digestion while minimizing any gas or bloating. You can buy peppermint tea at the store, or make your own at home. To make your own, simply buy fresh peppermint (choose organic, if possible), clean it, and then crush the leaves with a mortar and pestle (or the back of a spoon). Place the crushed leaves into a mug (put them in a tea infuser or tea ball if you have one), and add boiling water. Let steep for 7–12 minutes to desired flavor intensity, and then strain the leaves out (if applicable) before drinking.

Get Crafty

Virgo has many creative talents. If you haven't tried sewing yet, you might find it to be a peaceful, relaxing hobby—and a great way to express yourself artistically.

It might seem intimidating, but there are actually lots of easy sewing patterns that beginners can make. From shift dresses and boxer shorts to tote bags and pillowcases, you can find patterns and fabrics to fit your style and personality. Look for a used or hand-me-down sewing machine and read the instructions, or take a beginners' class to learn the basics. Then, set up your own sewing basket with your equipment (such as needles, thimbles, high-quality scissors, and pins) and start stitching!

Press Wildflowers

The simplicity and whimsy of pressed flowers can mesh well with many types of home décor. On your next trip outside, look for wildflowers that you can bring home, set between two sheets of wax paper, and store inside a large, heavy book for a week. Then carefully slide the flowers into a prepared frame that complements their color and style.

One wildflower that might speak to Virgo is Queen Anne's lace. It is said to represent sanctuary, and it has an interesting legend behind it: Queen Anne, wife of King James I of England, was trying to sew lace in a pattern as beautiful as a flower. In so doing, she pricked her finger. Her blood is said to be the purple-red center seen on some Queen Anne's lace flowers.

Spend Some Time with a Cat

Virgo loves pets, especially cats. These intelligent and low-maintenance pets offer friendship and can help you relax, re-center, and slow down for a while. If you don't have a cat at home, visit a local shelter to meet some potential pets and decide which breed might be right for you. Whether it's a lovable tabby or a regal Siamese, cats can add a wonderful dimension to your life.

If you already have a furry feline friend, be sure to make lots of quality time to spend together...and consider getting another one!

Organize Yourself with an Apothecary or Filing Cabinet

Virgo loves containers of all shapes and sizes, and for all sorts of uses. One useful storage spot for your house might be a Chinese apothecary cabinet, which features many drawers to keep everything in its place. It's perfect for storing small items like keys or brushes that can otherwise clutter busy spots in your house.

For your paper-based storage, look for a sturdy file cabinet. You can organize your documents with tabbed folders for easy access. And don't worry, file cabinets aren't only offered in heavy, gray metal anymore—you can find lots of visually interesting file cabinets online.

Take In a Ballet

Ballet isn't just for little kids in pastel outfits—adult ballet performances are a stunning show of physical beauty and skill mastery, accompanied by breathtaking music. As a Virgo, you can appreciate these accomplishments, along with the intricate costumes and spellbinding stories.

Check your local area for visiting professional ballet troupes, or watch a local college's or dance school's top ballet group.

Whether you watch a classic favorite, like *Swan Lake* or *Giselle*, or a newer dance production, like *Maple Leaf Rag*, you'll no doubt sit in awe of the dancers' strength, grace, and poise, and come away with a newfound appreciation for this elegant expression of movement.

Try the Extended Locust Pose

Practicing yoga is a wonderful way to build strength while calming your mind. For Virgo, poses that encourage good digestion are especially applicable.

One such pose is the Extended Locust Pose. It will strengthen your back and abdominal muscles, improve your posture, and massage your digestive tract. This is not a beginners' pose, so make sure to practice this with your yoga instructor for detailed technique guidance.

To do Extended Locust Pose, lie on your belly on a yoga mat, extending your arms out in front of you. Inhale, then lift your arms, head, and legs off the mat toward the ceiling. Hold for five breaths, and then release back to the mat and rest. Wait at least 30 minutes after eating a large meal before doing this pose.

Write a Gratitude List

Virgo is a very detail-oriented person, which is a big plus in many areas of life. Yet, even as you keep track of the little things, be sure to take a step back periodically to see the big picture as well.

As you unwind every night, try to push the little annoyances of your day out of your head and, instead, remind yourself of all that you have to be grateful for. You might want to write them down to please your record-keeping nature. Whether it's your good health, your great friends, a supportive family, a rewarding career, or even simpler things like a roof over your head and food to eat, you undoubtedly have a list of things in your life that make you feel blessed. Make sure to recognize them daily.

Put Clean White Sheets on Your Bed

Is there anything more inviting than a comfy bed that's just been freshly made with crisp white sheets? If your sheets are getting faded and threadbare, it's time to invest in new ones to ensure a restful night's sleep.

As you put the new sheets on the bed, be sure to tuck everything in very tightly—Virgo likes to feel secure in her bed. Make sure your nightstand contains only what you need to get through your night, like a book and some tissues. You might also consider spraying a relaxing essential oil (diluted according to instructions) onto your sheets before you go to sleep at night.

Recite Strength-Based Affirmations

Affirmations are short, powerful, positive phrases that you can recite aloud or silently to yourself to help bring about positive change in your life. They're easy to remember and simple to work into your day—you can recite them while you practice yoga, while you take a shower, or while on your morning commute.

Virgo is by nature analytical and hardworking. An affirmation like "I effortlessly make order in my world" speaks to where Virgo's strengths lie and how keeping order feels like an easy task to her, not a daunting struggle. Repeating these words can help you feel confident, empowered, and energized.

Plant Some Perennials

There's something so reassuring about the first flowers of spring. Prepare your garden for a riot of spring color by planting bulbs in the fall.

While it may seem like nothing is happening over the course of the winter and early spring, magic is taking place beneath the soil. When the snow has melted, you'll start to see green sprouts—your plants are growing! You've created your own mini-harvest (perfect since Virgo is the symbol of the harvest) of colorful blooms. You can consider tender purple crocuses, bright yellow daffodils, or bold red tulips. These flowers when cut will brighten your home and your heart.

Embrace Imperfection

Virgo is hardworking and wants everything to be perfect. And that goal is admirable—but also unattainable.

Instead, learn to love imperfection. Sometimes, you can teach yourself this by looking at a situation that seems imperfect from a different perspective. For example, if there are parts of your body that you aren't thrilled with, switch that thought and instead remind yourself of the astounding number of amazing things your body does for you every single day. Or, if you're unhappy with a decision you've made, think of it as learning a life lesson. And just as a baby learning to walk will fall dozens of times, so, too, will you "fall" as you learn things. And just as you wouldn't judge a baby for those spills, neither should you think harshly of yourself for yours. Love all the parts of yourself, imperfections and all.

Schedule Group Therapy Sessions

While bottling everything up inside might get you through a rough patch, it's not a long-term strategy for sound mental health. If you haven't already, consider talking to a therapist to unload and work through difficult situations.

Virgo tends to hold in her mental processes, which can backfire later when they build up and become overwhelming. Find a recommended therapist whose expertise matches your needs, and share your life concerns. They might even recommend that you attend a therapist-led group counseling session with other people going through a similar problem. Talking about your problems is a brave, mature, and healthy thing to do—so show your mind the same type of self-care you show your body at the gym and talk through your problems with those who can relate.

Add Fennel to Your Diet

Fennel is a strong-smelling herb known for its ability to soothe the intestines and digestive system. Stomachaches can be a problem for Virgo, but this herb can be a lifesaver.

You can chop raw fennel bulb into soups, salads, or vegetable dishes; use the feathery fennel fronds (the green tops) as an unexpected salad topper; or roast fennel bulbs for a tender texture. Fennel contains a lot of vitamin C, fiber, iron, and potassium, so fennel isn't just good for your stomach!

Relax with Lavender Spray

After a long day at work, coupled with regular home and family responsibilities, it can be difficult to quiet your mind. Reconnecting with the earth through a floral essence spray might be just the ticket.

Lavender is well known for its soothing, calming properties. Though you can use a lavender-scented candle, a diluted essential oil spray can be even more effective. Simply add some drops of lavender essential oil (diluted according to instructions) to a small spray bottle. Spritz it on your couch or pillow and proceed with your usual routine. The aromatherapy will work its magic as you go about your business.

Take Up Chess

If you're trying to spend less time in front of screens, you should consider some traditional methods of entertainment—like classic board games!

Chess, in particular, is a good fit for the analytical Virgo mind. Plus, you can play with a friend and enjoy some quiet social downtime as well. If you have never played, watch an online tutorial or read a book about chess strategy before you start a game. Then ask a friend to join you for a friendly match. Before long you'll find yourself looking forward to the precision of setting up the board and the intellectual challenge of making your moves.

Prepare Meals Ahead of Time

Virgo loves to plan, so be sure to extend that skill to your meal planning as well. Instead of leaving the decision 'til the last minute, try spending some time on the weekend (or whatever time you have free) figuring out what you'll eat, and when.

Meal planning like this is beneficial in so many ways. First, it makes your grocery shopping much easier and more focused because you'll know what ingredients you need to buy and can get them all at once—instead of stopping multiple times throughout the week. Second, you're more likely to try new recipes or foods because you can check out recipes ahead of time. Third, you can even start to prep certain ingredients on the weekends (for example, chopping carrots for a soup you'll make on Tuesday) or use timesavers like slow cookers to ease the pressure on weeknights. The time and headaches you'll save will leave you free for unwinding and relaxing.

Keep a Health Journal

Part of practicing good self-care is paying attention to trends and observations about how you feel physically and mentally. Luckily, Virgo loves statistics and data—so give in to your system-loving side and keep a journal of how you are feeling.

You can decide how to keep your records. Think about what aspects of your health you'd like to focus on—it might be blood pressure, heart rate, weight, stress levels, digestion—and then create a goal around that concern. In your journal, divide the space into columns or sections where you can track information, whether in numerical or written form. Periodically, go back over your notes so you can find patterns or celebrate your progress.

Play Number Puzzles

Number puzzles help keep your mind sharp, just like crossword puzzles do. Virgo often likes the exactness of numbers, so these activities are the perfect option for your logical mind.

You can find sudoku or other number puzzles in book format, through apps, or online. Instead of mindlessly scrolling through your social media feeds on your train ride to work, try these puzzles. Or fill in a few at your lunch break or while you're in the waiting room before a doctor's appointment. Your brain will appreciate the stimulation, and you'll likely find yourself progressing from beginner puzzles to expert level in no time.

Help a Friend with a Problem

Watching a friend go through a tough time can be a painful experience. One way to show support is to offer them help or advice, if your friend is open to it.

As a Virgo, you are very good at looking at problems and thinking of possible solutions. Your objective insights and potential answers might make a significant difference to your friend. Just remember to be sensitive to the big picture; don't push too hard, and, above all, listen and be compassionate. You'll show yourself to be reliable, thoughtful, and caring—traits that are valuable to your friend and can make you proud of yourself too.

Go Meatless (Sometimes)

You've probably heard that you should keep an eye on your meat intake. But does that mean you have to give up hamburgers forever? No. Instead, adopt a flexitarian ("flexible vegetarian") diet, devised by dietitian Dawn Jackson Blatner, and just go meatless periodically.

Flexitarians want to eat more plant-based food on a regular basis but also want the flexibility of eating meat once in a while. Your body—especially your digestive system—will be healthier when your diet consists of a higher percentage of plant-based foods.

Virgo needs to take good care of her often-troublesome digestive system—and Virgo's symbol is that of a harvest—so this plant-focused diet is a good match for you.

Visualize Letting Go

If you've ever endured an embarrassing situation or a difficult interaction with someone, you've probably also replayed it again and again in your mind: wishing you did something differently, wishing it didn't happen at all. Ruminating like this on the interaction isn't serving you well, though. In fact, the best thing you can do is learn from it and then let it go.

Virgo in particular can replay these situations far longer than is necessary. One way to move on is to close your eyes and visualize the situation tied to you with dozens of strings. Breathe deeply, and imagine yourself cutting the strings one by one and letting the situation gently float away forever. This exercise can help you free your mind of these mental blocks so you're not weighed down by them.

Sign Up for a POUND Class

If you haven't heard of a POUND class, Virgo, it's about time you give it a try. This drum-based exercise is a great workout. Plus, it's fun! If you don't think you have rhythm, think again. After all, Virgo is great at counting, and finding the beat in a POUND class is based on counting (think five, six, seven, eight!).

Whether you've played the drums in the past or have never played an instrument in your life, you're sure to find a local POUND class that fits your schedule and your pace.

Bring a friend along with you, or just get ready to meet new people. Either way, you'll probably leave class tired but laughing and feeling uplifted.

Keep a Bullet Journal

Ryder Carroll, a digital product designer, came up with the simple yet revolutionary idea of bullet journaling, or BuJo for short. Instead of logging long, cumbersome journal or calendar entries, just jot down bulleted lists. You can customize the bullets and lists how you want, but the key is that the process shouldn't be overwhelming. Writing in the journal is actually an act of mindfulness that helps you organize your thoughts quickly and easily.

Check out https://bulletjournal.com and see how easy the process can be. Journaling in this simple way will help you empty your mind of the responsibilities swirling around it so you can keep track of everything in an organized way that works for you.

Plan a Spring Bloom Trip

Spring flowers are a sign of rebirth and new beginnings. Taking time to enjoy them is a powerful way of re-centering yourself and enjoying the beauty of nature.

You can look at spring blooms wherever you live, or take a trip somewhere instead—maybe to see the bold colors of tulips in the Netherlands; the inimitable cherry blossoms in Japan or Washington, DC; the millions of cheerful daffodils in Gibbs Gardens in Georgia; or the Portland Rose Festival in Oregon. No matter what type of flower you enjoy, savoring them en masse is a humbling and relaxing experience.

Make Time to Read a Virgo Author

It can be difficult to fit books into your busy schedule. One easy way to find time is to swap some TV-watching time for reading time, even if it's just a couple of hours a week. Virgo is ruled by Mercury, who is the messenger god and ruler of the written word, so reading books is a particularly effective self-care practice for you.

In particular, look to fellow Virgo authors, like Leo Tolstoy, Stephen King, Agatha Christie, Mary Shelley, or D.H. Lawrence. You might find that their characters and plotlines are especially interesting to you. Whether you pop into a bookstore to grab a hard copy or download the ebook on an app on your smartphone, you'll find this pastime relaxing and intellectually stimulating.

Splurge Once in a While

Virgo is very organized and stays on budget, which is a skill you should celebrate! But every now and again, allow yourself to splurge on something you don't necessarily need, but would like to have.

Ask yourself what would make you happy—whether it is a new pair of shoes, a fancy watch, or a cool cordless speaker—and get it! And don't worry, you don't need to bust your budget completely. Just the act of treating yourself will make you feel joyful, especially if it's a treat you've been wanting for some time.

Do the Wind-Relieving Yoga Pose

Since Virgo rules the intestines, you might sometimes have trouble with gas, bloating, and indigestion. This yoga pose can work wonders on these issues (while strengthening your back and abdominal muscles), and it's simple to do.

Lie down on your back on a yoga mat. Bring one knee up toward your chest, holding your leg steady with both hands, and then lift your head forward toward your knee. Hold the pose for a few breaths, release your leg, and then switch legs. Do this as often as necessary, after meals or before bedtime.

Keep an Eye on Your Body Language

Some scientists believe that more than half of human communication is nonverbal—meaning, it's conveyed by body language. That means that facial expressions, hand gestures, and posture tell people a lot about how you feel—or might even project an inaccurate picture of who you are. Because Virgo can often live in her head,

her body language might show her to be cold, while she's actually just reserved and shy.

Try to be alert to this potential misconception and be mindful of your posture and facial expressions, especially when you meet new people. You are actually warm and caring, so let people see that side of you too. If it feels right, you can smile and offer a friendly handshake.

Add More Fiber to Your Diet

Taking care of her digestive system is important work for Virgo. Fiber is a crucial part of healthy digestion, and you probably already know a few whole-grain sources, such as oatmeal and barley. But did you also know you can get fiber from lots of other types of foods, such as split peas, black beans, artichokes, Brussels sprouts, raspberries, and blackberries?

Most adults under the age of fifty need 25–38 grams of fiber a day, so keep that number in the back of your head as you plan your meals. Throw a few raspberries on your lunch salad, add black beans to your taco, or whip up a split pea soup in your blender to add fiber to your diet in an easy and delicious way!

Cook Dinner for Someone Special

Getting together with friends and loved ones is one of the best ways to relax and truly be yourself. Virgo might enjoy cooking someone else dinner, because she likes to do things for other people.

Whether it's a romantic candlelit dinner for two, or a quiet meal with a longtime friend, you can extend the invitation, plan the meal, and then send your guest home with leftovers for the next day's lunch. The good company and the homemade food will leave you physically satisfied and mentally fulfilled.

Visit a Lilac Garden

The unmistakable, fresh scent of lilacs in springtime is like a breath of fresh air after the dull winter weather. When lilacs—a Virgo flower—are in bloom where you live, go visit a lilac garden to savor the beauty of your flower. Search online for a lilac garden in your area—you might not have even realized it was there. On your visit, take deep breaths and walk slowly, treating it almost like a meditative experience. While you're there, take the opportunity to learn about the many varieties of lilacs, which can actually vary in color from white to deep purple.

Indulge In an All-Natural Body Scrub

Body scrubs can rejuvenate tired skin, wake up your senses, and calm your mind—plus, they feel amazing! An all-natural version is ideal for Virgo because it will connect you to the earth itself. Simply start with organic sugar or sea salt as a base, then add an appropriate carrier oil plus essential oils (diluting according to instructions) that match your needs or preferences. For example, try a lavender-vanilla scrub to complement a soothing bath. Or, wake up in the morning with the bright smells of a citrus blend. To use, gently rub a coating of the scrub to areas that need smoothing or exfoliation, then rinse off.

Try a Bentonite Clay Mask

Bentonite clay is a natural volcanic ash found in Fort Benton, Wyoming. It contains minerals such as iron, magnesium, and potassium, and it holds an electric charge that might draw toxins out of your skin when the clay is combined with water. The clay can also soften your skin, decrease the size of your pores, and even out your skin tone. To make a mask, use a plastic spoon to combine equal parts sodium bentonite clay (bought from a trusted source) with water or raw apple cider vinegar to make a paste in a nonmetal bowl (or follow the specific instructions on the packaging). Apply the mixture to your face and let it absorb and harden for 15–20 minutes, then rinse off and moisturize as normal.

CHAPTER 13

Self-Care for Libra

Dates: September 23–October 22
Element: Air
Polarity: Yang
Quality: Cardinal
Symbol: Scales
Ruler: Venus

Libra is the second air sign of the zodiac. He is yang and a cardinal sign and begins at the autumn equinox when the day and night are in perfect balance. Libra also marks the beginning of the soul's journey toward relationships. The word *we* comes to Libra's lips more easily than *I*, as he thinks of life in terms of relationships and sometimes in his zeal assumes that his personal preferences are always enjoyable to his partners. Libra's goal is to balance *we* and *me*. Libra can become unbalanced because he sees all sides of every issue and everyone's opinion; he considers too many possibilities. This leads to conflicts of opinion within himself.

Libra's symbol is the Scales, and he is the only sign of the zodiac whose symbol is an inanimate object. Libra can sometimes be detached and superior to the chaotic feelings of other people as he weighs all thoughts. At its best, this tendency gives him a great ability to judge fairly and fight for equality between people. At its worst, it makes Libra aloof and condescending toward others.

The planet Venus is Libra's ruler. In Roman mythology, Venus (known as Aphrodite in Greek mythology) was the goddess who beguiled men and gods alike. The Romans believed that she brought laughter and love to the mortal world. Other myths stated that Venus was treacherous and malicious and exerted a deadly destructive power over men. The two parts of the Libran personality are described in these myths: the gracious partner who shares his joy with everyone, and the heartbreaker. Libra spends his life balancing these extremes.

There is grit and determination beneath the charm and smiles in both Libran women and men. In fact, Libra is often called the steel hand in the velvet glove. Additionally, the female Venus and male yang within Libra provide a balance of traditional feminine and masculine traits. Libran women can be very tough and politically minded, and Libran men often have an eye for aesthetics.

Self-Care and Libra

Libra understands himself through his relationships. In his quest to keep the peace, he can become very involved in figuring out the best strategies for achieving personal and communal goals and avoiding conflict—and Libra does not like conflict. Charming and full of grand ideas, he frequently stirs things up, but learns over time how to quell any high winds that may blow. The best self-care for him includes fresh air to calm his constant whirl of thoughts.

Since relationships are so important to Libra, he frequently needs time to himself to find his center, which can become lost in all of his generosity and focus on others. Finding this center requires checking in with the way he feels about things, rather than concentrating on what he thinks. Feeling does not come naturally, as Libra is a thinking sign. When Libra talks about something important, he will say "I think this," rather than "I feel this." He wants to get down to the concrete reasons for his reactions. Taking a time-out throughout the day to see if the Scales are tipping or are balanced will lead Libra in good directions for all of his self-care practices. Libra responds best to self-care that involves both mental and physical practices. As a positive yang sign, Libra is naturally an optimistic thinker. When something is not working out in his life, he can change his thought patterns easily to reevaluate what adjustments he can make to be successful.

When Libra is unable to reframe his mind-set or needs a little help in sorting out all of his whirling thoughts, he benefits from counseling and therapy. Libra wants to understand his psyche, so he needs someone with wisdom and patience who will help guide him through his many thoughts and questions. Libra already has dozens of relationships that require his time and energy, so if the therapist is too chummy and reveals too much of their personal life, it will not help him. Instead of exploring his own identity, Libra will be focused on what the therapist thinks of him. Once he finds the right therapist, Libra will commit to counseling for a long time.

The best physical self-care for Libra often involves toning exercises that improve his strength and posture without leaving him feeling sweaty and unkempt.

A motivating factor in exercising is what Libra wears. No ratty T-shirts here: Colorful and well-fitting exercise garb is a must. While Libra can give his all to a workout, he likes to make sure he looks good doing it.

Libra Rules the Kidneys

Libra rules over the kidneys, so self-care that focuses on this part of the body is especially important. In practical terms, Libra should take care that his lower back area is always warm. After swimming, he should change to avoid sitting in damp clothes. Drinking enough water is also very important, as it keeps the kidneys functioning properly. It can be hard to monitor care of your kidneys because they are internal organs, but Libra should be mindful of any kidney or bladder disturbances and have a doctor check them out.

Libra's rulership of the kidneys has both a physical and symbolic meaning. Physically, the kidneys purify the body, removing waste and moving clean blood up to the heart. In the psychological and spiritual realm, Libra's mission is to purify consciousness through his relationships and just decisions. Libra understands that through peace and balance the world will thrive.

Libra and Self-Care Success

A motivating factor for Libra in self-care is vanity! Libra likes to look good and will work hard to achieve that goal. Ideas about balance are all well and good, but when the reflection in the mirror looks healthy and well rested, Libra feels good. Sports that interest Libra have a touch of elegance about them. Tennis, golf, and ballet are activities that Libra will enjoy. Libra has a great deal of physical grace and enjoys fluid movement. However, there is hidden aggression in Libra that he is usually too polite to express. Graceful sports that give him an outlet for this pent-up energy include martial arts such as aikido, Tai Chi, and kendo.

Libra is also very involved with how other people react to him, and when he sees that something he is doing brings good attention and compliments, he will keep it up. The flip side of Libra's social nature—and a pitfall to good self-care—is too much socializing. This, coupled with his desire to impress, can lead to overindulgence with food, drink, and late nights. Because he wants the feeling of comradery and friendship, he can easily be swayed by the crowd—staying that hour or two more, having that additional drink. Before long, Libra is running on fumes. It may be boring to be mindful of balancing work, play, and obligations, but moderation is essential to Libra's success in self-care.

Another important element of Libra's self-care is sleep. If illness or agitation interrupts his sleep cycle, Libra wakes up feeling unbalanced. Sleep aids such as meditation tapes, stretching before bed, a glass of warm milk, or breathing exercises can help. And as soon as Libra is back in a proper sleep cycle, he feels in balance and in control of his thoughts.

Symbolized by the Scales, Libra values fairness for others and himself. While it is easy for Libra to be fair to others, he is learning to care for himself, and this skill will be a key to his success in overall self-care. When he is fair to himself, it makes the Libran Scales shine, and when he strikes a balance between others and the self, and justice and forgiveness, he gives his gifts of kindness, equilibrium, and joy to all. And the best way for Libra to keep those Scales balanced is by taking care of his own needs. So let's take a look at some self-care activities especially designed for Libra.

Give Your Décor a Luxe Touch

Ruled by Venus, Libra cannot abide ugly surroundings. All décor in his home or office should have a touch of luxury and beauty—both treasured elements of his ruling planet. Art Deco furniture especially appeals to Libra, as it evokes a sense of harmony and symmetry. Be sure to balance all pictures so they are symmetrical and the colors don't clash! Accents in shades of green will add an extra touch of balance and overall tranquility to your space.

Pay Someone a Compliment

Friendly Libra compliments freely and doesn't mind receiving a compliment—or two or three—himself. Cultivating connections with people, even if just for a moment as you pass a coworker in the hallway or hug a friend goodbye, delights Libra's outgoing and sociable nature.

Try to compliment not just outward appearance, but also character traits you admire. While "I love your shoes" is very flattering, "You are such a great listener" will stay with the person you compliment for a long time. You may just get some flattery in return—though sparking a positive connection to that person will be reward enough.

Treasure Your Romantic Keepsakes

Ruled by Venus, Libra is a romantic at heart, fond of revisiting memories time and time again. And no doubt you have had plenty of love in your life—whether in your current partnership or in your loving friendships. One great way to relive favorite memories is by keeping a collection of mementos that you can pull out and sift through whenever you want. Use a treasure chest to store all of your special keepsakes—a love letter from long ago, a movie ticket stub, a favorite photo or two. When you are feeling less than your upbeat self, you can take out your "treasure" for an uplifting trip down memory lane. It might just be the reminder you need of the love you have in your life. Look for a chest with sophisticated accents or an elegant wood finish to delight your aesthetic side.

Eat Black Cherries

Boasting a sweet flavor and rich color, black cherries should be the mascot for Libra's sensual ruling planet, Venus. Not only are they a delightful treat, but they are quite healthful! A compound in black cherries helps prevent inflammation and premature aging by fighting free radicals that can cause inflamed tissue and cell damage. Cherries also contain melatonin, a natural relaxant that will help ever-active Libra go to sleep.

How can you not feel posh reclining on your sofa with a bowl of cherries? Venus approves of this sensual act of self-care.

Snack On Almonds

Almonds aren't just a tasty snack! They also contain tons of antioxidants that lower blood pressure, curb hunger, and maintain healthy kidney function. Healthy kidneys are especially important to Libran wellness, as they are the part of the body that he rules. Your kidneys remove toxins and other waste from your blood and send the purified blood back up to your heart. They also release erythropoietin, a hormone that stimulates the production of red blood cells; renin, an enzyme that regulates your blood pressure; and active vitamin D, which maintains calcium levels for healthy bone growth. (If you suffer from kidney problems, check with your doctor to see if almonds are beneficial for you.)

Almonds are an easy snack to take on-the-go, so be sure to slip a packet into your bag before you head out for that next social gathering.

Display Your Totem

Libra is symbolized by the balance scale, an ancient tool of measure featuring two bowls suspended from a support beam. Display a small brass spice scale on your desk or in your living space. This Libran totem will serve as a reminder of the essential balance in life. If you are having trouble finding harmony or working out what is right in a particular situation, look to your scale for inspiration and a boost of confidence. Try balancing out objects in the scale to symbolize your ability to always find an equilibrium.

Enjoy an Elegant Bath

As a sign ruled by Venus, Libra enjoys the sensual experience of a warm bath. A regular relaxing bath is not for Libra, though. You need to turn the sophistication level up a notch! Create an opulent space for your bath with sweet-smelling candles, lots of bubble bath, and music turned to a low volume. Waltz rhythms are a sophisticated and calming choice. Try "The Blue Danube," a classic by Johann Strauss II; you may recognize it from popular films such as *Titanic* and *2001: A Space Odyssey*.

This elegant, pampering act of self-care will leave you feeling renewed and ready for whatever is in store—whether it's an outing with friends, or bedtime.

Treat Yourself to Silk Pajamas

Venus, Libra's sensual ruling planet, is in charge of all plush textures, including silk. Invest in a pair of silk pajamas. This cool, smooth fabric feels heavenly on your skin—and it's impossible to not feel fabulous in it. The soothing effect of silk will also help you slip into dreamland, which can be difficult for airy Libra, whose mind is always busily swirling through the clouds. Look for pajamas in light pink or deep blue shades, as these colors promote serenity and restful sleep.

Dive Into the Words of a Fellow Libran

As a generous and social sign, Libra is always busy helping others. While your compassionate nature is part of what makes you wonderful, it is also important to make the time to tend to your own needs. Nurture your intellectual side and reconnect with your celestial roots by enjoying a thought-provoking book by a fellow Libran. Try a work by one of the many great Libra authors: F. Scott Fitzgerald, Anne Rice, or Philip Pullman. You can also get your diplomatic wheels turning with a biography on an influential Libra political figure such as Eleanor Roosevelt or Margaret Thatcher.

Create a Love Potion

Oh, how Libra does love love! As a relationship-oriented sign, Libra feels balanced and happy when his relationships are flourishing. Feeling stuck in a romantic rut? Having trouble with a friend? Revitalize your love life with a special potion!

You can make your own love potion with the following simple recipe! Just mix 1 cup (8 fluid ounces) milk with 2 teaspoons honey in a small pot over medium heat. Then think of what you desire as you add in ½ teaspoon ground coriander, 3 drops vanilla extract, and 1 drop rose flavoring. Stir the ingredients until they are hot but not boiling, then pour into a wide cup and drink as you meditate once again on the love you seek.

Manage Your Worries Before Bed

Sleep is important to Libra's well-being, as it brings him back into balance after each busy day. If stress upsets his sleep routine, he'll feel unbalanced, which can lead to a lack of confidence, and an inability to make even small decisions. Experiment with ways to manage your anxieties before bed to avoid this imbalance. This might involve writing out a to-do list for the next day, so you don't need to dwell on your schedule at night. If you have worries you are repetitively thinking about, write them out before you head to bed; resolve to set time aside the next day to tackle them. You could also try different aids, like yoga poses and soothing music, to find what works best for you.

Restore Romance with Strawberry Begonias

A sophisticated plant with wide, red-hued leaves and soft light-pink flowers, strawberry begonias are the perfect addition to Libra's home. Pink is a Libran power color, invoking his warm, loving nature. If an imbalance has caused you to lose that loving feeling, or you want to set the mood for a romantic night, give your begonia plant a little extra care. Water it, trim away dead leaves, or add a bit of liquid fertilizer to the soil. You'll be feeling the love in no time.

Own Your Libra Mantra

The perfect mantra for Libra is "We balance ourselves and each other." Symbolized by the Scales, Libra is all about creating balance in all things, especially his relationships with others. It's important for everyone around Libra to be balanced in order for him to feel the same way, and as a giving sign, he is naturally more than willing to help out. This can lead Libra to focus all of his energy on the needs of others, neglecting his own necessities. In the end he may feel like his friends and family members are balanced, but he will also feel burned out and unsteady himself.

This mantra will serve as your reminder that it is not your sole responsibility to balance everyone. Other people are perfectly capable of helping themselves, and they can also help you find your own equilibrium—if you let them.

Socialize Responsibly

Charming Libra loves to socialize, but this can sometimes lead to overindulgence and late nights. In order to stay in balance, it's important for Libra to mind those late nights and take care to not eat or drink too much at gatherings.

If you can, ask a trusted friend or partner to help you keep track of your tendencies, or set a limit ahead of time that you know will satisfy your needs and still allow you to wake up the next morning well rested and energized. Responsibility and fun aren't necessarily mutually exclusive!

Nurture Your True Self

While glamour is important to Libra (given that Venus is his planetary ruler), it's also vital to maintain a balance between material and inner beauty, and avoid becoming too focused on what others think of you. Practice self-care habits that are focused solely on you, and not on impressing others. Don't worry, you don't have to go crazy with it—try dipping your toes in with a couple of small adjustments. If you typically wear makeup, or cologne, try going one or two days each week without it. Reveal your true face and scent!

This can also mean tossing pride to the wind in exchange for something others may not understand. If there's a shirt or sweater in your closet you really like, but have been reluctant to wear because it isn't "in style," pull it out and go for a walk!

Balance Your Emotions with Opal

Ruled by passionate Venus, Libra is a sensual, romantic sign—though his emotional side is sometimes ignored in favor of logic and diplomatic thinking. The opal is the perfect gem for balancing your quest for justice and harmony with your need for emotional expression and love. Opal has long been associated with romance and passion. As a reflective and somewhat soft gemstone, it can both absorb *and* express emotion, releasing any inhibitions or stabilizing intense feelings.

Do you feel daring? Black opals are a more dramatic take on the traditional milky-white color. You'll balance your emotional and logical sides—and turn heads while doing so.

Accept Your Role As a Leader

While Libra may be seen as a mediator, seeking peace between everyone, his quest for harmony actually makes him a strong team leader. Don't let your ability to see both sides stop you from taking the lead.

Use your ability to your advantage. Libra is known as the steel hand in a velvet glove; there is grit in this charming sign, so others should not be fooled.

Practice taking the reins on solving a small problem between friends or at work. Follow your gut instinct, and then apply your diplomacy skills to lead the group to a solution. In taking these small steps, you can work your way up to a larger leadership role.

Breathe Deeply for Relationship Balance

Libra is the sign of harmony, but it's important to not lose yourself in your romantic pursuits and partnerships. In fact, this tendency for Libra to try to please others at the expense of his own desires creates a lack of true harmony. Use a breathing exercise to step back from a situation where you may be headed toward this imbalance. You might also like to try a loving-kindness meditation to encourage compassionate feelings for both yourself and others. Pausing to take a few deep breaths while you meditate will allow you to refocus your attention to a more balanced goal for both your needs and the other person's needs.

Embrace Your Romantic Side

Ruled by Venus, Libra is the sign of romance, so be sure to share the affection! Leave a love note in your partner's pocket. Wear a locket with a special person's picture inside. Or show the love on a larger scale: On Valentine's Day send valentines to everyone you know. Not only will you be nourishing your own loving side, but you will be deepening your bond with those around you. Plus, a little romance goes a long way in keeping your relationships balanced—the ultimate goal of diplomatic Libra.

Take Someone Ballroom Dancing

Ballroom dancing is the perfect blend of exercising and spending quality time with your partner. As an air sign, Libra will love the fluid movements of the dance, while his need for strong, harmonious relationships will be fulfilled by the intimate experience. As you and your partner move in harmony to the music, you'll feel your connection deepening—not to mention all of the great memories you'll be making together!

Ballroom dancing is also a balancing act, using complementary steps to create a passionate presentation. If you have the space to dance in your own home, try a flirtatious fox-trot to Frank Sinatra's "I've Got You Under My Skin," or a passionate tango to Carlos Gardel's "Amargura."

Lie Out in an Open Field

Libra loves open spaces, as he has a touch of claustrophobia due to his air element. Take a trip out to an open field where you can lie down, either on a blanket or directly on the grass, and soak in the fresh air. Take deep breaths in and out to establish balance. Enjoy the harmony of nature in its blended colors and sounds. Give yourself time to daydream. A simple act of self-care, this trip into nature is just the thing to recharge your batteries for your next adventure.

Drink Plenty of Water

Libra rules over the kidneys. The kidneys are an important part of your overall health. These small powerhouses work to remove toxins and other waste from your blood before it is pumped up to your heart. In order to promote proper kidney function, you should make sure you're drinking the recommended amount of water each day (depending on gender, lifestyle, climate, and health). Drink up, Libra!

Strike the Extended Triangle Pose

The Extended Triangle Pose is perfect for Libra as it promotes balance, which is essential to his well-being. To do this pose, stand up straight with your arms at your sides. Next, slide your feet out to the sides until they are 3–4 feet apart. Raise your arms out to the sides, palms facing down. Next, turn your left foot just slightly to the right and your right foot to the right a full 90 degrees. Inhale, then as you start to exhale, bend at your hip to the right. Place your right hand on your shin, your ankle, or the floor, and extend your left arm toward the ceiling. Turn your gaze upward to your left hand (if it feels comfortable to do so). Hold this pose for five to ten breaths, then move out of it as you slowly inhale. Reverse your feet and repeat the pose on your left side.

Plan a Trip to China

China is the perfect location for a Libran holiday. Ruled by Venus, Libra has a great appreciation for beauty—especially beauty rooted in history and long-standing tradition. He easily gets swept up in the romance of a place and its people. And with China's winding Great Wall, legendary Yellow Mountain, and other breathtaking sites, there is a lot to get swept up in! Even if your trip is far off in the future, just planning this amazing experience will have you feeling energized and in full Libran spirits.

Gain Confidence with Centaury

Compassionate Libra is always ready to help others. Sometimes, however, his focus on other people can lead to anxious thoughts as he tries to please everyone. A helpful flower remedy for Libra's anxiety is centaury.

Created by Edward Bach, the Bach Flower Remedies are solutions of brandy and diluted wildflower materials that retain the healing properties of that flower. Specifically, the centaury remedy helps kind, sensitive people like Libra who can become anxious in their desire to please. The Bach Flower Remedies can be used by adding a couple of drops to a glass of water and sipping slowly throughout the day (follow the directions on the bottle).

Get a Swedish Massage

Soothing healing practices like massage are very Venusian—perfect for Venus-ruled Libra. And an ideal massage for relaxation is the Swedish massage: the sensual experience of circular strokes and pressure on your muscles and joints is heavenly. Have the masseuse focus on your lower back, which can be a problematic area for Libra. For ultimate relaxation, be sure to select a location that is aesthetically pleasing. A spa that is undergoing renovations or is beside a building eyesore will affect your ability to completely focus on your massage.

Nurture Your Nervous System with Cauliflower

Cauliflower is a good source of vitamin B and calcium, which promote a healthy nervous system. Air signs like Libra have especially sensitive nervous systems, so it is important to give special care to this part of your body.

Cauliflower is also a delicious treat that is experiencing somewhat of a resurgence in popularity. There is a vast array of recipes online that offer new and intriguing ways to incorporate cauliflower in your diet. You can enjoy cauliflower rice, cauliflower soup, and even cauliflower pizza!

Window-Shop at Fancy Locations

Feeling a little less upbeat than your usual bubbly self? Go window-shopping. As a sign ruled by the alluring planet Venus, Libra has a deep appreciation for beauty. A trip to a charming shopping mall or sophisticated store is the perfect boost of positive energy. You don't need to buy anything to feel the uplifting effects (though you certainly can if you want to). Just window-shopping in a beautiful place is therapeutic for luxe-loving Libra.

Wear Pastels

Pastels are the perfect representation of Libra: welcoming and oh-so beautiful. Soft yellow, blue, and pink shades create a stylish and elegant look that Venus-ruled Libra will love showing off at his next party. Pastels also provide a fresh, airy vibe for this air sign.

Be sure to choose the right color for each occasion. Yellow and pink are perfect for an energizing afternoon of fun with friends, while blue works best when you are looking to relax or encourage communication within your relationships.

Practice Tai Chi

Tai Chi, short for *Tàijíquán*, is a martial arts practice focused on fluid movements and breathing. As an air sign, Libra needs to incorporate graceful motions and deep breathing into his self-care routine. Tai Chi is also deeply rooted in the philosophy of balance, something that Libra places great value on. In fact, the term *taiji* in *Tàijíquán* refers to yin and yang: the opposing forces of the universe that together create balance. Tai Chi incorporates these forces into its moves.

Tai Chi has also evolved into a seated exercise that you can use to reduce and manage stress. Described as "meditation in motion," this modern form of Tai Chi promotes calm through modified elegant, flowing movements. You can find countless Tai Chi lessons and routines online!

Boost Your Creativity with "Imagine"

Libra is one of the most imaginative signs of the zodiac. Ruled by Venus, he has a special connection to the five senses, which enables him to envision (and create) amazing things. But sometimes even the most creative Libra could use a little extra inspiration. Play "Imagine" by fellow Libran John Lennon when you need a spark to ignite your next big idea, or more fuel to finish your current project. The soothing rhythm will also act as an opposing force to your vigorous energy, providing more balance to your day.

Splurge on a Haircut

A motivating factor for Libra in self-care is pride in his appearance. When the reflection in the mirror looks healthy and well rested, Libra feels good. Take care of your lovely looks by treating yourself to a haircut. The sensual experience of having your mane shampooed and trimmed is hard to beat. You could even treat yourself to an add-on conditioning or restorative treatment. Plus, when you walk out the door with a stylish new do, heads are sure to turn.

Balance Your Spending

Libra likes nice things, which can come with not-so-nice price tags. Keep your finances in order so that your earnings and spending are in balance. This could mean balancing your checkbook after each transaction, or designating one day each week (or month) to going over your finances and tracking them with a spreadsheet or other detailed document. There are also many phone apps available that can sync with your credit and debit cards and automatically categorize how you are spending your money.

Donate Unused Clothing

A lover of the latest trends in clothing and accessories, Libra can easily end up with a stockpile of things that wind up collecting dust. Devote a day to sorting through all of these possessions and donating the items that you don't use. You may think that you'll someday wear that sequined jacket, but if you haven't worn it yet, you most likely never will.

Decluttering your space can help reduce stress. And it can create more room for some new stylish purchases!

Volunteer for a Social Justice Cause

Symbolized by the Scales, Libra is passionate about fairness for all. Find a national or international cause that allows you to bring more fairness to the world. Social justice movements that you can join include everything from gender equality to access to education. You can march at a rally, work at a fund-raiser, or spread the word about a great cause. As the astrological diplomat, you have the ability to see a perspective and express it clearly to others—so use it. Your voice can make the difference, Libra!

Sip a Cup of Warm Milk

Always on the go and meeting new people, Libra needs to be well rested. Ready to wind down but feeling a bit too energized after the excitement of the past day? Try having a cup of warm milk! In fact, Libra could make this a regular bedtime ritual! Soothing and traditional, warm milk is a wonderful natural sleep aid. It is especially beneficial if you were given this as a child; the comforting memories will also relax you. You will be drifting off to dreamland in no time.

Buy a Pair of Leather Driving Gloves

If there is one thing Libra knows, it's how to do everything with a touch of class. Leather driving gloves may not be necessary in the modern vehicle, but they are certainly sophisticated. Ruled by Venus, Libra will especially love the smooth, somewhat daring feel of leather (real or fake).

Something that people may not realize is that Libra also has a tough side and has an urge to drive in the fast lane. Sure, you are a gentle sign with a knack for making others feel at home, but you also know how to get down to business. Slip on your gloves and go for a whirl—just be sure to keep to the speed limit and buckle up first.

Ease Overactive Thoughts with St. John's Wort

Libra cares deeply about his relationships. In fact, part of the Libran identity is tied to balance within his family, friendship circle, and romantic connections. Sometimes, Libra can get caught up in trying to make everyone happy, leaving him feeling overwhelmed and unbalanced himself. St. John's wort is a natural supplement that may help calm the anxious thoughts that Libra sometimes experiences. Talk to your doctor to ask if it may help you (St. John's wort is not suitable for everyone and can interact with other medications), as well as to discuss specific dosing recommendations.

Playact

Ignite your creativity and give yourself a confidence boost with a little playacting. It may seem counterproductive, but sometimes the best way for Libra to feel like himself is by pretending to be someone else. The time-out from his own thoughts and feelings is the perfect way to recharge and gain some perspective. Step into someone else's shoes for the afternoon: Dress in a way you normally wouldn't dress, and try out personality traits that don't come as naturally to you. At the end of the "show," you'll return to yourself with a creative reminder of all of the things that make you amazing.

Plant Morning Glories

Few appreciate beauty quite like Libra does. Ruled by Venus, he has a keen eye for aesthetics, particularly the grace and class of a flawless floral arrangement and striking outdoor blossoms. Morning glories are a perfect vine to accent the Libran home. This traditional flower will evoke a sophisticated atmosphere, while the soft blue color of the petals will promote calm and communication. Consider using morning glory blooms as a centerpiece in your living or dining room, where they are sure to

impress your guests and encourage open, relaxed conversation.

Bring On the Kiwifruit

Having trouble sleeping? Airy Libra can be quite the tornado of energy, which is great for a productive day, but not so great come bedtime. Don't fret; simply add more kiwifruit to your diet! Kiwifruit contains a number of powerful compounds, including serotonin, which is an important chemical in sleep regulation.

Kiwifruit is also loaded with vitamins and minerals, such as vitamins B_6 and B_{12} and magnesium. These vitamins and minerals are key in relieving and managing stress. Plus, kiwifruit is a delicious, colorful treat, perfect for topping frozen yogurt or salad, or enjoying by itself.

Toast with a Grasshopper

Venusian Libra loves cocktails that offer a complete sensory experience. Combining a rich blend of tastes and aromas, as well as a striking green color, the grasshopper cocktail is the perfect Libran refreshment.

Making your own grasshopper cocktail at home is simple. In a shaker filled with ice, combine 1½ tablespoons (¾ fluid ounce) cream, 1½ tablespoons (¾ fluid ounce) white crème de cacao, and 1½ tablespoons (¾ fluid ounce) green crème de menthe. Shake vigorously, then strain into a chilled cocktail glass. Top off the glass with a shaving of dark chocolate and voilà!

Find Balance with Ametrine

Ametrine is the perfect meditation stone for Libra, due to its inherent stable nature. This eye-catching orange and purple crystal is made of a combination of amethyst and citrine. Amethyst represents spiritual enlightenment, while citrine represents physical expression and grounding joy. Ametrine's unique blend of the metaphysical plane of amethyst and the physical plane of citrine creates perfect balance. Keep this stone with you always in the form of a bracelet or ring, or use it to meditate in your home.

Restore Joy with Lavender

Above everything, Libra values harmony in all things. From his relationships to his home, he seeks balance. As a compassionate sign, he tends to take on the full responsibility of creating and restoring balance for both himself and those around him, which can lead to him feeling overwhelmed and run-down. If you need a little release, the scent of a lavender candle is the perfect way to ease stress and recharge your batteries.

Boasting a sweet, floral scent, lavender has a soothing effect that calms anxious thoughts and promotes relaxation. You can light a lavender candle in a communal space. Not only will the qualities of lavender restore balance to yourself, your home, and your relationships, but its pleasing scent will be a popular choice for all who encounter it.

Create a Libran Grounding Space

With so many people to see and exciting plans in the works, Libra needs a space that allows him to touch back down to earth once in a while. Design a room in your home where you can pause and refocus before dashing off on your next adventure. Use darker colors such as indigo blue and burgundy, combined with a soft neutral like ivory or cream, to create a sense of calm and balance. Earthy accents like wood and potted plants will provide a feeling of stability. And, in keeping with the Scales, make sure there are equal numbers of all home accessories!

Visit a Teahouse

Sophisticated Libra knows a get-together over tea is the civilized thing to do. Not only that, but it provides the perfect setting for deep conversation with close friends. Libra places great importance on relationships, so he will appreciate the opportunity to strengthen his friendships even more.

Book an afternoon at a teahouse. Treat yourself to some pastries, and maybe ask for recommendations on a tea blend you have never tried before. Or go to a fancy restaurant for an upmarket afternoon tea treat. It can also be an excuse for you and your friends to wear your fanciest of clothes. Who knows? It might become a regular thing!

Savor Buttercrunch Candy

Libra adores indulging his senses. Ruled by luxuriant Venus, he understands the healing powers of even a small treat—especially when it comes to his taste buds. Splurge on a box of buttercrunch candy—or make your own at home! The rich, sugary sweet flavors are sure to lift your spirits and encourage a bit of relaxation. This delicious candy also makes for a lovely surprise to share with friends and neighbors, which generous Libra enjoys.

Keep a Loved One with You Always

For Libra an important part of happiness is close interpersonal relationships. Feeling less than your usual bubbly self? Having a picture on hand of someone you love is a simple yet effective way to brighten your mood and put you back in a positive mental space. Wear a locket with a special person's picture inside, or keep a photo tucked into your wallet where you can easily see it. Your loved ones give you strength, so keep them close!

Eat Honey

Rich and sweet, honey is the perfect indulgence for Venus-ruled Libra. But what you may not know is that, as long as you are not allergic to bees or bee products, honey is also healthy! Pure honey is full of health-promoting antioxidants that are linked to heart health. It also lowers blood pressure, improves cholesterol, soothes sore throat, and promotes healthy skin and hair.

To enjoy the benefits of honey, you can stir a little honey into your tea, or relish a spoonful straight from the jar. You can also make a rejuvenating face mask by mixing 2 teaspoons of honey with 1 teaspoon of aloe vera gel.

Decorate with Gold Mirrors

As an air sign, Libra needs plenty of open space for his creativity to shine. Mirrors are an easy way to make your home feel twice as big—even if home is a studio apartment with one window and a closet-sized bedroom.

Ruled by Venus, Libra also needs décor that expresses style and luxury, so your mirrors should have a touch of gilt, such as a gold frame or gold foil accents. Experiment with the mirror placement to find the best locations for ultimate openness in your space.

Keep an Emotions Journal

Libra has so many thoughts and feelings—and so much pressure to set them aside for the sake of being amiable! Libra has a talent for making others feel relaxed and happy, but sometimes his own feelings can be lost in his quest to please everyone else. Keep a journal to help you register and express your emotions on a daily or at least a weekly basis. While you may have the urge to swallow your feelings, this will only cause them to be bottled up until you eventually burst. Taking the time to write out all of your thoughts allows you to fully experience them, and then reflect on them. As you release them onto the page, you'll feel yourself released from their weight.

Make a Rejuvenating Libran Playlist

Libra is the life of the party, but even he could use an extra boost of energy once in a while. Make a playlist to get you back into the partying mood. Your playlist should include fellow Librans, such as Bruce Springsteen (his hit "Hungry Heart" may just be Libra's theme song), Bruno Mars, Gwen Stefani, Sting, and Ray Charles. Who knows how to energize a Libra better than a Libra does? So crank up the tunes and show off your dance moves!

CHAPTER 14

Self-Care for Scorpio

Dates: October 23–November 21
Element: Water
Polarity: Yin
Quality: Fixed
Symbol: Scorpion, Eagle, Phoenix
Ruler: Mars, Pluto

Scorpio is the eighth sign of the zodiac and the third fixed sign of the zodiac. Like the other fixed signs—which come in the middle of each season—she is strong, passionate, and stubborn. Scorpio is the strongest sign of the zodiac in terms of her creative energy and her ability to transform herself, and she has a latent power that waits until it's needed to reveal itself. Scorpio meets the battle between the personality and the soul head-on throughout life. Those born under this sign can experience the highest manifestations of this and the lowest: Scorpio is not a mild person; she is very magnetic and interested in the extremes of life.

Each astrological sign has a symbol. Scorpio has three: the Scorpion, the Eagle, and the Phoenix. The Scorpion represents the worst tendencies of this sign: an unevolved Scorpio who would rather sting herself to death than forgo the pleasure of the sting. Here is a personality that can become locked into the "too much" syndrome: too much alcohol, sex, exercise, or dieting, or too many drugs, or too much discipline that cuts off the joy of life. Scorpio often passes through this phase and transforms her habits into helping others overcome addictions and find meaning in life. The second symbol is the Eagle: a bird representing spirit that can fly closer to the sun than any other and yet is also a fierce hunter. Here, Scorpio is moving from the low to the higher spiritual life. Scorpio's final symbol is the Phoenix: a mythical bird that rises from its ashes to create a new self. This quest of transformation is the one Scorpio aspires to, and self-care is a way that Scorpio can achieve this quest.

Scorpio has two planetary rulers: Mars and Pluto. Originally, Scorpio was ruled by Mars, god of war, because of the fierce and strategic intensity astrologers observed with these personalities. Mars could be seen by the naked eye in ancient times and through observation was associated with Scorpio. In 1930, coincident with the development of atomic power, Pluto was discovered. Pluto is now considered the ruler of Scorpio because Pluto represents the transformation of the self at the deepest level. Pluto also represents the riches, including psychological, spiritual, and material, that Scorpio craves.

In Roman mythology, Pluto was the god of the underworld. He was a passionate god, and one deeply connected to the power, fecundity, and riches of the earth. *Pluto* in Latin means "the rich one," and while the riches of Scorpio may not always be material, she is a very charismatic person who always has the wealth of her strength and focus to re-create herself. In Greek mythology, Pluto was called Hades. One of Hades's powers was granting the use of a helmet that made the wearer invisible. Scorpio would love to have such an object. She loves being enigmatic and does not like to reveal herself to others.

Self-Care and Scorpio

Scorpio's focused energy must be expressed in creative activities, which are so important to this sign's self-care. Some unevolved Scorpios may linger on the darker side of life, but all are ultimately moving toward transformation. These descriptions may sound dramatic, but Scorpio isn't interested in living a superficial life. She wants to deal with the profound questions of life and death, head-on. Scorpio does not reveal herself easily and is convinced that she is the best judge of what she needs, which makes it difficult for her to accept self-care advice from others.

However, as a water sign, Scorpio is tuned in to her body, mind, and spirit and can be a fount of knowledge about medicine, herbs, alternative cures, and a healthy lifestyle. She just needs to use this knowledge to prioritize herself and her needs.

Oftentimes, Scorpios are therapists, doctors, or counselors, and those born under this sign have a deep understanding of the world's ills. She is used to having others come to her and tell her all about their problems. Scorpio doesn't say anything, just listens, but after a short time the other person might say, "Thanks, I feel a lot better." Scorpio has energetically helped them see something in a different way or transform their dark problems into the light. If Scorpio does this for herself, then there is no limit to the ingenious and successful ways she can pursue well-being and self-care.

One major area of self-care for most Scorpios is spending time engaging with pets. This very private sign has a wordless communication with animals that is healing and pleasurable. Scorpio also likes being a pet's master. Scorpio can be a very good animal trainer, or dog or horse whisperer. Pets offer uncomplicated love and Scorpio can return this.

Scorpio is usually able to easily incorporate sports into her self-care programs. She recognizes the need to move her energy around and keep it moving. Water sports (for this water sign) and martial arts are good choices. Taking a POUND class or moving to a drumbeat speaks to the primitive part of Scorpio. The social aspect of sports has limited appeal for Scorpio. Scorpio is sometimes solitary and may enjoy long-distance or endurance sports.

Psychological health is entirely up to Scorpio. Unless she decides to seek help or sees the need, she sees no point to counseling. And a therapist must be as complex and strong as the Scorpio client for any therapy to work. The most important part of a therapeutic relationship for her is that it allows spiritual, even religious, growth. Scorpio isn't fooling around this lifetime. She wants to purify her soul and will work with anyone who can offer that kind of growth.

Scorpio Rules the Reproductive System and Organs of Elimination

Scorpio rules the reproductive organs as well as the organs of elimination, basically everything from the navel to the tops of the thighs. This is the powerhouse of the body, the root and sacral chakras in yoga. Problems with the reproductive organs can sometimes mean that there is an energy block in the body. In addition to seeking medical advice, Scorpio might consider yoga exercises to keep this area of the body relaxed and unblocked. However, Scorpio must beware of satisfying her desires without thinking about the consequences. Even for the sign ruled by the reproductive organs, there is a difference between healthy sex and wanton sex for power.

The elimination organs are not as much fun to consider but are essential for the body's health. Keeping the colon and urinary tract healthy ensures that impurities can be eliminated from the body. Someone born under this sign might ask her doctor about taking probiotics, which keep the balance of flora constant in the body. A Scorpio woman might consider asking her doctor about taking a daily dose of cranberry juice, which may help ensure that the urinary tract remains healthy.

Scorpio and Self-Care Success

One major pitfall for Scorpio's self-care program is that Scorpio sometimes confuses care with pleasure. Everything that feels good isn't necessarily self-care, which can be difficult for this water sign to accept. If Scorpio spirals into a cycle of self-destructive activity, it will take some time for her to recoup and find herself on the side of light. But that is the power of this sign; more than any other sign, she can pull herself from the depths and make a truly remarkable transformation.

Another pitfall for Scorpio's self-care program is the very opposite of the first. Scorpio can become so rigid and obsessive about self-care that there is no flow to life or spontaneity. Too much discipline is too much control, and eventually there is a rebellion. When Scorpio follows her instincts and moderates her extremes, she is able to practice self-care to her best ability.

The most successful aspect of self-care for Scorpio is her desire to engage in these types of rituals. Once she decides on a program, a routine, or practice, she will continue it until it no longer serves her. Her motivation is simple: "I create a healthier me." This is why Scorpio will not benefit from a quick fix. She wants to understand the root of the problem, be it physical, mental, or spiritual. Meditation, spiritual practices, dance, and exercise are all ways she can move her considerable energy into balance so she heals herself and provides self-care.

Humor is a big factor in Scorpio's outlook on life. She has a biting wit and is often sarcastic, but wildly funny. Laughing at the world—and at herself—is a good self-care practice and a way of sharing with other people. Scorpio can be a loner and sharing a joke is a way to keep connected.

Whether she's laughing, engaging in physical activity, or looking for a creative space, Scorpio, like all water signs, is intuitive. And she uses this trait when deciding which self-care rituals are right for her, which is why it is imperative for her to make her self-care choices based on her astrological sign. So let's take a look at some self-care activities that are tailored specifically for Scorpio.

Treat Yourself to Tiger's Eye Jewelry

Scorpio is fiercely loyal and very brave, but she also tends to be intense. Keep grounded in tumultuous situations by wearing tiger's eye jewelry. Due to her passionate nature, Scorpio must always focus on staying centered. While it can be difficult to do so at times, carrying or wearing tiger's eye is an easy way to keep emotions in check.

It represents a wise, all-knowing eye and brings clarity to an individual's vision—essential when trying to keep a level head during emotional times.

Stay Healthy with Red Ginseng

Immunity is important for all of us, but is particularly essential for Scorpio for a couple of reasons. First, Scorpio rules over the elimination organs. Keeping the colon and urinary tract healthy ensures that impurities can be eliminated from the body. Second, Scorpio sometimes has a hard time expressing emotions. During times when she feels sad or angry, she can turn inward, and her emotional unrest can affect her physical well-being.

Look into boosting your immune system by taking red ginseng. Not only does it have anti-inflammatory and antioxidant effects, but it is claimed it also strengthens the immune system and can help fight fatigue.

Ask your doctor (who is familiar with your health and medications) about making red ginseng a part of your self-care routine on a short-term basis either by enjoying a cup of tea or taking a supplement. It's an easy way for Scorpio to keep wellness at the top of her mind.

Collect Glass Figurines

Scorpio is the ruler of transformation, a characteristic that makes her appreciate transformation in other beings and objects.

If you'd like to bring a talisman of transformation into your home, consider collecting clear glass figurines or abstract shapes. Hold the glass in front of natural light and enjoy the rainbows that light makes when shining on the figures, as you note the transformation that happens right before your eyes. When light hits the glass, it bends, and is transformed into a rainbow. Pause and take a moment to appreciate the transformative beauty and power.

Get Away from It All

In the swamps! While it may not sound like your typical vacation, consider visiting a swamp. A water sign, Scorpio rules all swamplands, so in a way you'd be visiting your own kingdom.

The next time you'd like to take some time away, consider a high-speed airboat adventure in New Orleans. Or head down under and take a floatplane to Australia's remote Finniss River floodplains. Or, off the coast of the Bulgarian Black Sea, discover Alepu, a swamp and nature reserve home to a large variety of rare waterbirds.

Exploring these swamplands will satisfy your adventurous side, and you may find you'll feel at home at these mysteriously beautiful and watery places.

Carry Black Tourmaline

Scorpio is the third fixed sign of the zodiac. The fixed signs come in the middle of each season; they are strong, passionate, and stubborn. All the fixed signs partake of serpent or kundalini power. In Scorpio this power waits within until needed. If you ever need a reminder of how powerful you are, consider carrying a black tourmaline crystal.

A black tourmaline crystal in your left pocket promotes a sense of power and self-confidence, and the dark color will remind you of your sometimes dark tendencies. It can empower you during challenging times, when you may most need a reminder of your innate power. It is also an excellent crystal for meditation, and for promoting healing.

Keep one close at hand to help ensure you are capitalizing on your power as a Scorpio.

Respect Snakes

Do you cringe when you see a picture of a snake? Consider changing your opinion of your serpent sister.

Ruled by Scorpio, snakes symbolize the transformative life force that Scorpio has. Just as a snake can shed her skin, so too can Scorpio transform her being. Rather than fearing these slithery creatures, reflect on how alike you are. Scorpio desires growth, rebirth, and metamorphosis. Scorpio is not afraid of reaching deep within herself to summon change and encourage soul transformation. Even though you may not want to have a pet as a snake, next time you think of your spiritual sister, respect your commonalities.

Beautify Your Kitchen with Apothecary Jars

Scorpio rules all pharmacists and medical equipment. Honor your spirit and give a nod to this alignment by keeping grains and spices in apothecary jars.

Scorpio makes a wonderful pharmacist or physician, since these careers combine passions, essential medical knowledge, and personal interactions aimed to benefit others. While it might not be the perfect job for you personally, you can give a nod to this part of your Scorpio nature by decorating your home with apothecary décor. The kitchen is the easiest space to accomplish this in, though you can also find appropriate furniture for your bedroom or living room—interesting bureaus and shelves that hark back to a time before modern pharmacy practice. Whenever you beautify your space, you are performing an act of self-care, and also setting the stage for those times in the future when you can relax and enjoy your space.

Visit a Labyrinth

Scorpio always rises to a challenge, and she enjoys the complex and mysterious. Why not add a little fun to your self-care and visit a maze?

Simultaneously fun and exhilarating, mazes are a great way to add mystery to your day, without any drama. Get a group of friends together and make it a competition—who can escape first? Or go on your own for a personal challenge. Either way, you will leave feeling accomplished and inspired.

Adopt a Ferret

Scorpio is typically very private, and has a wordless communication with animals. Their relationship not only is enjoyable, but also can be healing. Pets offer uncomplicated love and Scorpio can return this.

If you're considering adopting a pet, why not try a ferret? A ferret may be an unusual pet, but their cuteness and strangeness are perfect for Scorpio. A less common choice than a cat or dog, this very active animal can be a wonderful companion for you. Additionally, they love to play, which can add a spirited and fun element to your daily care. Just make sure to

get expert advice on adopting (and properly caring for) your ferret from a local animal shelter before you commit.

Enjoy Flamenco Music

If you haven't tried listening to flamenco music before, you may be missing out. The rhythmic qualities of this Spanish-based music speak to Scorpio's passionate soul.

Flamenco music can be part of your self-care routine in a myriad of ways. You can use it to unwind at the end of a stressful day, or make it part of your physical fitness regimen and use it as the soundtrack of your dance-based workout. If you're feeling daring, why not try flamenco dancing on a date? The sensual music can be both soothing and seductive.

Add Alexandrite to Your Jewelry Collection

One of Scorpio's ruling planets is Mars: the red planet. Due to its red color, a beautiful stone for Scorpio is alexandrite.

Compared to many gemstones, alexandrite's discovery was relatively recent, as it was found only in the last two hundred years. Despite this, it has already gained a reputation as having mystical properties. One possible reason for this is that the miners who originally discovered the stone reported that it changed color from green to red, depending on the light. Its red shade is often described as fiery, and it can be a beautiful addition to Scorpio's wardrobe.

Listen to the Music of Your Scorpio Brothers and Sisters

As a water sign, Scorpio is naturally creative, and it comes as no surprise that many musical artists were born under the Scorpio sign.

Expand your playlist and take a listen to the many songs of Scorpios who create music in all genres, from rock to rap to country to folk to pop, including:

- Drake (born October 24)
- Katy Perry (born October 25)
- Keith Urban (born October 26)
- Brad Paisley (born October 28)
- Frank Ocean (born October 28)
- Anthony Kiedis (Red Hot Chili Peppers front man was born November 1)
- Joni Mitchell (born November 7)
- Diplo (born November 10)
- Jeff Buckley (born November 17)
- Björk (born November 21)

Treat Yourself to Sexy Nightwear

Every astrological sign rules a certain area of the body. For Scorpio, this includes the genitals. Naturally passionate and intense, Scorpio enjoys spicing things up in the bedroom. Why not set the stage for an exciting and romantic evening with your partner by showing up in sexy lingerie or nightwear?

Experiment with bold colors such as black or red, and alluring, silky fabrics. Make your bedroom an ideal setting for romance by dimming the lights and dressing your bed in lush fabrics. Enjoy your partner, and your time together. Self-care can be mutually enjoyable.

Immerse Yourself in the Works of Scorpio Artists

An afternoon in the museum can be a simultaneously relaxing and inspiring act of self-care. Next time you have the opportunity to spend some time admiring great works of art, pay particular attention to artists born under the Scorpio sign. A few notables include:

- Pablo Picasso (born October 25)
- Roy Lichtenstein (born October 27)
- Claude Monet (born November 14)
- Georgia O'Keeffe (born November 15)

If you're unable to visit a museum, check out their works online. If you're particularly drawn to one artist, consider decorating your home with prints of their work—a tribute to a fellow Scorpio.

Honor Eagles

The Eagle is Scorpio's second symbol (the other two being the Scorpion and the

Phoenix). These beautiful birds are majestic and spirited, much like Scorpio herself. This bird represents spirit that can fly closer to the sun than any other—and yet also is a fierce hunter. The Eagle can also represent Scorpio moving from the lower to the higher spiritual life.

Learn more about these regal animals. You may find that you identify with other qualities they possess. Consider putting their likeness in your home, or keeping a picture of an eagle in your desk drawer at work. Their strength and perseverance are wonderful reminders that you are stronger than you think, and capable of soaring to great heights.

Give Mastic a Try

Mastic is a spice exclusively (it is true; the only place it grows is on Chios) found on the southern side of the Greek island of Chios. It has a pungent taste that Scorpio loves. While the tree that produces mastic is closely related to the pistachio, the flavor is a refreshing cedar or pine taste. Mastic has been used as a natural remedy for a range of discomforts, including many digestive ailments. Why not give it a try in some traditional Greek recipes? Better yet, take a trip to Chios to visit the home of this intriguing spice. While there, you can also tour medieval villages and visit beautiful beaches.

Attend a Masquerade

One of Scorpio's ruling heavenly bodies is Pluto. In Greek mythology, Pluto was called Hades, and one of his powers was granting the use of a helmet that made the wearer invisible. Scorpio would love to have such an object; she loves being enigmatic and does not like to reveal herself to others. If you can't have a helmet of invisibility, why not try for the next best thing—a disguise!—and attend a masquerade ball?

These balls are mysterious and sometimes romantic, both of which appeal to Scorpio. So, if you're looking for a fun night out that is suited to your astrological tendencies, attend a masquerade ball. If you can't find one near you, host your own!

Try Your Hand at Cartooning

Creative and humorous, cartoons can be both a source of humor and a thought-provoking statement on current affairs. If you find that you enjoy reading cartoons, why not try creating your own?

Drawing cartoons and writing witty captions will appeal to Scorpio's sense of humor and creativity. Not only that, but the act itself is a productive and cathartic form of self-care. No matter your talent level, cartooning is a worthwhile hobby to look into.

Host a Murder Mystery Night

Scorpio is the sign of all things mysterious. Feed your creativity and create a true mystery by hosting a murder mystery night.

Whether you create the mystery yourself or buy a package from a website like www.mymysteryparty.com, this is a great opportunity to flex your creative side, unwind, and socialize with friends. To ensure that the evening maintains an authentic, secretive energy, invite guests who share your creativity and love of mystery. Assign roles ahead of time so that guests can arrive already in character. Not only will this evening be thrilling and fun, but you will stimulate your brain in a wonderful way—an unorthodox yet exciting act of self-care.

Learn to Dance the Tango

Dance in any form is an intimate expression of the dancer's feelings. The tango is the perfect dance for Scorpio as it puts your sensual side on display, allowing you to channel your inner desires through movement. The dance creates a connection between the partners and allows for an exciting intimacy that you can continue off the dance floor.

If you have a partner, sign up for a couples' class and learn together. If you're single, you can still bring the heat and have some fun, learning alongside others who are looking to master the dance as well. It's a fun way to exercise and get your heart rate going—and depending on your connection with your partner, it may even get your heart racing!

Take a Dip in a Mud Bath

Why not get dirty to get clean? The many cleansing and detoxifying properties of mud baths make them an amazing spa-day treat for Scorpio. It's a transformational experience of heated water and earth that relaxes your body, soothes your muscles, and exfoliates your skin. Scorpio will emerge from the bath refreshed and ready to take on the world.

Find a spa close to you that offers mud baths, and book yourself some time to enjoy the treatment. Try to make a full day of it, as you don't want to unwind only to tense up afterward due to a tight schedule. If you can't sneak away for a full day or find a mud bath treatment in your area, research and buy a luxurious mud mask online and enjoy it on a smaller scale at home.

Try Bach's Holly Remedy

There's an intensity to Scorpio that burns bright and provides strength to those born under this Sun sign. Sometimes, though, Scorpio's passion can burn a little too bright and may benefit from some calming. One option to ease this intensity is the original Bach Flower Remedies, which are made from wildflowers and, according to the company, "gently restore the balance between mind and body." (The Bach Flower Remedies are available online.)

Bach's holly remedy is meant to help those who are "attacked by thoughts of such kind as jealousy, envy, revenge, suspicion," which can sometimes be the case for Scorpio. If and when you do feel yourself in such a state, try adding a couple of drops of holly to a glass of water (follow the directions on the bottle) and drinking slowly throughout the day.

Dine On Natural Aphrodisiacs

As Scorpio rules the reproductive organs, it's only natural for those born under the sign to have a heightened sexual energy. When Scorpio wants to turn up the heat, she's very capable on her own—but indulging in some natural aphrodisiacs can increase desire for all parties involved.

Next time you're planning a romantic night, find a high-quality restaurant that specializes in shellfish and order a dozen oysters for you and your date (as long as neither of you is allergic to shellfish). The zinc and amino acids (which increase dopamine) will aid in arousal.

You may also want to have some saffron ice cream in your freezer for when you return home. The spice is another known aphrodisiac, and the ice cream will cool things down before you heat things up.

Investigate Your Past Lives

Who's to say we only have one life to live? For those who believe our souls have inhabited other bodies and lived other lives, a past-life reading is a potential way to unlock the histories and mysteries of those lives gone before. Scorpio's interest in mysticism and spirituality allows for an openness to this type of belief—at least enough to question and investigate if it's true.

There may be something more to that old familiar feeling, and there's one way to get to the bottom of it. After doing your research and receiving recommendations from a trusted source, visit a past-life expert and have a reading. See what memories from your former lives can be recalled and how those past lives can affect your present and future.

Open Yourself Up to Spiritual Study

There's a difference between religious and spiritual. As someone who is in touch with her spiritual side, Scorpio recognizes and appreciates that difference, and finds herself looking to deepen her understanding of her spiritual leanings. It's through fully understanding and appreciating a spiritual ritual or belief that Scorpio will adopt it and incorporate it into her life.

Is there a spiritual practice that has always piqued your interest? If so, delve into its origins, discover the power it possesses, and, if it truly speaks to you, make it a part of your life. You are in charge of your own spirituality, and you can incorporate it as you see fit.

Try White Magic

Have you ever cast a spell? As an intense and transformative person, you may find that a simple white ("good") magic spell may help you feel empowered. While it is important to limit spellcasting to white magic to avoid hurting anyone, consider how magic could help you create meaningful life changes.

If you are looking to manifest a change in your personal or professional life, research a spell that could help move the needle. *The Modern Witchcraft Spell Book* by Skye Alexander offers beginner spells you could try, or you can look online for a spell to help you reach a specific goal. Regardless of which spell you choose, be sure to keep your intentions pure, and enjoy the experience as an emotional and mental act of self-care.

Go for an Aqua Jog

A lot of people assume Scorpio is a fire sign; it may be because Mars is one of her ruling planets, or it may be due to her passionate personality. However, as you know, Scorpio is a water sign and the pool is a great place to get your exercise. Swimming laps isn't the only option though. Scorpio's determined demeanor makes aqua jogging another perfect form of in-pool workout.

Aqua jogging is a great cardiovascular activity, like its on-land counterpart, but by exercising in the pool, you cut down on the stress on your joints. So, next time you're looking for a fun way to de-stress, buckle into a buoyancy belt and break a sweat in the pool.

Get Back in Black—Head to Toe

Dressing well is not always about looking good: It's about feeling good. Luckily, Scorpio knows how to feel good while looking good. Why not embrace your dark side while doing so? Next time you're getting ready to go out on the town, opt for an all-black outfit, and give it even more of an edge by working in at least one leather (real or faux) accessory or article of clothing—whether it's boots or a belt, a skirt or pants. It's not that you necessarily need the confidence boost that comes with such an ensemble, but it's just one more way to embody the mysteriously seductive Scorpio. Now you can look good, feel good, and be *bad*.

Have Yourself a Stinger

While it's a reference to the venomous appendage of a scorpion, the stinger is also the perfect cocktail for Scorpio, as the minty mixture makes for a pointed libation. As an after-dinner drink, the stinger is a perfect way to segue into your next nighttime activity—whatever that may be.

Here's your simple recipe for a stinger: 4 tablespoons (2 fluid ounces) brandy and 1½ tablespoons (¾ fluid ounce) white crème de menthe. Shake ingredients with ice and strain into a rocks glass with ice.

Soar in Eagle Pose

While Scorpio is tied closely to its Scorpion symbol, the Eagle is also a symbol of the sign. The Eagle Pose lets you work on your balance while improving blood flow. This is not a beginners' pose, so make sure to practice this with your yoga instructor for technique guidance.

To begin, stand in Mountain Pose (standing straight, feet together, arms by your side). Bend the hips, knees, and ankles. Cross the left leg over the right thigh and wrap the top of your left foot around the right calf as best you can. Bring your arms to the center in front of you and entwine them, crossing the right elbow over the inside of the left elbow. Bend your elbows. Turn the palms to face each other and join them. Lift the elbows to shoulder height and move the forearms away from the face to bring the wrists over the elbows. Gaze straight ahead. Remain in the pose for several breaths, and then repeat on the other side.

Wear Topaz

This stone—one of Scorpio's birthstones—is available in a number of shades and contains healing properties that work well for Scorpio. Its colors shift and change in different angles—replicating the mysterious qualities of this sign. Topaz is often used to help ground people and clear negative energies. Since Scorpio can sometimes let her emotions get the better of her, topaz is the perfect accessory to clear those toxic feelings and remain levelheaded.

It's beneficial to wear topaz (in a ring or pendant, for example) when you are in situations that may trigger negative emotions—whether those are feelings of jealousy, anger, or frustration. Research the various colors that this calming stone comes in; each offers different healing qualities that can benefit Scorpio.

Get Yourself a Scorpion

A pet scorpion? That is a little much, even for you, fearless Scorpio. But you can still keep a totem of your Sun sign's symbol—maybe a small figurine or a scorpion in amber—nearby as a source of strength. Scorpions have been around for millions of years in one form or another—adapting and adjusting to the world around them to survive, similar to Scorpio herself.

While a fierce predator who can pack a punch with its venomous stinger, the Scorpion symbolizes the unevolved form of Scorpio, the one who can do damage to herself with too much excess—whether that's too much drinking or extreme dieting, or some other destructive behavior. A scorpion totem can act as a reminder of who you can become if you're not careful and remind you to take care of yourself rather than suffer your own sting.

Visit a Hot Spring

While a hot bath is always nice and relaxing, Scorpio could use something a little more exciting than warm water in her bathroom. Why settle for a warm bath when you can enjoy a hot spring? As a water sign with a hot temper (occasionally), Scorpio is well suited to bathing in a hot spring. The water is heated naturally by the earth and can contain a number of beneficial minerals like calcium, magnesium, potassium, and zinc—meaning your dip will help relieve stress, smooth your skin, increase circulation, and more. Research the health considerations of hot springs before you go.

If you're not within driving distance of a hot spring, plan a trip and make it an all-natural adventure. You deserve a break, and this will soothe your body and your soul.

Do Something Daring

Scorpio is known for being bold, but sometimes you need to remind yourself of that fact. It's healthy to test your limits and try something new. What other people consider daring is probably a little everyday for you, Scorpio. You need to find something that will push you out of your comfort zone. What about a trip to a nudist resort? Or lessons in windsurfing? Or something else that might make others blush, or back away in fear? The goal isn't to be uncomfortable to the point of not participating, though; it's about pushing boundaries. Choose something you'll ultimately enjoy, but that will be a thrill while you're doing it.

Give Yourself a Scare

Some people turn to their favorite comedies when they need to relax. Others get lost in an old Hollywood classic. Scorpio though? Bring on the horror movies—the darker, the better. Scorpio has an interest in the macabre and the mysterious, making horror movies an obvious go-to, whether you're looking to stay in and Netflix and chill or take in an all-night horror-fest.

There are actually also some health benefits to all the jumps and scares—not that Scorpio scares easily. A study funded by a UK movie subscription service found that watching horror movies can actually burn calories; the study's participants burned 184 calories while watching *The Shining*.

Try Clove Tea

Clove, the aromatic spice from Asia, works twofold for Scorpio, who rules over both the elimination and reproductive organs. Cloves may help the digestive system and alleviate gas. And cloves are also known to be a natural aphrodisiac. While these are two separate benefits, the fact that cloves can accomplish both makes it the perfect spice for Scorpio to select after dinner. Before you do so, check with your doctor (who is familiar with your health and medications).

A simple way to make a clove tea is by adding a teaspoon of ground cloves to boiling water. You can include other spices if you desire. Let it steep for 15 minutes, strain, and serve. Whether you're looking for relief or action, the cloves will work their magic.

Visit a Graveyard

There's a connection between Scorpio and the afterlife. Being ruled by Pluto, the celestial body named for the god of the underworld, Scorpio has a proclivity for the other side. It's not something to be ashamed or afraid of though, as a powerful link to the afterlife allows for greater knowledge here on earth. By taking a respectful and reflective walk through a graveyard, you're honoring your connection to Pluto as well as the souls of those who've passed.

If you're able to track down and travel to a graveyard of your ancestors, bring a sheet of paper and some rubbing wax or a crayon to make a gravestone rubbing. It's a sentimental connection to your past. Just be sure rubbings are allowed in the cemetery and you remain respectful during your visit.

Hula for Your Health

An ancient Polynesian dance form passed down generation by generation, hula is as much about storytelling as it is about movement. Each move helps to tell a greater story while getting your heart rate going, your hips and other joints moving, and your mind focused. It's a low-impact exercise that can work your entire body, and it's perfect for Scorpio, who prefers there to be an intention behind her moves.

Check out your local gyms and cultural centers to see if they offer any hula exercise classes. If there aren't any classes held locally, you can find many beginners' instructional videos online.

Embrace Your Inner Phoenix

While Scorpio is most immediately identified by the Scorpion symbol, that is only the first of her three symbols. Whereas the Scorpion is the start of the sign's evolution and the Eagle symbolizes the transitional period, the Phoenix is the symbol of its complete transformation. The mythological bird is the embodiment of Scorpio's journey from darkness to light. No matter where you are on your own path, it's important to keep this symbol in sight. Look for a piece of art depicting the phoenix in flight, or perhaps a pin or carving; whatever you end up choosing, the importance is the meaning—you are the Phoenix and you will rise.

Kick a Bad Habit

Scorpio is extreme. This can be extremely beneficial for Scorpio, or it can be extremely detrimental. Unfortunately, in the case of vices, this extreme nature can be quite harmful. Scorpio's bad habit isn't a once in a while type of thing. It often leads to too much—too much smoking, too much drinking, too much junk food, whatever the particular tendency. The good news to this black-and-white behavior is that once Scorpio sets her mind to it, she'll be extremely determined to stop.

You know what you need to stop doing. It can be risky behavior or negative thinking. Whatever it is, make a plan on how to overcome it, and stick with it. Turn that darkness into light.

Be Cautious of Secrets

Some signs are sunny extroverts who want everyone to know everything about them at all times. Not Scorpio though. While Scorpio is a deeply devoted friend, she enjoys keeping an air of mystery and a bit of distance between herself and other people. Such a secretive side keeps people guessing and crafts an enigmatic persona, welcomed by this sign ruled by Pluto.

Embrace your mystery, but don't let it wall you off from other people. As you know, when you do connect with others, you forge a strong connection. Allow people to see you for the fiercely loyal friend you can be—even if you do have a secret or two.

Practice Deep Meditation

Scorpio isn't looking for 5 minutes of mindfulness or 10 minutes of sitting peacefully to practice breathing exercises. No, Scorpio is searching for meaningful transformation and is willing to work for it. Your focus should be on transforming the darkness into light and then carrying that lightness with you. Scorpio likes to live in the extremes, so a next-level meditative practice makes sense.

Deep meditation is its own practice in itself. In order to start practicing deep meditation effectively, you should look up a recommended class or follow instructions from a trusted teacher's app or online courses.

Give Muay Thai a Try

Scorpio likes her workouts to be as intense as her personality. What better way to get an intense workout than by training in this combat sport? Muay Thai is a sport from Thailand that's made its way around the world as both a fighting style and an exercise opportunity. Similar to a scorpion's stinging strike, Muay Thai is built around a combination of strikes delivered from the "eight limbs," or the eight points of contact allowed: hands, shins, elbows, and knees.

To exercise with Muay Thai, you don't necessarily need to get in the ring and square off against an opponent—though that might be welcomed some days. You can look for a beginners' workout class with expert coaches in your area that teaches the boxing-martial art hybrid, and ask the trainer to adapt the practice to your needs and fitness.

Balance Your Root Chakra

Chakras are spinning energy centers that directly influence your well-being, and how consciously and happily you create your life's path. There are seven chakras in your body, starting with the first chakra, or the root chakra. This is located at the base of your spine and is in charge of grounding you. When your root chakra is out of balance, you can find yourself feeling aggressive and reckless. Given Scorpio's tendency to fall victim to those kinds of feelings, it's a good idea to try and balance this chakra.

One of the best ways to balance your chakras is by visiting an energy healer. For instance, a Reiki healer can identify whether or not your chakras are out of balance and then aim to transfer energy to heal the imbalance.

Add Probiotics to Your Diet

While Scorpio is better known for ruling over the reproductive system, she also rules over the elimination organs. As important as the mouth is to the digestive process, so too are these body parts. Scorpio's governance over this particular part of the tract means she should be mindful of what she does and doesn't eat. Consider adding probiotics into your diet; these microorganisms found in different foods may help balance the good and bad bacteria in your system and may help with digestion and elimination.

Foods and drinks to try that are rich in probiotics include yogurt, pickles, and kimchi. Probiotics are an easy way to be good to your digestive system. If you are suffering from any health conditions, check with your doctor first.

Watch That Sarcastic Sting

Scorpions have their stingers, and Scorpio has her wit. It keeps her entertained and people laughing—until they're not. Occasionally, Scorpio can go a little too far, so it's best to keep your sarcastic comments in check. You're a water sign, after all, and are very in tune with others' emotions, so hurting them and setting fire to a bridge will ultimately hurt you.

Like a scorpion's stinger though, your wit is your best defense. Keep it sharp! Just know when to use it.

Help Others Evolve

It's true: By helping others, you can help yourself. As a Scorpio, your role in the world is to help others evolve. You're a deeply intuitive spirit whose connections with others can help them grow and transcend their current state, especially if they are stuck. This guidance not only benefits the other person; it benefits you as well. Creating this type of spiritual connection with another person will help you develop your own sense of self. It also breaks down the wall you can sometimes build to the outside world. Help others find out the cause of their problems by asking questions and sharing your confidence.

Remember, though, not everyone is as determined as you are, Scorpio. Guiding others along this path will be a good lesson in patience.

Create a Scorpio Sanctuary

You are a passionate soul, Scorpio, who likes a little danger. Your living space should reflect that part of your personality. Home décor isn't just decoration; it's an expression of who you are and helps to make you feel at peace in your place. Blacks and deep burgundies are great colors for your bedroom and can be punctuated with bright whites and reds. These color choices speak to your mysterious yet sensual persona.

Even if this color palette isn't exactly right for your home, you can still sneak a little Scorpio into your décor. Pyramid paperweights are great for your desk—whether at home or at the office; the shape is harmonious with Scorpio power. You can also add a little danger to your living room with snakeskin patterned pillows, or maybe even a Venus flytrap plant. It's up to you how far you take it, but the most important thing is to make your space your own.

Draw Power from Your Planets

Scorpio is ruled by two different planets: Mars and Pluto. You can draw strength from both. Mars can be visible from earth during close approaches between the planets. At those times the planet burns bright in the night sky and is visible by the naked eye. Find out online the next time Mars will be on one of these close approaches, and then plan a night under the stars. Burn bright like your red planet, Scorpio.

And while Pluto may not be visible by the naked eye, you can still draw on its energy. Pluto's still a bit of a mystery—like you. Embrace that enigmatic power to keep people guessing.

Investigate Pendulum Power

Refine your innate transformative abilities by purchasing a pendulum in a stone or metal of your choosing.

Historically, the pendulum has been used as a way of gaining spiritual insight. It can provide you with healing and spiritual growth as it locates blocks in energy. By asking questions of the pendulum, you can receive guidance and awareness to clear your body and spirit.

It's important to understand what the swings of a pendulum can mean, so be sure to purchase your pendulum from a reputable business, and seek guidance on its proper use through an instructor or a book on pendulum dowsing.

Have Fun—but Be Safe

There's a sexual energy possessed by Scorpio that the other signs just can't match. It's not your fault that you were granted this gift, and you shouldn't feel any shame in enjoying it. However, it's important for you and your partner to always be safe. Take the necessary steps to ensure that your adventures in (and out of) the bedroom don't put either of you at risk—and then enjoy! Try out new positions, locations, and situations; spice things up any way you want. Embrace this prowess and let the physical manifestation of your passion deepen your connection.

Beware the Sting of Stubbornness

Scorpio's strong will suits you well in many endeavors. However, if you're not careful, that strong will can sometimes become a stubborn streak. Don't let stubbornness get the best of you. You have too much to share with the world to wall yourself off from it. It's important to be open to other people's opinions even if they contradict your own. Rather than write a person off in that situation, allow yourself the opportunity to discuss your viewpoint, and then hear them out on theirs. You're very sharp, Scorpio, and you know when you're right—but it's wrong to let a disagreement ruin a relationship.

CHAPTER 15

Self-Care for Sagittarius

Dates: November 22–December 21
Element: Fire
Polarity: Yang
Quality: Mutable
Symbol: Centaur
Ruler: Jupiter

Sagittarius is the third (and final) fire sign of the zodiac. His time period ushers us from autumn to the winter solstice on December 21. He is yang and mutable, and his preferred self-care rituals line up with the traits associated with these cosmic designations. Sagittarius is the open, adventuresome, optimistic, good-humored sign of the zodiac, and his breezy ease attracts people and luck.

Sagittarius's symbol is the Centaur: half horse (beast) and half man. The centaurs figured in Greek mythology as a band of beasts given to riotous living and fighting, representing the unruly forces of nature. However, the leader of the centaurs was Chiron, a wise and skilled teacher and healer. He tutored the hero Achilles as well as the healer Asclepius.

Like these two different versions of the centaur, Sagittarius metaphorically straddles two poles: one representing instinctive natural animal instincts and one the higher mind that quests for meaning and understanding. This sign's symbol outlines the soul journey of Sagittarius: from an instinctual and perhaps unruly character to a perceptive truth-seeking healer, teacher, and philosopher, like Chiron. Additionally, the arrows that the Centaur shoots were not part of the original Greek myth, but in astrology, the Centaur shoots an arrow symbolizing truth despite not knowing his destiny.

Self-Care and Sagittarius

Sagittarius is ruled (and protected) by Jupiter, the planet and, in Roman mythology, chief god. The optimism of Jupiter (the planet is known as the Greater Benefic in astrology) is boundless. Jupiter also represents bigness and excess, and Sagittarius loves having and doing more than enough—which means that taking some time out for self-care is necessary for the Centaur. Roaming the big wide world is Sagittarius's joy. He may not know why he wants to keep moving, but like a nomad he keeps going forward. Sagittarius is wonderful to be around because he rarely says, "We can't do that." His response is usually, "Let's go." The types of self-care that really speak to Sagittarius are typically ones that are full of physicality and movement.

And at some point, as with Chiron, those born under this fire sign will seek out wisdom and become interested in the workings of the higher mind. The wanderlust, the urge for new horizons, turns inward. Sagittarius is not interested in any one particular religion or practice and is not dogmatic about his beliefs. His great interest is how to live life in accord with the wisdom of the ages and the super-conscious mind, rather than the everyday conscious mind. Intuitions become very strong, and Sagittarians frequently become counselors, teachers, philanthropists, or humanitarian workers. Sagittarius wants to practice self-care because more restoration and well-being means more energy for life.

Sagittarius is generally rather unconcerned about his appearance, and vanity will not motivate him to practice the ritual of self-care. Looking good for him is the result of an interesting life and not a goal in and of itself. His style is casual. Any self-care item or practice has to be easy and portable. If Sag can put it in a suitcase, he will probably bring it along; if there is too much effort involved, whatever the helpful device is will be left on the hall table.

Sagittarius Rules the Hips and Thighs

Sagittarius rules over the hips and thighs, so self-care related to these parts of the body is especially important. For Sagittarius these muscles and bones are essential for free and easy motion. Even in a petite Sagittarian, the thighs may be very well developed. This is the first area to address in terms of self-care. Stretching is essential and usually something that Sagittarius forgets to do. If he can remember to stretch and then exercise, it will save trouble down the road.

Sagittarius is prone to sciatic stress because the sciatic nerve runs from the base of the spine through the buttocks and down the lower limbs. The best exercise for Sagittarius, at any age, is walking. He needs to imagine he is going on a journey, even if it is just around the block.

Sagittarius and Self-Care Success

Pitfalls for Sag self-care fall mainly around his habit of procrastination. He gets involved in the next adventure or trip, while putting off focusing long enough beforehand on his self-care requirements to see that taking good care of his body, and mind, will only enhance the pleasure of traveling. He is too likely to say, "Oh, I didn't know that flight was 15 hours" as he unkinks his back.

He accepts these things with good humor, but taking the time to actively tune in to his body's needs will save a lot of stress and wear and tear.

Sag is also in the habit of talking about something (including self-care) before doing it. There seems to be a direct ratio between how much Sagittarius speaks about something and how little he does about it. If he directs his focus to think, meditate, and imagine the desired goal, then there is a good chance he will follow through. If he dissipates his energy in describing, telling everyone what he is going to do, or verbally speculating if he should do it, probably not much will happen. The best advice for Sag is this: Do it; don't talk about it.

Sagittarius is usually not interested in delving into his emotional past and finding reasons for current behavior. But he does like to talk out his thoughts and, in this way, a therapist and good listener can be helpful. Many communication or getting-along-with-people problems for Sagittarius are because he has a peculiar habit of "foot-in-mouth" syndrome: Whatever comes to mind comes out of his mouth. His blunt way of speaking rubs most people the wrong way, even though he never intends to be mean or hurtful. He just calls it like he sees it and is incapable of lying. This is a characteristic of Sagittarius, but everyone usually forgives him because he is so genuinely surprised that he has given offense. Awareness of this tendency may push away some of the worst blunders. Jupiter, Sagittarius's ruling planet, is the culprit here. Jupiter rules all excess, whether it is speaking too much, or eating and drinking too much. Sagittarius expresses himself widely and fully, and the more energy he has to give to everything the better. When this energy is used for more hospitality and generosity, everyone is pleased. But if it leans toward the more destructive feelings, this energy makes chaos and the Centaur can get out of control.

A primary factor in self-care is for Sagittarius to avoid sitting at a desk all day long. This will give back problems, make the Centaur unruly and fidgety, and put him and everyone near him in a bad mood. A standing desk, or a cubicle where he can move around, is the solution. Sagittarius is one of the most common signs of professional athletes. Sagittarius's quick-fire power gives him a fast reaction time as well as stamina. Self-care is easy for a Sagittarian professional athlete because his performance is tied to his profession. And his strength is that he never hews to a rigid schedule or regime. His instincts tell him what needs stretching and strengthening. This is a good reminder for non-athlete Sagittarians too.

Perhaps the most important pathway for self-care success for Sagittarius, however, is laughter! If a Centaur can see and feel the humor in whatever self-care activity he is involved in, then the practice will be successful. Sharing jokes and laughter with buddies will encourage Sagittarius and everyone around him. His laughter is contagious and self-care is the best way to increase it. So let's take a look at some restorative self-care activities designed especially for Sagittarius.

Promote Strong Bones and Muscles with Figs

Delicious and full of potassium, figs are the perfect ingredient for healthy, energized Sagittarius. Sagittarius controls the hips and thighs, and a strong body is essential to the adventurous Centaur. If he doesn't move around enough during the day, the pressure on his hips can lead to muscle pain and cramps.

You can help to prevent these aches and discomfort with the potassium found in figs. Figs are a Sagittarius fruit, and the potassium strengthens muscles and preserves the calcium in your bones. Cut fresh figs into a salad with leafy greens and other restorative ingredients such as almonds and pure honey.

Begin (and End) Projects with a Bang

Sagittarius is motivated by the energy and excitement of his surroundings. While others might get by with a quick crossing out of a completed task, Sagittarius needs something with a bit more panache to celebrate the small victories—or get in the zone for a new project. Decorate your work area with a small gong and strike it before and after completing a task. The simple but energizing melody will be just the motivation you need to get things done.

Strike a Pilates Pose

Pilates is the perfect exercise for the athletic Sagittarius. It stretches and builds lean muscles, and it provides a ritual of discipline that keeps him grounded. As the sign that rules the thighs and hips, Sagittarius will delight in exercises that target these parts of the body. Ask your instructor about a great exercise for your thighs and hips: the leg bridge combined with leg dips. Form a bridge with your legs by lying on your back with your knees bent and feet flat on the floor (arms at your sides) and lifting your hips off the floor. Extend one leg up and out, straight up in the air, and then lower and repeat with the other leg.

Learn a New Language

Curious and energetic, Sagittarius loves to learn and travel. Learning a new language will challenge your mind, while arousing your wanderlust. Many smartphone apps offer language lessons for users of all skill levels. There are also countless books and classes out there if you prefer a more traditional approach to learning.

Before jetting off on your next adventure, take some time to learn at least the basics of the native language in that region. Not only will you enjoy learning something new, but an understanding of basic words and phrases will open you up to meeting and communicating with people of different cultural backgrounds during your travels.

Engage In a Little Philanthropy

Jupiter, Sagittarius's ruler, governs generosity and involvement in worthy causes. Sagittarius loves helping those in need, and also appreciates the different perspectives he gains through his philanthropy. Make a conscious choice to contribute to any organization or charity that you feel reflects your values and ideals. No matter how much you have to share, spread your generosity with the world! Your help will be greatly appreciated, and you may learn a few new things in the process.

Communicate with Your Fellow Equine

The Centaur, the symbol of Sagittarius, is half horse and half human. Realign with your celestial heritage—and also feel the wind through your mane—by taking a horseback ride (or if you are a beginner, consider a lesson). An adventurous gallop on the back of a horse will delight your playful side and celebrate your love of the natural world. Too hot or cold outside for a ride? Visit a horse ranch or farm rescue and devote an afternoon to grooming or mucking out the stalls for your hooved companions.

Calm Your Mind with Jasmine

Keep a jasmine plant in your home, preferably in your bedroom or any other room where you like to relax. It's the perfect plant for Sagittarius as it promotes calm and restful sleep, which will leave him well rested and ready for the exciting day ahead.

A simple flower, jasmine brings a touch of nature's beauty into the Sagittarian home. Caring for your plant is simple: Just water weekly, or as needed, and add a wire frame or wooden pole to the pot for support once the vines have started to grow out.

Relax in Velvet

Jupiter, Sagittarius's ruling planet, is linked to the love of things a bit indulgent and luxurious, including silky, plush fabrics. Restore your Jupiter roots with the most luxe of all textiles: velvet! Spend an afternoon wrapped in a velvet robe—enjoying the smooth, soft fabric on your skin—to feel like the planetary royalty you are. You can also go a bit further by purchasing velvet bedding, but beware: It won't be easy to get out of this heavenly bed in the morning.

Visit a Place of Worship

Sagittarius represents the quest for spiritual enlightenment and the celebration of different religious traditions. Refocus your quest by experiencing a devotional ceremony at your chosen place of worship. Meditate in a Buddhist temple, pray in a mosque, sing a hymn in a church pew, or chant in front of a Hindu shrine.

No matter which devotional practice you observe, your experience will activate your crown chakra (the connection between your own consciousness and the energy of the universe around you) and further you on your journey to spiritual understanding.

Check Out a Sacred Historic Site

Combine your Sagittarian wanderlust and quest for spiritual enlightenment with a pilgrimage to a sacred location. Researching thoroughly first, you could visit the Temple Mount in Jerusalem, Israel; one (or all four) of the Char Dham pilgrimage sites in India; the Great Mosque of Muhammad Ali Pasha in Cairo, Egypt; Saint Peter's Basilica in Rome, Italy; the Bodh Gaya in Bihar, India; or the city of Bethlehem in Palestine—or plan an extended trip to visit them all! These are just a few of the myriad of famous spiritual locations across the world that you can explore.

Plan an International Getaway

Always keep your passport up to date and ready to use. Sagittarius is the king of adventure, so a trip abroad is the perfect balm for a chaotic or dull workweek. If a release from the hustle and bustle of the office is what you seek, opt for a soothing beachside retreat with a tropical beverage and plenty of sunscreen. Looking for some excitement after an uneventful week? A revitalizing trip to the colorful avenues of Barcelona, or a zip-lining excursion through a rainforest, will be just what the doctor ordered.

Visit the Racetrack

It's a thrill to watch, connects you with your equine symbol, and employs your Sagittarian luck. For an added layer of excitement, attend one of the big races: the Kentucky Derby, Preakness Stakes, or Belmont Stakes. Taking place in the spring each year in Kentucky, Maryland, and New York respectively, these races have deep roots in American tradition. Racegoers often dress up in eye-catching pastels and oversized hats, and enjoy signature cocktails like the Mint Julep, Black-Eyed Susan, and Belmont Breeze.

Set a Long-Term Fitness Goal

Sagittarius has a sustained fire power that few can hold a flame to. When a busy work schedule pushes physical self-care to the wayside, that fire longs to get out and you may feel tension in your muscles from the lack of exercise. Having a long-term fitness goal will push you to dedicate that much-needed time each week to taking care of your body, so you can achieve whatever dream you set your sights on. Consider training for a marathon, a trek up Mount Kilimanjaro, or a CrossFit competition.

Shake Those Hips to Zumba

Sagittarius rules the hips and thighs. Give these parts of your body a proper workout to keep them strong and ready for adventure. Ideal workouts that allow you to really shake those hips (and thighs) in a fun way are those that incorporate quick-paced dancing, such as Zumba and Buti Yoga. These faster routines get your blood pumping and your muscles working in an exciting way that you'll forget is exercise. You can also bring friends along for even more fun! If working out in a group setting isn't your style, there are many online videos and entire video games out there for dance-focused fitness that you can do in your own home.

Read a Classic

A classic novel is a perfect way to stimulate the Sagittarian love for philosophical and reflective thought. Great places to start include the works of Jane Austen,

Mark Twain, and Charles Dickens. During or after your read, you can spark further thought with online guided questions (some books also include discussion group questions right in the back of the book). Consider having a friend or two read the same title as well so you can discuss your thoughts and insights with one another after reading.

Take a Staycation

Sagittarius has a natural sense of wanderlust, but sometimes the excitement is happening right outside your door! Don't miss out on what your town or region has to offer. A staycation is the perfect way to explore locally and without stress. Check out any websites for your area that list upcoming events—or host an event of your own for neighbors. You can also invite friends who don't live locally to visit and share the wonderful aspects of your area with them!

Find a Sagittarius Totem

A totem is a small object that represents anything from a person or group of people, to a personal value or ideology. Whether it's tied to the equine symbol (a Centaur or horse) of your astrological sign, or to the archery element (a bow or arrow), find a totem that encapsulates your zodiac sign. Your totem will be a unique symbol of your amazing Sagittarian qualities, from your humor and warmth to your intelligence and courage. Look to it when you need a little reminder of just how exceptional you are.

Take the Horse Stance

This yoga pose is perfect for Sagittarius—and not just because of the name! The Horse Stance improves posture and strengthens the thigh muscles, which are ruled by the athletic Centaur. From a standing position, move your feet apart slightly wider than shoulder-distance apart, toes pointing outward. As you inhale, reach your arms overhead wide, pressing your palms together. As you exhale, bend your knees 90 degrees and pull your hands to your chest, sliding your shoulder blades downward. Keep your knees pointed over your feet and your tailbone tucked under your body. Hold this pose for 30 seconds, or however long you can manage, and remember to breathe.

Take an Archery Lesson

With his name translated from Latin as "the arrow," Sagittarius's signature sport is written in the stars! Learn the basic techniques of archery one afternoon—or turn it into a regular hobby! Requiring precision and practice, this sport is the perfect way to release your Sagittarian energy—and a few arrows too. Archery also enhances physical strength and concentration (hitting your target is not as easy as the Centaur makes it seem), so on-the-go Sagittarius will be ready for anything.

Ask Yourself

Both philosophical and curious, Sagittarius understands the need for reflection between adventures. Take a moment to pause and let your mind wander. Start by asking yourself a question: What are my current life goals? Who do I look to for advice, and why? Where would I go right now if I could travel anywhere on (or beyond) earth? Be as specific or vague as you want, and invite in any thought that arises. You might be surprised as to what comes up!

Ride a Bike

Unable to take a horseback ride? Go for a spin on your bicycle. Look for a hill that is safe for riding so you can really fly. Whether racing a friend or yourself—down a mountain trail or a driveway—the feeling of speed and of fresh air swirling past your face is made for Sagittarius. Just be sure to put on a helmet before you start training for the next Tour de France!

Keep a Dream Journal

Sagittarius rules the higher mind, which gains insights into your deeper consciousness and purpose through dreams and other internal experiences. Use a dream journal to keep track of your dreams so you can better understand your needs, desires, and fears—and how they influence your daily life.

Note the main elements of your dream: Was there a recurring item or emotion? How does this dream relate to past dreams? Is this the first time that a certain animal has appeared in your dreams, or has it emerged before? Dozens of websites and books out there can then help you decipher what specific dream elements mean. For instance, take a look at how color in your dreams can be interpreted by reading Dr. Betty L. Thompson's fascinating book *By the Light of Your Dreams* (available on www.bythelightofyourdreams.com).

Enjoy a Night on the Town

Your Sagittarian humor and buoyant spirit attract many different kinds of people to you, but sometimes even the magnetic, warm Sagittarius can feel a little less than his awesome self. Invite a group of friends out for a night of lighthearted fun—and maybe a dare or two—to remember just how loved you are. Whether it involves a trip to the latest "it" club or the act of ordering one of every appetizer at a favorite restaurant, it will be a night that neither you nor your friends forget.

Take a Sagittarian Class

Sagittarius is the sign of curiosity and learning. Exercise your mental muscles with a continuing education class at a local college, or an online course that piques your interest. Topics that Sagittarius will enjoy exploring include philosophy, spirituality, elements of the natural world, and different cultures. Try a class on the teachings of Plato, the notion of reincarnation, the identification of different plant species in a certain region, or the rites of passage in the Apache culture.

Relax under an Oak Tree

Sacred to the Sagittarian ruler Jupiter, oak has represented the link between the spiritual and natural worlds since ancient Greece and Rome. Reacquaint yourself with the great outdoors—and your planetary ruler—by stretching out under an oak tree or climbing its branches (you do love adventure).

Those past civilizations also saw oak as a protective charm, and the mythological Greek warrior Jason of the Argonauts used a sacred oak branch in the building of his ship *Argo*, before sailing off to battle. Part archer himself, Sagittarius has a unique connection to nature that can easily be forgotten in the chaos of everyday life. A simple afternoon enjoying the shade and splendor of an oak will leave you feeling refreshed and realigned with your Sagittarian spirit.

Create a Vision Board

Sagittarius is a dreamer. Create a vision board to capture all of your big plans and desires onto something tangible that you can keep in a place such as your bedroom or office to look at on a daily basis. When you are constantly reminded of the things you aspire to, you will feel motivated to continue taking steps to reach those goals, even when they may feel far away. No matter how big or small, those steps add up, and before you know it, you will be manifesting the dreams on your vision board into reality.

Rest Before (and After) Your Adventures

As the vivacious explorer, Sagittarius is always on the move. Make sure you get a good night's sleep before and after your adventures. No Centaur can perform his best when he is constantly yawning and needing caffeine pick-me-ups! Consider investing in a humidifier or dehumidifier if too much or too little moisture in the air makes it difficult for you to fall or stay asleep. You can also diffuse lavender oil or spray it (diluted according to instructions) onto your pillow to help you relax and get into the bedtime mind-set. If you are still tired from all your adventures, consider taking a quick power nap!

Burn Myrrh

An ancient spice connected to Sagittarius, myrrh has been a part of spiritual practices and worship since ancient Egypt. The sign of spiritual enlightenment, Sagittarius will feel opened to the intangible elements of the universe when burning this herb. Jupiter, Sagittarius's ruler, also governs the liver, which myrrh has been used to detoxify since the beginning of traditional Chinese medicine. You can burn myrrh gum powder and myrrh resin incense with an incense bowl or censer and a charcoal tablet. Myrrh can also be found as an essential oil to diffuse or, diluted according to instructions (use with caution if you have sensitive skin), to massage into the skin.

Go Adventuring with a Sagittarian Friend

Share your sign with a friend? Take them on an adventure that will invigorate both of your fun-loving personalities. Whether it is a surprise afternoon hike near home or a birthday trip to another region, your friend will cherish the memories always—and you will too. As one of the curious signs of the zodiac, your fondest moments will be in discovering something new together— be it a nest of newly hatched birds along the mountain trail, or a delicious regional cuisine.

Refocus with Amethyst

The amethyst represents the third eye (connected to personal insight) and spirituality, but also temperance and concentration with a clear mind. With so many exciting things to do, Sagittarius can get caught up in a constant shift from one task or thought to the next. A little focus will allow him to keep track of things that need to be done, and to see those projects through to the end. Place an amethyst geode prominently in your work space or living room. Avoid bringing it into a sleeping space, though, as it will be hard to fall asleep when your gears are still turning.

Clear the Path to Abundance with a Turquoise Ring

A good luck charm for health and abundance, turquoise is ruled by auspicious Sagittarius. Look for a turquoise ring for an added boost of luck (yes, you may be quite fortunate already, but a little extra help never hurt).

Throughout history, turquoise has also been believed to have metaphysical healing powers. Desiring spiritual understanding and knowledge, Sagittarius may find divine secrets in turquoise. Believed to absorb the energies of the universe, this gem can help you by realigning your own energy centers and balancing them with the energies of the world around you.

Spice Things Up with Nutmeg

Intrepid Sagittarius doesn't have time for bland foods—he loves spices and exotic flavors that take his taste buds for a spin. Restore your vibrant energy by adding a delicious nutmeg kick to your warm morning oatmeal or savory dinner casserole—or look into new recipes where you can use this spice. Even just a sprinkle in your coffee will get your adventure gears turning. Tasty and revitalizing!

Nourish Your Spiritual Side

Sagittarius seeks spiritual understanding, and historically he has been associated with positions in the clergy. Many influential clergy members were Sagittarians, including Pope Francis, Saint Junipero Serra, and Pope John XXIII (also known as the "Good Pope"). Feed your spiritual curiosities by reading a book on theology or philosophy. You can explore a traditional text such as the Bible, the Tanakh, or the works of Plato; or modern philosophical fables such as *The Alchemist* or *Life of Pi*.

Keep Moving Forward

This mantra, "Keep moving forward," is the spirit of Sagittarius. No matter what has occurred in the past, or what may be in store for the future, Sagittarius takes everything in stride, just like his intrepid astrology symbol, the Centaur. But, sometimes, a difficult day or situation can catch even the most confident and optimistic Sagittarius by surprise. Adopt this mantra, and repeat it to yourself whenever you need a little boost of encouragement and a reminder that no matter what obstacles may come your way, you have the strength and ingenuity to keep going forward.

Top Your Toast with Lingonberry Jam

Bright, sweet lingonberries are ruled by Jupiter, and both the Native American history and medicinal properties of the berry will delight Sagittarius. Some traditional Native American cultures use the berries or juice to ease colds and sore throats, and in folk medicine they are believed to treat nerve issues. Just like Jupiter these berries are colorful orbs of vitality, promoting a healthy Sagittarius. Look for lingonberry jam in stores, and spread it over your morning toast, or use it to make thumbprint cookies with a twist when you need a sweet treat.

Use a Standing Desk

Sagittarius is an active sign that can experience back pain or other muscle tension when sitting still for too long. After all, your muscles were made for adventure! Use a standing desk (or ball chair, if standing isn't an option) for short periods to keep your spine straight and avoid these physical aches. The frequent movement will also keep you feeling refreshed and focused on the task at hand so you can get things done with ease. Many companies have inexpensive desk attachments to raise your computer or surface work space to whatever level is best for you.

Practice Leg Stretches

Sagittarius rules the thighs and also the legs. To avoid strain, be sure to stretch these muscles well before exercising—you'll need them strong for your next adventure! Great stretches that target the thigh and leg muscle groups include the hamstring stretch and the standing quadriceps stretch.

To do the hamstring stretch, stand straight and bend over, coming as close as you can to touching your toes without bending your knees. Hold for 5 seconds, then stand up straight, and repeat the stretch once or twice more.

To do the standing quadriceps stretch, stand straight and bend one leg back, grabbing your ankle with one hand. Bend your knee back as far as possible and hold for about 30 seconds. Repeat with your other leg.

Find Joy in "Ode to Joy"

Playful and optimistic, there is no sign better suited for such a celebration of joy than Sagittarius. In fact, Sagittarian Beethoven's "Ode to Joy" should be the Sagittarius theme song. However, even the vivacious Sagittarius experiences a few bumps in the road that can make remaining positive a bit more challenging. Keep this song on your phone and hit the play button whenever you need a little reminder of the things that make you—and the world around you—so amazing.

Enjoy a Mai Tai Punch

This tropical treat captures the Sagittarius sense of adventure. All you will need are 3 tablespoons (1½ fluid ounces) spiced rum, 3 tablespoons (1½ fluid ounces) coconut-flavored rum, 1 teaspoon grenadine syrup, ⅜ cup (3 fluid ounces) pineapple juice, ¼ cup (2 fluid ounces) orange juice, 1 cup (8 ounces) ice cubes, and 1 maraschino cherry. In a cocktail mixer filled with ice, combine the spiced rum, coconut rum, grenadine, pineapple juice, and orange juice. Shake and strain into a rocks glass filled with fresh ice. Top with the cherry and a festive drink umbrella or two.

Find the Funny Every Day

Ruled by jovial Jupiter, Sagittarius exults in laughter and the friendly practical joke. Sometimes life can get a bit overwhelming—even for optimistic Sagittarius—and finding the whimsy in a situation is more of a challenge. Feed your inner comedian by watching a funny video on your phone, playing a joke on a good friend, or listening to a comedy podcast on your way to work in the morning. Taking the time to delight in something humorous every day will keep your positivity stores brimming.

Pause with Purple Jade

Sometimes Sagittarius can get a bit over-enthusiastic, and the words tumble out before he has a chance to think them over. Carry a purple jade stone to encourage taking that much-needed pause before saying what is on your mind.

Purple jade taps into your connection with the world and people around you by opening your crown chakra, which controls how you perceive and react to your surroundings. Carrying this stone with you will encourage well-thought-out responses to every situation.

Travel Through Your Taste Buds

A favorite spice in Mexican and Indian cuisine (and also a signature Sagittarian flavor), anise will jump-start Sagittarius's energy, while taking him on a one-way trip to the bustling streets and luminescent shoreline of Mumbai.

For the full exotic experience whenever your wanderlust emerges, make an easy curry powder to season soups, rice, sauces, and more. Simply toast 1 tablespoon whole anise seeds, 2 tablespoons whole

coriander seeds, 1 tablespoon whole cumin seeds, 1 tablespoon whole mustard seeds, 1½ teaspoons whole fenugreek seeds, and 1½ teaspoons whole allspice berries in a pan until very fragrant. Grind the toasted seeds together, toss in 2 tablespoons turmeric powder, and store in a sealed container until ready to use.

Detox with Clove Essential Oil

It is claimed that clove essential oil protects the liver, which is also governed by Sagittarius. The liver flushes out the toxins that can lead to many health problems, so a healthy liver is crucial to a healthy you. Being a spice, clove is also the perfect essential oil for fiery Sagittarius. Clove also prevents the inflammation that may occur when you are out trying all of those exotic foods during your travels. Sparingly rub the (diluted according to instructions, and use with caution if you have sensitive skin) oil onto your skin or diffuse it to aid detoxification and other benefits.

Honor Commitments

Make a commitment to honoring commitments! Sagittarius gallops through life, with so many things to do and so much energy behind each step. Keeping track of every promise and every important date can be tricky in all of the excitement of your upcoming plans. Whether promises are romantic, work, social, or family oriented, staying true to your promises is essential in respecting both your time and the time of others. Keep a calendar, set phone reminders, and implore friends and family to work with you to ensure that you uphold your commitments.

Go for a Hike

Get out and get moving in nature. A hike through a nearby forest or mountain trail is the perfect combination of the Sagittarian love of adventure and love of the great outdoors. Savor the lush, organic colors, sounds of birds or other critters, and earthy smells you encounter on your hike. Once you've had the chance to get some sun and physical activity, and to delight in Mother Nature's beauty, you'll feel renewed and fully recharged for whatever may lie ahead.

Watch a Documentary

Sagittarius loves to learn—and a fun, informative documentary is the perfect way to learn something new while relaxing, or staying dry on a rainy day. Always searching for spiritual enlightenment and the secrets of the intangible world, Sagittarius will enjoy documentaries on different religions and experiences with the metaphysical. UFO sightings, documented encounters with spirits, and accounts of miraculous healing will all catch his eye.

You can also experience the great outdoors—even when the weather outside your window is less than ideal—with a nature documentary. Learn about the intelligence and social habits of different animal species.

Revisit an Unfinished Project

Sagittarius is full of exciting ideas and has ample energy to hit the ground running. However, sometimes in his enthusiasm for finding the "next big thing," he can get caught up in a new project before finishing the previous one. When you find yourself on the lookout for a new venture, ask yourself, "Is there a project I have started in the past but haven't yet completed?" Once you pinpoint an unfinished project, you can come up with a revitalized plan to see it through to completion.

Watch Out for Jupiter

Jupiter, the ruling planet over Sagittarius, represents knowledge, justice, prosperity, optimism, and personal growth. Be mindful of where your celestial ruler is currently positioned: when it will be visible from your location, which planets it will be aligned with when, and on what dates it will transit the sun. Your natal chart can provide more details on what each position means for you, and which positions will affect your life the most (these will be the ones to be especially mindful of).

Subscribe to a Podcast

Sagittarius loves to learn—and stay on the move. A podcast allows you to do both with a quick, often free, subscription. With the big wide world at your fingertips thanks to ever-advancing technology, you can find an overwhelming range of podcasts on a variety of topics, so you can choose just what excites you. The philosopher and theologian Sagittarius will love topics such as ethics, the teachings of Socrates, personal experiences with spirituality, and different spiritual beliefs. Download podcasts that catch your eye and listen to them during car rides, while out for a run, or in your downtime.

Practice Honesty with Yourself

Sagittarius prides himself on being honest. While honesty with others comes naturally, being honest with yourself can be a bit more challenging, whether it is to celebrate the things that make you great or acknowledge the things that you can work on. Practice being more honest with yourself. Take the time to pay yourself compliments, while also looking into the things you can improve. It may help to write things down so you can further explore these truths, and also return to them when you need a refresher.

Encourage Healthy Liver Function with Berries

Sagittarius rules over the liver, which flushes the body of toxins and stores iron and a number of important vitamins. Blueberries and cranberries are full of liver-promoting properties, including antioxidants like anthocyanin, which also gives them their striking colors. They are also delicious sources of vitamin C, and may inhibit tumor growth.

You can make a simple jam with the berries to top your morning toast, give the traditional PB&J (peanut butter and jelly) sandwich a twist, stir into plain yogurt, or pour over meat. Just simmer cranberries from one 12-ounce package and ½ cup (4 ounces) sugar in 1 cup (8 fluid ounces) water for 10 minutes, then mash slightly. Stir in 1 teaspoon cinnamon, ¼ teaspoon nutmeg, and ⅛ teaspoon ground allspice, then remove from heat and add 2 cups (16 ounces) blueberries. Enjoy!

Decorate with Your Spirituality in Mind

Sagittarius is deeply connected to spirituality. Living in a home that personally connects you to your spiritual side is essential for Sagittarius self-care—whether it's creating a designated meditation space, or adding spiritual items throughout your home. Decorate your bedroom with personal spiritual items that you may not want to share with visitors, but that will create a comforting and mindful atmosphere for private reflection.

Create a space in your home and decorate it with small objects that spiritually motivate and uplift you. These objects can include photographs, elements of nature, or an oil diffuser with your favorite scents. You could even extend the theme to your garden for meditation and reflection outdoors.

CHAPTER 16

Self-Care for Capricorn

Dates: December 22–January 19
Element: Earth
Polarity: Yin
Quality: Cardinal
Symbol: Goat
Ruler: Saturn

Capricorn is the last earth sign of the zodiac. She is a powerful cardinal sign, and her season begins at the winter solstice (the winter solstice represents the nadir of the sun with the shortest days). Ancient peoples celebrated the winter solstice because it marked the pivot of the sun's motion from darkness to light. Shortly after the winter solstice, the sun gains seconds, minutes, and then hours of light. Ancient sacred spaces such as the Karnak Temple, in Egypt; Stonehenge, in England; and Newgrange, in Ireland, were built to catch the solstice light as it beamed through specially designed architecture. The return of the sun was a religious and spiritual renewal that blessed all people. The winter solstice is still celebrated today in these sacred spaces.

The cardinal fire sign, Aries, begins the astrological year and the cardinal earth sign, Capricorn, ends the calendar year. Metaphorically, the leadership spark that Aries initiates can only be realized in the world through the practical and structural orientation of Capricorn. Slowly and steadily, Capricorn will build structures and get where she wants to go.

Saturn is Capricorn's ruling planet. In ancient times, Saturn was the farthest planet that could be seen with the naked eye. In Roman mythology, Saturn (Cronos in Greek mythology) was the lord of time. He also ruled challenges, delays, and old age. He was a powerful god, but not a cheery one. The Romans respected him for the power of his wisdom and patience. Indeed, in Roman mythology, when Saturn fled from Mount Olympus to Italy, his rule there initiated a golden age and time when people lived in perfect harmony.

The feast of Saturnalia was held every year during the winter. During this time, it was forbidden to declare war; slaves and masters ate at the same table; and people gave each other gifts. Saturnalia eventually developed into the Christian holiday of Christmas. Many contemporary holidays have their origins in the progression of the astronomical cycles (which forms the basis for the astrological signs). The winter solstice, the beginning of Capricorn, marks the return of the light, and Christians believe that the birth of Christ brought light to the world.

The planet Saturn is called a malefic planet in astrology because its influence delays or hinders activity. People don't usually enjoy the effects of Saturn, because under his influence we are forced to think concretely, to plan, and to consider all the real-world ramifications of our actions. But we all need the reality check Saturn offers. Capricorns have this quality naturally. Capricorn patiently, diligently, and steadily climbs toward her goal.

Capricorn considers life serious business and is very interested in achieving success. Sometimes the success she achieves is in intangible, spiritual realms; sometimes success is purely material. The best of Capricorn's qualities blends practical realities with a sense of mission and high-mindedness. The worst of Capricorn traits can be ruthlessness and obsession to achieve her ambitions at any cost. Capricorn's most significant trait is the fervor with which she approaches all her endeavors and causes. Capricorn's strong power instinct, drive, patience, and work ethic sustain her while she climbs toward her goals.

Self-Care and Capricorn

In terms of self-care and well-being, Capricorn is enigmatic. She realizes that she must be strong, fit, and healthy to achieve her goals, but launching self-care and being mindful of her own needs do not come naturally. She is devoted to action and self-improvement, but may need lessons in how to temper her drive with softness and kindness to herself.

The best approach for success is for Capricorn to realize that "things must get done." And in her case the things that must get done are taking care of her health and learning to relax and laugh. If Capricorn sees self-care as a mission she must accomplish, she will learn to implement and perhaps even enjoy self-care. It is merely a matter of applying her strong will to the necessary goal of self-care.

Once Capricorn realizes that self-care is useful to her, she is very pragmatic and successful. Capricorn rules structure and hierarchy, and if ill, she has a talent for finding good care. She usually knows qualified medical people, and through diligence she will connect with professionals who can truly help her. For everyday care Capricorn tends to know where to find the best products for well-being and maintenance. She loves to share this knowledge with her acquaintances, family, and friends.

Capricorn Rules the Bones

Capricorn rules the skeletal structure, all the bones, the joints, the knees, and the teeth. Maintaining calcium and good nutrition is an essential habit for her. Frequently Capricorn has dental problems and should follow through on all checkups. In the skeletal system Capricorn's weak area is the knees. Heavy-impact sports are not the best for Capricorn. If Capricorn is a jogger, she needs to be vigilant about sneakers. They should specifically be for jogging and should be changed frequently. When possible, she should jog on earth rather than concrete. If she uses a treadmill, she should alternate with the elliptical jogger, which is softer on the joints.

Capricorn is not casual about exercise and sports. She pursues her goals in the same determined fashion as with work, love, or money. Capricorn needs to be aware that it will be hard for her to back away from her goal even if it is causing pain and difficulty. Too much bodily stress will not be beneficial in the long run. If Capricorn tunes into her body, she will have the answer to whether to press on or stop. Developing this sense of "enough" is a crucial skill in self-care.

Capricorn and Self-Care Success

Capricorn can get so involved in her own work that self-care falls by the wayside. She pushes herself and then becomes exhausted. And, of course, all the good striving she has done must stop while she regains her balance and well-being. She should try asking herself, why not prevent burnout before it occurs? Capricorn's disciplined approach and persistence can easily be adapted to taking care of herself. And then she will truly be of use to herself and to others.

A way to keep in healthy balance is to make room for laughter. It sounds silly to say make room for such a natural human reaction, but the problems and injustices of the world can gnaw at Capricorn's sense of responsibility, and she feels she must go out and rescue the situation. Laughing at the entire array of human weaknesses and strengths is the antidote to an overserious approach to life. There is a guru known as the laughing guru; he and his followers get together and have laughing sessions. This would be a great activity for Cap and would put her on the road to success in self-care and whatever else she wants to do.

Psychological counseling is of interest to Capricorn only in so far as it makes her more effective in her work life. She may consider therapy, unless in crisis, an indulgence. She is always interested in ways to improve her usefulness in the world and more efficient methods of getting to her goals, but a leisurely examination of childhood traumas or her home life only becomes important if her life is not functioning the way she would like it to. Capricorn is a leader and not particularly interested in the complexities of how someone else is feeling. She says, "Let's just get the job done." Capricorn avidly reads books about the habits

of successful people, and this can form the basis of her inner therapy and sense of well-being.

The soul work for Capricorn usually involves lessons in the exercise of power with humility. Pride and domination are qualities that can hinder Capricorn's true power and leadership abilities. When she uses her strength to be of use to others, rather than using people and situations for her own expedience, Capricorn can be very evolved.

Capricorn is also very loyal to friends and family. Her loyalty extends to her principles and devotion to causes. Once she commits to a set of beliefs, she does not waver. If she has the means, she is extremely charitable—but only after thoroughly researching the charity's business structure and how the donated money is spent. Capricorn doesn't treat money or commitments lightly.

Capricorn shares a sense of duty and engagement that benefits us all. She feels responsible to do her best to improve the world. If we follow her lead, we can all reach the summit of whatever mountain we attempt to climb. Now, let's take a look at some self-care practices designed specifically for Capricorn.

Plan a Family Reunion

Capricorn feels strongly about the past and family traditions; reliable and stable, she often takes on the responsibility of being the glue that holds family (or friends or loved ones) together. So why not embrace that family-centered side of yourself and plan a reunion dinner for your loved ones?

Get everyone together to share in stories, memories, and fun times. As a Capricorn, you will feel rewarded and comforted by the feeling of connection, and it will also be a whole lot of fun! Remember, it doesn't have to be a fancy gathering (although you do love a sophisticated get-together). Any size and style of dinner will do. It's all about taking time and reconnecting with your family and loved ones, and letting them know how important they are to you.

Get Your Calcium

Capricorn rules over the bones and skeletal system; therefore, regular consumption of calcium is an important factor for you. Calcium is important because it strengthens bones, regulates blood pressure, aids in the secretion of hormones, and helps boost your metabolism. Without enough calcium, your body can be prone to osteoporosis, teeth problems, and pains in the knees, toes, and joints.

The easiest way to get more calcium is through dairy products like cheese, yogurt, and milk, but you can also find it in foods such as spinach and other leafy greens, nuts, grapes, oats, sardines, and calcium-fortified soy milk or tofu to name just a few.

Or you can also try one of the many available calcium supplements; just check with your doctor before choosing one.

Buy Some Black Tulips

The black tulip is a unique flower and one that appeals to Capricorn's love of the finer things in life. Once thought to be only a myth, the black tulip came into existence in the 1980s through the labor of a Dutch grower named Geert Hageman. Because black is one of Capricorn's signature colors, it fits perfectly to have a black flower. Like many things worth having, the black tulip may be harder to find, but it makes a special and unique gift. Treat yourself to a bouquet of black tulips and appreciate the beauty in something both individual and simple.

Buy Good Sneakers

As a Capricorn, you need to take extra special care of your joints, especially the knees as yours are prone to stress. One way to take care of your knees is to make sure you buy good supportive sneakers for working out, particularly if you are a runner. Capricorn tends to only go for well-made, high-quality clothing pieces, so make sure you extend this habit to your workout footwear as well. Do your research (something Capricorn loves to do) and find the best brands and styles for your workout regimen. Don't forget to change your exercise shoes regularly, too, to always have the best support possible.

Seek Out Terra-Cotta for Your Outdoor Spaces

Terra-cotta is the perfect material for Capricorn to use in her garden, terrace, or other outdoor spaces. Terra-cotta is a kind of earthenware used since ancient times, and its name translates to "baked earth." Not only is it made from the earth (and Capricorn is an earth sign), but its dark red, burgundy, orange, and brown hues are all colors that Capricorn is drawn to. Add some terra-cotta pots to your terrace, put some terra-cotta statues in your garden, or hang a simple terra-cotta sculpture on an outdoor wall space. Feel the warmth of the color and the earth elements resonate with your Capricorn roots.

Meditate On the Color Nut-Brown

As a Capricorn, you are driven and resilient, and always searching, but sometimes for your own mental happiness it is necessary to relax and just *be* for a few minutes. At least once a week (or more if your schedule allows), try to spend 10–15 minutes musing on one of your signature colors, nut-brown. At first you may think brown is a boring color, but nothing could be further from the truth. Brown symbolizes warmth and the earth, and nuts symbolize the bounty of the earth. Brown is found in nature at all times of the year and represents stability and practicality. Brown is dependable and simple. Picture yourself in a forest in autumn surrounded by shades of warm brown and allow yourself to unwind and relax.

Decorate with Pewter

Capricorn's home should be decorated in the style of the things she values, including permanence, reliability, structure, and tradition. She also has a love of fine things, and this will be obvious in the ornamentations she uses in her home. Because she rules over pewter, décor items for the Capricorn home should include some kind of pewter element as well. Pewter appeals to both Capricorn's love of history and her love of simple quality pieces in her home. Try a set of pewter candlesticks on a dark wood table or a few pewter accessories like picture frames or mirrors. If you know a fellow Cap, something pewter would also make an excellent gift for her home too.

Find Some Black Amethyst Glass

Capricorn loves history and especially antiques. Objects that harken back to a simpler time give her a feeling of stability and comfort. Embrace that part of your sign by buying some black amethyst glass. Amethyst glass is a type of depression glass, glass given away by companies with purchases during the Great Depression as an incentive for consumers to do business with them. The glass would range in colors from the common pink, green, and amber to the rarer cobalt blue, purple, and black. Not only is this depression glass—now considered a valuable antique—simple, sophisticated, and useful (all things you love), but its black to purple hue is one that Capricorn is also especially drawn to.

Find some black amethyst glass for your home; its form and function will match your Capricorn taste perfectly.

Use a Blackboard

Sometimes a little nostalgia is good for the soul. Capricorn loves tradition and history, so why not play on that theme a bit in your home (or even office) décor. Buy a small blackboard and some chalk, and put them in a central locale in your space. Use the board to write reminders, notes, doodles, and even jokes on. Revel in the feeling of nostalgia: the feel of the chalk in your hand, the sound of the chalk moving along the blackboard, the light smell of the dust. It will bring back memories. Embrace the old in a new and fashionable way with a blackboard in your living space.

Make a Family Tree

Capricorn has a strong sense of family tradition and history. Why not expand on that trait and make a family tree! Discovering where you came from can give you great insight into who you are today.

There are so many websites that can help you trace your ancestry, or you can ask relatives and loved ones to help you fill in the blanks. You can also find public records online that can give you clues about family members who have passed on or who lived long ago. Once you've collected all your data, you can compile it to create a beautiful piece of family history to display in your home.

Calm Your Mind Before Bed

Capricorn is a work-centric person; you love to give things your all and are never one to back away from a challenge. But, as a result of all this strength of will and drive, you often find yourself burned out by the end of the day. After a long day of climbing those mountains, your body and mind need a break before falling asleep. It's important for Capricorn to take some time to quiet her mind before going off to bed.

Turn on a soft light or flameless candle, lie down or sit in a comfortable position, and close your eyes, exhale through your mouth and inhale through your nose three times, and think about nothing. That's right, nothing. Focus instead on relaxing every part of your body: from your head down to your toes. Visualize each part of your body letting go of its tension and releasing stress. Now turn off the light, and go enjoy a peaceful night's rest.

Indulge Your Inner Goat

The symbol for Capricorn is the Goat, so keep connected to your sign and indulge in some goat's milk and cheese. Goat's milk is high in calcium and helps build strong bones—and Capricorn is also strongly associated with bones and the skeleton. Goat's milk is also easier to digest than cow's milk, and since many a Capricorn suffers from some stomach issues, this is a plus. Goat's milk is a promising treatment for people with malabsorption issues like osteoporosis, a condition that Capricorn is often susceptible to. So try a little goat's milk for both your sign and your health.

Buy Some New Shoes

Nothing would honor your sign like indulging in a new pair of boots or shoes, because Capricorn rules over the knees—and also the shins. Not only does Capricorn rule over these areas, but she must also take special care with them as Cap tends to suffer from knee and joint pain. So when you buy those new boots, make sure they are a high-quality product and made well. Cheap shoes will only lead you to foot and knee problems down the road, so splurge for a good pair. And being a sensible Cap, you won't go crazy buying a whole closetful of shoes; you'll go for a pair you can match with a variety of outfits and styles.

Go for the Sour

Capricorn, though she loves food and cooking, often does not do well with certain types of foods, especially the spicy ones. She does, however, have a taste for sour and fermented foods: vinegars, pickles, soy sauce, wine, even "sour" milk products like sour cream and certain cheeses, and more lemony tasting foods. Any food that gives you that little bit of pucker is a good fit for Capricorn. So indulge in a plate of sour pickles or put out a bowl of sour balls; your Capricorn taste buds will thank you.

Try Some Teak Furniture

With her hardworking nature, Capricorn has an appreciation for fine craftsmanship and respects when something is well made. With that in mind, when decorating your home and outdoor spaces, you could invest in some teak wood furniture. Teak is valued both for its durability and its water resistance. The natural oil in teak gives it a greater natural water- and weather-resistance than many other types of wood, meaning your outdoor furniture will last longer, be protected from rot and many pests, and continue to look good for years to come. Longevity like that is important to Capricorn, so if you're looking for furniture that suits your tastes and also matches your sign qualities, go for teak.

Commune with Birches

Birch trees are often associated with Capricorn, especially in Celtic druid astrology. The druids thought that "birch babies" were always stretching themselves in search of light. A birch baby is also highly driven, ambitious, and resilient, and is a natural leader—all Capricorn traits! So embrace your birch heritage and plant one in your yard. Don't have a yard, or have a yard that can't accommodate a tree? Then go to a place where you can find birch trees (your local state park perhaps, or a nearby arboretum), and take some time to sit beneath them and feel the presence of these glorious trees.

Embrace Your Inner Elvis

Elvis Presley, "The King," was a Capricorn. Known as a consummate perfectionist who always set the bar high for himself (hello Capricorn!), Elvis dug all types of music from rock 'n' roll to country music. So embrace your fellow Capricorn and put on some Elvis tunes as you do your chores around the home, or any time you need a boost. Capricorn loves traditional rock 'n' roll, and there could be no better example than Elvis.

Stop the Hurried Pace

Capricorn feeds on challenge: When others quit, she pushes on. *Resilience*, *determination*, and *drive* are all words that describe the mighty Capricorn. Unfortunately, all that pushing and striving can take a toll on your mental health. It is especially important that Capricorn self-care involves some kind of mindful moments during the day. Being mindful simply means being aware of the present.

Stop for a moment and savor that steaming warm cup of coffee, take a moment to watch your kids playing, or pause and really listen to that song on the radio. Stop for at least 10 minutes out of your fast-paced day and enjoy your life right in the moment. A little mindfulness can lead you to a more peaceful life.

Buy an Hourglass

Capricorn's ruling planet is Saturn and in mythology Saturn was the god of time. Saturn the planet was named so because not only was it the farthest planet able to be seen with the naked eye (in ancient times), but it has the longest observable orbit in the sky (around thirty years) and so was thought of as the keeper of time, or Father Time. Embrace your ruling planet's timely mythology and purchase an hourglass. The earliest of time-keeping devices, its connection to time-related symbolism is unmistakable. Hourglasses are also a symbol of balance and symmetry, things near and dear to the Capricorn heart, and to sit quietly and watch the rhythmic cascading of the sands through the hourglass is itself a form of relaxing meditation.

Buy an hourglass and add it to your home's décor as a reminder of your ruling planet. Or if an hourglass isn't your speed, you might prefer collecting antique clocks and watches as a good Capricorn hobby.

Find Strength with Black Hematite

Hematite is a shiny dark stone with a strong metallic luster and is one of the best stones you can use to harness the energy of the earth for strength and to dispel negativity. It is a grounding stone that will help you feel more focused and less stressed. Capricorn tends to work herself to the point of exhaustion, and hematite can help bring you back in balance and ease the symptoms of stress and anxiety.

Hematite is an attractive stone and relatively inexpensive, so it can be often found in jewelry. Wearing a necklace or bracelet with hematite will keep the stone near your pulse points, maximizing the stone's protective energy. Or if jewelry is not your thing, you can carry some hematite in your pocket. This strong protective stone will keep you emotionally and spiritually safe as you go about your day.

Play an Instrument

While Capricorn's practicality often makes others think that she is not creative or artsy, the truth is that Capricorn is typically an excellent musician. Capricorn is not deterred from the challenge of learning an instrument, nor is she afraid to put in the hard work necessary. In fact, Capricorn is quite efficient at playing instruments and can master them quickly. One of the best instruments for Capricorn is the bass guitar. It allows her to be the steady rhythm of a musical piece. Try your hand at learning an instrument. You might be surprised how playing it can give you both the structure you love and the fun you need.

Climb a Mountain

No, not a metaphoric mountain, a real mountain. Just as it is for your symbol the Goat, mountain climbing is an ideal physical activity for Capricorn. Many people think mountain climbers are risk-takers, but in actuality mountain climbing takes a large amount of planning, training, and forethought, things that Capricorn is great at. Mountain climbing also relies on the Capricorn traits of determination and drive, and the ability to be present in the moment.

In addition to the mental benefits of this activity, there are also major physical benefits including stronger muscles and improved cardio strength. Try and find an instructor or course in your area, or try a course at one of the many indoor rock-climbing facilities. Remember, if you can climb a mountain, you can do almost anything!

Find Your Way

Capricorn is known for her determination. Once she has carefully considered her options and decided which is the best path for her, Capricorn will not be daunted by any obstacle. Though her progress may be slow and steady, she will find her way.

A good way to reinforce this determination is to use a mantra. A mantra is a phrase that helps keep you focused on what your goals are and what matters to you. Mantras boost your self-love because they help you focus on all that you are capable of doing. As you are pursuing your goals, remember to repeat this Capricorn mantra: "I find a way." Because once you set your mind to it, there is no mountain you can't climb.

Sip a Martini

The famous superspy 007 is known for loving his martinis, and it turns out this is also the perfect cocktail for you, Capricorn. Based on the balance of its ingredients, martinis are well suited to your meticulous nature. Capricorn loves to be in control, and this classic and respectable drink often represents power and class. To make your classic dry martini, fill a cocktail shaker with 5 tablespoons (2½ fluid ounces) dry gin, 1 tablespoon (½ fluid ounce) dry vermouth, and ice. Shake (or stir) for about 20 seconds and then strain into a martini glass. Try your classic dry martini with a lemon

peel garnish, as this scent appeals to Capricorn's spirited earth nature.

Find Healing with Turquoise

Capricorn's birthstone turquoise is known for its healing properties. Turquoise also acts as a purification stone that can dispel negative energy, and it can be worn to protect you from outside influences. As a Capricorn, you like (and sometimes need) to be in control of situations and when you aren't, you can become fierce. Meditation with turquoise can help you keep calm when things aren't going your way.

Either hold some turquoise in your hand, or—even better—wear a turquoise necklace, as turquoise is associated with the throat chakra. Unlike standard meditation where you sit in silence, when you meditate with turquoise, you should chant a mantra such as "I am healed" out loud. You should also visualize a stream of energy from your heart to your throat to your crown and back again in a loop. Try this meditation for 10–15 minutes.

Surround Yourself with the Scent of Pine

Capricorn's season is winter, so it's no coincidence that the scent of pine is a great choice for you to have in your home or work space. The aroma of pine is thought to encourage self-confidence, positivity, patience, and strength, all qualities

Capricorn embodies. Pine also stimulates the circulation and helps with fatigue, so you can keep on task and going strong as goal-orientated Capricorn loves to be. Try using pine essential oils in a diffuser, burning pine-scented candles, or even bringing fresh greenery into your home as decorations.

Read Some Realism

Not only does reading improve your imagination, your memory, and your vocabulary, but also it is a known stress reliever. As a Capricorn, you often take on too much and can work yourself to the point of exhaustion. When you need to take your mind off the stress of your work or personal life, try reading as an excellent way to relax and release tension. But what does Capricorn like to read?

Like in all areas of your life, as a Capricorn you tend to gravitate to the reality based. You are also a dedicated and persistent reader (huge volumes of works never intimidate you!). When you are not reading books related to your trade or profession (or books on successful people), you tend to lean toward books with characters who get to the bottom of things in practical ways. Books about struggles against poverty and other real-life obstacles are also preferred. Authors like J.D. Salinger, Zora Neale Hurston, Stephen Hawking, and Charles Dickens may top your list.

Add Some Rosemary and Thyme

Capricorn loves to cook. The precise nature of a recipe and the balance of ingredients and flavors go naturally with her disciplined nature. You are also a traditional person and so you love homemade food, especially family recipes and comfort foods.

Next time you are cooking up a batch of winter stew (a classic Capricorn comfort food), try adding in some spices suited especially to your sign: rosemary and thyme. The earthy smells of these spices appeal to your earth sign nature. As an added bonus, rosemary is known to boost alertness and focus, and thyme—in addition to having one of the highest antioxidant concentrations of any herb—helps reduce stress.

Get Thee to a Nunnery (Literally)

Capricorn loves history. She also feels a special connection with places connected with stone, land works, and buildings from the past. Aligning with this affinity for the historic and the traditional, Capricorn rules over old churches and cloisters. So go visit one! Choose a historical church or cloister made from earth and stone, nothing too modern or showy (remember Capricorn loves classic and simple). If your budget doesn't allow you to venture off to sites around Europe, then research the history and tradition of churches in your area.

Get a Simple Tattoo

Capricorn is fiercely independent. So why not show your independence permanently by getting a tattoo (once you find a trained artist with a good reputation). Of course, being a Capricorn, the design you pick will be simple and elegant—no full back tattoos happening here. A small understated design in a simple color will showcase your individuality, your strength, and your uniqueness in a way that nothing else could.

You could ink the Capricorn zodiacal symbol or even the Capricorn constellation if you want to keep with your sign, or pick a personal design that carries a meaning for you. As suits your Capricorn taste, you'll most likely want the tattoo in a discreet place where only those you choose to let see will do so—not that you would care about the opinions of others anyway. After all, you are not getting this tattoo for them. You are getting it for you!

Buy the Best (but Only Buy a Few)

When it comes to her wardrobe, Capricorn's closet may seem sparse by other signs' standards, but she is not concerned by it. Capricorn's wardrobe is comprised of practical, multifunctional pieces. She may not have as many pieces as other people do, but what she does have is well made, stylish, and elegant. Go with simple pieces that you can use in several different situations, and don't be afraid to stick to the basics; it is what makes you so down-to-earth and relatable. You'll be better off with a smaller amount of expensive but exquisite outfits than a multitude of cheaply made pieces.

Is your budget a little too tight to go for the high-priced stuff? Capricorn is not afraid to go hunting for designer finds at consignment or resale stores either. After all, it doesn't matter how you got it as long as you and it look good!

Heal Anxiety with Amber

Amber, though not usually associated with Capricorn, is a stone that can be beneficial for Capricorn's personality. Amber is said to promote relief of anxiety and stress, aid with mental exhaustion, and help eliminate worry. Purchase a piece of amber jewelry and wear it like a healing talisman to boost your positive energy and protect you from the bad energy. Amber is best worn directly against the skin so your body can absorb its healing properties, and it often feels warm as opposed to other stones or glass.

Find Your Inner Ballet Dancer

Capricorn's self-control and discipline are unmatched by any other sign, so it makes perfect sense that she is well suited to the rigors of ballet dancing. Ballet dancing takes both great ambition and a work ethic to succeed, two things for which Capricorn is known. Capricorn's methodical goal setting and unrelenting attitude when faced with a challenge make her able to put in the hard work necessary to succeed in ballet dancing. Sign up for a class yourself and experience the challenge and the beauty of ballet.

Get Your Hands Dirty with Clay Modeling

Being an earth sign, Capricorn naturally loves things associated with the earth and physical realm, and she's not afraid to get a little dirty. Try creating your own earth product where the emphasis is more on form than function. Find and join a local class on clay modeling, one where you get your hands in some clay; there are many types of class and many forms of clay to choose from. Art studios often offer these classes—and, once properly trained, you can make your own unique ornamental sculptural creation for your home. The use of the clay and the free-form nature of the technique stimulates Capricorn's artistic side and brings her closer to the earth.

Get a Deep-Tissue Massage

Capricorn's ligaments and joints take daily wear and tear, and problems with them can become an issue for her. To combat this, try a deep-tissue massage to help your body relax. Deep-tissue massage impacts deep layers of muscle and connecting tissues known as fascia, and it has been used to treat pain and musculoskeletal ailments, and strain in joints and tendons, for thousands of years. Deep-tissue massage can lead to improvements in pain, stiffness, range of motion, and the overall function of your joints. Contact a local massage therapist and schedule a deep-tissue massage for your joint health!

Learn to Delegate

If there is one thing Capricorn dislikes doing, it's handing off a part of her workload. To Capricorn there is only one right way to do something, and *her* way is the right way. But rather than work long hours poring over a complicated and difficult project, it is critical to your self-care to learn to delegate. Capricorn is prone to letting her work life overshadow her home and personal lives—all of which is not good for mental well-being! Next time you are assigned a project, take it and break it down into smaller parts. Then find some of those smaller parts to delegate out to your coworkers. Perhaps one of them is very apt in an area that isn't your forte. This self-care task may be difficult for you, but it is essential to reducing your stress levels at work.

Boost Your Business Look

Capricorn is a big career person. She is a hard worker who loves to lead and succeed. She can often be (although not always) found in the business world, but no matter where she works, she is usually the driven, determined, and dedicated leader. When it comes to fashion and style, she gravitates toward simple, sophisticated, and often business-like attire, so why not further embrace that idea and buy yourself the ultimate in business chic: a briefcase.

Not only does a briefcase suit your uber-organized mind-set, but its style and function fit perfectly with your no-nonsense personality. Try a briefcase in your signature colors like brown, black, or burgundy.

Try an Exotic Flavor

Capricorn is a traditionalist and that normally goes for her food preferences as well. You tend to like traditional foods, and will balk if someone tries to change them on you—may the stars help anyone who tries to serve you anything but turkey on Thanksgiving! But, just this once, break out of your food comfort zone and try something different or exotic.

Korean kimchi would be a good bet for Capricorn, as it is filled with vegetables and on the salty side—a flavor that Capricorn usually gravitates toward. Kimchi can be found at almost any supermarket, or find a good recipe and follow the directions carefully to make your own at home (a challenge any Capricorn would be up for!).

Visit an Ancient Tree

Capricorn tends to love history, whether that be in the form of learning about historical time periods, collecting antiques, or researching family ties. She has a love of all that is old and historic. Explore that love of history in a new way by visiting ancient trees throughout your area. Trees and the earth are tightly tied to Capricorn, and the history associated with a long-standing tree will add to her enjoyment. Or take an ancient tree vacation. For example, the Woodland Trust (www.woodlandtrust.org.uk) keeps an ancient tree inventory of the oldest and most important trees in the UK. Plan a trip around visiting some of them and revel in the history!

Add Some Zing with Vinegar

Capricorn loves to cook and her dedication and patience make her an excellent chef. But, being a traditionalist, she often doesn't stray from her standard recipes or flavors. Next time you are in your kitchen whipping up a meal for your family or friends, try adding some vinegars to your dishes to bring them up to the next level. Adding an acidic component like vinegar to savory foods can up the flavor and do wonders for your dish. Drizzle some balsamic vinegar on your pizzas or flatbreads, add strawberry vinaigrette to fruit salad, or make some blueberry balsamic barbecue sauce—the options go on and on.

Cuddle with a Panda

Cuddle with a panda stuffed animal, that is! Despite appearances, a panda actually has a lot in common with Capricorn. In addition to the simple and basic color scheme of a panda (something any classic Capricorn can appreciate), as a spirit symbol, pandas are also associated (like Capricorn) with tenacity in the pursuit of a goal. The panda also represents privacy and personal boundaries, things that Capricorn also values. Bring the spirit of the panda into your home by keeping a panda stuffed animal in your bedroom. The comfort and peacefulness it brings will resonate throughout your room and make it a perfect place to relax and retire.

Decorate with Granite

Capricorn is the ruling sign of minerals and rocks; you are an earth sign, after all. So, when decorating your home, especially your kitchen and bathroom spaces, you should choose materials made from stone for your countertops. Both granite or marble would make excellent choices and stay in line with your Capricorn desire for well-made but versatile items. You could also try soapstone countertops as well.

Recharge Yourself with Smoky Quartz

Smoky quartz crystals are a natural grounding stone. Associated with Capricorn, they are variations of quartz crystal that come in hints of gray, brown, or black—all earth colors for this earth sign. They are thought to stimulate the digestive system and ease pain and stiffness in the body. They can also help with anxiety, headaches, and feelings of pessimism. In many healing traditions, smoky quartz helps remove distractions and improve concentration. With Capricorn's concern for intellect, self-discipline, and balance, this is a perfect stone for you to use in your home. It will provide your living space with the positive vibrations you need to recharge your energy and find balance.

Ease Your Body with Tea Tree Oil

In addition to many other areas of the body, Capricorn is also the ruling sign over the skin, so skin problems are often issues for you. Luckily, tea tree oil (diluted according to instructions) may help certain skin conditions; ask your doctor for guidance.

Tea tree oil is a common and readily available essential oil, and Capricorn is often drawn to its spicy earthy scent. It is also claimed diluted tea tree oil is good for arthritis pain in joints, another area of concern for Cap, as it is able to penetrate and desensitize irritated nerve endings.

Keep a Tuxedo

This may seem like strange advice, but for Capricorn it fits perfectly. Capricorn takes everything in her life seriously and that includes fashion. Capricorn sticks to classics in and out of the workplace, and traditional business attire is the cornerstone of her wardrobe. Capricorn, regardless of gender, also tends to lean toward traditional menswear elements, like formal pants, suit jackets, and military-inspired styles (for women, think of the wardrobes of Diane Keaton or Marlene Dietrich). With that said, one of the best ways to exemplify your classic style and taste is to wear a tuxedo (tailored perfectly, of course) to your next posh event. The structured lines and impeccable look of a well-made tuxedo will make any Capricorn feel like a star.

Try an Empowering Mantra

With Saturn as her ruling planet, Capricorn is often self-disciplined and hardworking. She is highly organized, highly efficient, and highly dedicated to becoming a success. With those traits in mind, here is a mantra you can repeat to yourself or out loud to reinforce your inner power. Simply sit in a quiet place and clear your mind. Take a few deep breaths and start saying the mantra "I build the structure of my life" out loud several times. Then take a few minutes to think about what that mantra means in your life. If you find your mind wandering, simply refocus it. Try this meditation for 15 minutes each day and feel your self-confidence grow.

Wear More Leather

Capricorn likes her clothes to be of high quality and versatile in many different situations—multitasking outfits that are just as multitalented as she is! She likes clothing that is practical and has a purpose, but she cannot bear shoddy workmanship. As a result, Capricorn does well in fabrics like leather that can be equally at home in a chic restaurant or a trendy cocktail bar.

Leather (real or faux) is also ideal for Cap because it is most often seen in earth tones, especially brown and black, which are perfect for the simple yet sophisticated Capricorn style. Whether it be gloves, belts, jackets, or coats, you should try incorporating more leather into your wardrobe both for ease and appropriateness, but also for elegance and glamour.

Incorporate Your Life Into Your Décor

Capricorn loves her job or main hobby and is often very passionate about it. So use that passion in your décor as well! Try and find pictures or paintings of people doing what you do, or things related to it. Or, if that's not possible, try framing your achievements and your family's achievements, things like degrees, photographs of winning awards, or noteworthy actions.

Of course, you'll want to make sure all your frames match and fit into your classic and refined taste. Coming home and seeing these things will make you feel more at ease and put a smile on your face.

Try a New Spin on an Old Favorite

Capricorn enjoys salty flavors, and that can lead to you overdoing it on the salt in your recipes. Try a new twist on salt with sour salt. Sour salt is actually citric acid and adds a nice pucker to certain recipes during cooking (it should not be used as a table salt substitute however). Sour salt is sometimes used as an addition to lemonade and is perfect for making sourdough bread (which appeals to Capricorn's earthiness). Make sure to research appropriate recipes and follow the sour salt directions for correct use of this interesting ingredient. Jazz up your taste buds and give sour salt a try.

Breathe Away Worry

Worry is a Capricorn trait. You are always striving for more and worrying about what mountain you will need to climb next. But all that worry is not healthy for your mental well-being, so breathe it away! Try this simple breathing exercise to release some worry from your life.

Sit down in a comfortable chair or on the floor. Sit with a straight back and rest your hands on your lap. Close your eyes and just sit for a moment, getting accustomed to how you feel. Now it's time to get breathing. Take a deep breath in through your mouth or your nose, fill your lungs completely and hold the breath for 1 second, and then exhale deeply, emptying out your lungs. Pay attention to the slow, steady rise and fall as you breathe. Continue breathing with this method for 3 minutes, or at least twenty breaths. Notice how much calmer and more collected you feel afterward!

Discover Calm with Sandalwood

Sandalwood has a deep, woodsy smell that resonates well with Capricorn. The earthiness of sandalwood can help both slow your mind and improve your sense of clarity. As a Capricorn, you work tirelessly (almost stubbornly) toward your goal and push yourself sometimes beyond your limits. Sandalwood can work wonders on healing the emotional and psychological impact of this stress, and can help with feelings of anxiety and burnout. An especially popular scent, sandalwood features in a wide array of products. Try lighting a sandalwood candle to boost your feelings of calm.

Stand As Strong As a Mountain

Mountain Pose is an ideal yoga pose for Capricorn. Capricorn is as sturdy and strong as the mountains, and this pose helps personify that lofty image. Capricorn also rules over the joints in the body, and this stance works on strengthening those areas.

To do Mountain Pose, simply stand tall and proud with your feet together. Soften your kneecaps so you don't lock or hyperextend your knees. Next, imagine a line of energy all the way from your legs, up your spine, and out through the crown of your head. Your entire body should be straight on this centerline; tuck your tailbone and bring your pelvis into a neutral position. Press your shoulder blades back, but don't squeeze them together. Keep your arms straight, fingers extended, and triceps firm. Breathe slowly and feel your spine elongating. Keep your eyes on the horizon and visualize the strong impenetrable mountain that you are.

CHAPTER 17

Self-Care for Aquarius

Dates: January 20–February 18
Element: Air
Polarity: Yang
Quality: Fixed
Symbol: Water Bearer
Ruler: Uranus, Saturn

Aquarius is the most unpredictable sign of the zodiac. He is the sign of invention, individuality, group consciousness, and genius. There are two distinct Aquarian personality types because before the discovery of Uranus, Aquarius was ruled by cautious and conservative Saturn. Ancient astrologers had predicted a planet farther out than Saturn that could not be seen by the naked eye. They called this planet Ouranos, after the mythological sky god. With the electrifying discovery of Uranus by William Herschel in 1781, astronomers verified what ancient astrologers had predicted.

Astrologers then observed that many people born under the sign of Aquarius had characteristics that were not saturnine, but something different. These characteristics are now called Uranian, and they speak to the uniqueness and future-oriented personality of this most individual sign. Today, as we move toward the Age of Aquarius, we see some Aquarians who harken back to saturnine influences, but the majority (especially among the last two generations) are those who are moving forward into the unknown, unpredictable excitement of Uranus's influence.

The planet Uranus in mythology was symbolized by Ouranos, the sky god, who had an unusual and dramatic debut in the pantheon of the gods. His mother was the Earth Mother, Gaia, who gave birth to Ouranos (both her husband and son). So passionate was their relationship that Gaia could not give birth to their children. One of these children was Cronos, who decided to overthrow Ouranos and, while in the womb, emasculated his father. Ouranos later regained prominence, but his shattering beginnings are symbolic of the Aquarian rebellious and antiauthoritarian streak.

Aquarius is an air sign, and his symbol confuses some people. His sign is called the Water Bearer, and the symbol shows a young boy pouring something that looks like water from a large vase. Ancient sources record that when the constellation of Aquarius rose in Egypt and Babylonia, it corresponded with a period of floods and rain; hence, the symbol may pertain to weather patterns in the ancient world.

The symbol, however, also symbolically portrays the youth pouring rays of knowledge for all humanity. Aquarius's purpose, astrologically speaking, is to pour forth knowledge and ideas that benefit all people. For example, the Internet is Aquarius-ruled and a perfect example of individual ingenuity in service of the collective. The Internet is also theoretically egalitarian, a cherished value for Aquarius.

The planet Uranus represents the breakthrough force that shatters old forms. Aquarius's soul mission is to coordinate spirit and matter in new and revolutionary ways. His humanitarian principles can lead him to promote actions that are personally beneficial and beneficial for humanity. He thinks and acts for others as though we were all joined together in the common endeavor of living on this planet...which, in fact, we are.

Self-Care and Aquarius

Of all the air signs, Aquarius is the most blasé about self-care. He has a sensitive nervous system, but doesn't like to get bogged down in physical minutiae. He lives in future possibilities and frequently can forget that the here and now requires tending. Aquarius also has an "electric" nervous system that is erratic: He is either on or off. It is as if someone pulled the plug on his energies when they are off, but when he is on, it's like someone ramped up his voltage. Tuning into this rhythm is essential for Aquarius self-care.

One of the manifestations of Aquarius's supercharged mental activity is insomnia. It can come in waves or be chronic. Physical exercise is very good for balancing the energy, as is meditation and breathing exercises. But if Aquarius is riding the wave of creativity, it is best for him to go with it and sleep when the inspiration wanes. Some Aquarians simply do not need as much sleep as other people do.

Taking drugs to sleep or relax is often a bad idea, but especially so for Aquarius. Dampening his natural spirit shuts down his imagination. Over time he can become lethargic and dull because his life flow energy has been thwarted.

Aquarius, like all air signs, is a thinking sign rather than a feeling sign. He often has a detached quality and does not understand his more emotional brothers and sisters. It is as if feeling people are speaking another language. Like Spock in Star Trek, to him emotions are illogical and get in the way of useful activities that could improve any situation. However, the more evolved Aquarius understands and respects the intuitive knowledge that the more feeling signs have. This type of Aquarian may not be a gushy person, but he can learn to respect those qualities in others. Those Aquarians who remain detached can sometimes come off as cruel, distant, and impossible to sway.

Aquarius is the sign of the rebel. He doesn't like constraints. In terms of self-care, this is a problematic impulse. But, if Aquarius thinks, "I could have much more impact on the world if I were fitter or ate better," that is the opening into motivation for his self-care. Aquarius is not lusting for fame or fortune necessarily, but he needs to know that his ideas are traveling to other people (like the rays of knowledge in his symbol).

Aquarius might start a blog about whether or not self-care is productive for the planet. For example, the statistics on meat eating and the amount of energy it consumes might sway Aquarius to become a vegetarian. Doing something good for humanity is more of a motivator than self-care for his own sake. This is not altruism—just an indication that he is interested in breaking through standard practices that are outmoded and potentially harmful to the group as a whole.

Aquarius Rules the Circulation

Aquarius rules the circulation of blood and energy, as well as the calves and ankles. In Chinese medicine the life force of the body is called chi. Acupuncture and acupressure techniques balance chi to restore health to the whole body. It is a very old practice and particularly beneficial to Aquarius, as his energy can get dammed up and cause circulatory problems.

The ankles are also vulnerable to stress for Aquarius. An Aquarius jogger should tape his ankles to increase his strength. Activities such as in-line skating, ice-skating, or snowboarding require special care to keep Aquarius's ankles strong and injury-free. A muscle-building exercise that can help is to work with leg weights in the exercise room.

Sports and exercise are essential for Aquarius to keep blood and energy moving. He excels at both team and individual sports. In fact, among the top fifty athletes of all time, Aquarius is the most represented sign. Aquarian athletes apportion their energy well and enjoy the flow. Mindless aerobics or exercise classes are not good outlets for bursts of Uranian energy. Aquarius gets bored, and repetitive motion actually tenses his muscles. If he is in an exercise rut doing this type of exercise only because he thinks it is good for him, then he can cause himself physical damage with these repetitions. The best exercise choices for him are martial arts, Bikram yoga, jazz dancing, and Zumba.

Psychologically, Aquarius may have a hard time with therapy, because he resents anyone trying to "normalize" him. If a therapist says, "Well, this is the way the world works," Aquarius just doesn't believe it and walks away. Aquarius is not abnormal, but definitely marches to the beat of a different drummer. Counseling that incorporates methods such as cognitive behavioral therapy (CBT), neuro-linguistic programming (NLP), or hypnotherapy could be more beneficial than classic therapy. Aquarius has to be sold on the need to do therapy and the type of therapy he will engage in. He generally wants to solve a problem, not get lost in stories of his childhood or difficulties. Besides, Aquarius can think himself imaginatively in and out of problems, so he may think he can cut out the middleman and skip the therapy.

Aquarius and Self-Care Success

Consistency in anything is usually not Aquarius's forte. If he is in an active phase, then a new self-care program would be appealing. However, if he is "off," nothing will motivate him to do the things he knows he should. He truly resents thinking that he *should* do anything. He is not lazy, just too busy doing something else. Once he can place taking care of himself in a broader context, then he can be disciplined: Self-care becomes self-knowledge and might even benefit other people!

Self-care is productive when Aquarius can follow his own rhythm. Consistency usually doesn't work, but over time with activity and fallow times, he gets the job done.

In self-care, he is also not swayed by socializing routinely with groups, although he advocates group activities. For Aquarius, boring people are cautious and regular about self-care. If Aquarius finds a group that enlightens and challenges him, then he will be part of it and probably will become the leader. Leading his own self-care New Age group is the single best way for Aquarius to take care of himself. It partners with the idea of everyone working together, plus he benefits personally. Now, let's take a look at some self-care acts that will appeal to Aquarius.

Join an Exotic Food Club

One of Aquarius's fun qualities is a love of experimentation and trying new things. Apply that trait to your diet and find a way to explore new flavors and tastes regularly.

You can join a convenient subscription-based club that sends new foods right to your door once a month, or go to a local meeting of a group of people who like to try unique foods. (They might meet after work once a month for a quick meal, offer weekend dates for longer tasting sessions, or rent out restaurants for special events.) Search online for such groups and ask the moderator if you can join. Your adventurous personality will likely be a perfect fit!

Try the Camel Pose

The Camel Pose is a backbend posture that can improve circulation, which is especially important for Aquarius. Camel Pose also stretches the whole front of your body and can feel energizing after you've been sitting for a long period of time. This is not a beginners' pose, so make sure to practice this with your yoga instructor for detailed technique guidance.

To do the pose, kneel down on a yoga mat with knees hip-distance apart and the tops of your feet pressed into the mat. Rest your hands on your lower back and gently lean back toward your feet. If you are flexible enough, you can then reach back and touch or hold each heel with your hands. And, if it feels comfortable, allow your head to drop back without straining your neck. Hold the pose for about three breaths (or whatever feels comfortable), then slowly come up, bringing your head forward last. Breathe deeply.

Adopt a Unique Mantra

Feeling comfortable in his own skin is everything to Aquarius. A proven way to build self-confidence is through adopting a mantra that you can repeat aloud or to yourself to improve the way you think about yourself. Best of all, they're easy to work into your day—you can say them in the shower, in your head during your commute, or during your meditation practice.

Because Aquarius is so unique, sometimes the world might try to convince you to stop being you and instead join the crowd. When you need that boost of self-confidence in your special qualities, repeat "I go my own way" as you breathe deeply. Your individuality is something you should celebrate and cultivate, and these powerful words can remind you of that if you're feeling doubtful.

Dye Your Hair a Crazy Color

Getting bored with your regular hair color? Embrace your daring side and dye your hair with streaks of a bold color like purple or blue. You can visit a hair color professional to do the job or grab an at-home kit at a drugstore if you're feeling brave (make sure to follow all the instructions carefully).

Changing your hair color will keep your life fresh and help you feel like you're embracing who you really are—a rebel! You might even inspire others to try something similar when they see how great your hair looks.

Make Art at Midnight

Yes, you need your sleep, and it's important to rest when you feel tired. But Aquarius's super active mind can also be plagued by insomnia every once in a while. When those bouts hit, experts advise that you get out of bed and do a soothing activity to calm your racing thoughts.

For Aquarius, this is a great time to tap into your creativity and paint, draw, write, or try some other quiet pursuit. Keeping your hands busy will lessen the stress of not sleeping, and allowing your mind to wander as you freewrite or paint might make you feel drowsy eventually. You'll climb back into bed exhausted and wake up to the masterpiece you created!

Be Weird

In a sea of boring gray fish swimming in the same direction, you're a riot of color swimming the other way. While this uniqueness is something to revel in, it can also draw unwanted feedback from those gray fish. In these moments remind yourself that you are a gift, and you're perfect just as you are. What other people see as weird or different is actually exactly what makes you so special.

The truth is that Aquarius can be eccentric, but it's better to embrace and flaunt that trait than to try to hide it. The world needs a little color, and you're just the person to provide it.

Find an Acupuncturist

Acupuncture is a method of traditional Chinese medicine that involves a trained practitioner inserting tiny needles into specific points on the body to treat a wide variety of health issues. It's based on the concept that the energy, or chi, in your body needs to flow freely and be balanced in order for you to feel well. When your energy is blocked or imbalanced, you feel physically ill or mentally out of sorts.

Acupuncture is especially useful for Aquarius because his energy tends to get dammed up, causing circulation problems. Find a local skilled acupuncturist, and try it out the next time you don't feel well. Explain your issue to the practitioner, and they will arrange a personalized session that focuses on your specific concerns.

Protect Your Ankles

Aquarius rules the ankles, so you need to make sure you take good care of yours. If you play sports that put strain on your ankles—such as skating, skiing, snowboarding, and running—visit a sports medicine facility to ask experts the best way to take care of your ankles both in the short and long term. Ask if you should wear stretchy braces or tape your ankles to give them extra support. You can also learn specialized stretches, precise healing methods, and preventative exercises to keep your ankles in top shape for years to come.

Consider Alternatives to Traditional Therapy

Traditional talk therapy is a great resource for some people. But Aquarius might have a harder time aligning with that particular method because of his reluctance to have anyone tell him what's "normal" or "typical."

That doesn't mean that you should bottle up your feelings either though. Instead, trying therapy that incorporates cognitive behavioral therapy (CBT), hypnotherapy, or neuro-linguistic programming (NLP) might be more of a match for your personality. They are all innovative ways to change behavior. These methods are particularly effective at purposeful problem-solving (not necessarily diving into long-ago childhood stories), which is usually in line with Aquarius's preferences. Make sure to ask your primary care physician for a local recommendation, and try one of these therapies for a mental health check-in.

Color Outside the Lines

The adult coloring book craze seems to celebrate very traditional coloring—applying perfect shades of grass green, staying within the outer lines of the picture, using amazing types of shading and intricacy. And that's certainly one way to color.

But the Aquarius way is to forget all those "rules" and color your way. Make the grass bright blue. Turn the page upside down. Rip a page out, cut it in half, and connect it to another half-page to make a unique picture. Push color beyond the boundaries of the design in any way that speaks to you. This way of coloring is still meditative and calming—it just better reflects your Aquarius personality.

Embrace Your Inner Unicorn

Unicorns may be mythical, but they still symbolize the purity of Aquarian ideals. Therefore, try to incorporate unicorns in your life in one way or another. It shouldn't be too difficult—unicorns are currently a favorite theme in décor and clothing.

You can put unicorn stickers or decals in your bedroom or bathroom, or grab a tote bag or T-shirt with a unicorn on it. If you're feeling more cultured, take a special trip to visit The Met Cloisters (a museum in New York City that specializes in medieval arts), where you can see a beautiful decorative medieval tapestry that features unicorns.

Wear Batik Fabric

Batik is typically a type of Indonesian fabric made by applying wax to certain sections of the fabric, then dyeing the rest. The areas that had wax do not accept the color and thus you can make lots of intricate patterns. It is an ingenious way of creating a very individual fabric. Batik suits Aquarius because of its bold color palette and unique designs.

In addition to wearing batik clothing, you could also plan a fabulous trip to tropical Bali, one place where this gorgeous fabric is made. Visit local studios there to see the rich fabrics being created right in front of your eyes—or ask for some expert instruction and assist in making your own personalized design and color scheme!

Flaunt Iridescent Colors

That shimmery, multicolored shade you see on certain seashells and soap bubbles is iridescence—and it's a great match for Aquarius. The unique way iridescent materials look when light hits them represents your individuality and eccentricity.

Whether you wear iridescent accessories like cuff links or gemstone bracelets, or go bold and don a shimmery iridescent minidress or shirt, you're sure to garner compliments and turn heads. Iridescent home décor is also a good option—look for modern picture frames, sparkly hanging charms, or a shimmery shower curtain. Iridescence is timeless, spellbinding, and unique—just like you.

Accent Your Outfit with Blue Sapphires

The rich, deep blue shade of sapphire harmonizes with Aquarius's electric nature. These precious gemstones are one of the hardest minerals on earth and can actually be several shades of blue or violet. You can find men's and women's polished sapphire jewelry, or check out raw sapphire stones, which can take on an almost iridescent hue and are most often light blue.

If you'd like to see a stunningly large and flawless blue sapphire, visit the Smithsonian National Museum of Natural History in Washington, DC, which houses the almost 423-carat Logan Sapphire, mined from Sri Lanka.

Invent Something!

Aquarius rules all inventions and inventors, so if you have a unique idea, run with it! Many people think of interesting ideas but then don't follow through—instead, look up patents to see if anything similar has been done, then brainstorm how you can make your idea come to fruition.

Even if you just treat this idea as a hobby that you work on in your free time, it can be an exciting and motivating way to build confidence and have fun! And who knows—you might just think of the best invention since sliced bread.

Sample Some Black Popcorn

Sure, the commercialized yellow popcorn you've seen for years is a classic snack food. But it's also boring, and Aquarius isn't boring!

Black popcorn, on the other hand, is a gourmet treat. It's made from a different type of kernel, one that is smaller and mostly disintegrates when popped. (So you get far fewer hull pieces stuck between your teeth!) It has lots of flavor, and you can still season it with butter or oil and salt.

Black popcorn (look for organic types if you prefer) is available at specialty grocery stores or online.

Wear an Ankle Bracelet

Ankle bracelets are a timeless fashion statement that can call much-deserved attention to an often-forgotten part of your body. Since Aquarius rules the ankles, what better way to pay homage to your sign and show off your ankles than wearing an ankle bracelet?

You can find an ankle bracelet to match any style preference—thin and delicate, chunky and eye-catching, and everything in between. They're perfect for warm-weather wear, but don't forget about them in the colder weather—a little shine between your pants and your shoes is an unexpected delight.

Brighten Your Home with Bird-of-Paradise Flowers

When the weather is gray for an extended period of time, you might need cheering up. A surefire way to bring a smile to your face and a splash of color to your home is by filling a vase with fresh flowers.

Bird-of-paradise flowers are one especially amazing choice. These brightly colored, stunning flowers have pointed petals (they're usually yellow or orange) and incredible height and are native to South Africa. They almost resemble origami in their simple beauty. A tall, narrow vase would help showcase their shape and makes a real statement on an otherwise empty table.

Highlight Your Eyes with Glittery Eye Shadow

When you're headed out for a crazy night on the town, let your face match your excitement! No matter who you are, anyone can apply some glittery eye shadow for a night out. Try it and let the music move you.

Shades of blue, purple, and green work especially well for Aquarius, so visit your favorite beauty supply store and choose a glitter shadow that matches your outfit. The light at the nightclub will catch and reflect your glittery accents and add to the party atmosphere. Your individuality will shimmer and shine through the noise—so everyone knows you're *you*.

Take a Pilot Training Course

If air travel gets your heart racing in a good way, don't just settle for being a traveler squished into a middle seat. Put yourself in the cockpit with a pilot training course!

It's not as far-fetched as it seems. Aquarius rules air travel, so it's a good match for your sign—and your desire to find your own way in life. Search online for a reputable pilot training school near you, and then ask about their introductory programs. (You'll likely get ground training and then flight training.) The adrenaline rush of soaring above the world as you pilot the plane will keep you motivated to finish the course and receive your pilot's license.

Indulge In New Coffee Flavors

If your morning cup of coffee is starting to become boring, mix things up by asking a knowledgeable barista for new coffee bean recommendations. Whether you prefer sweet, earthy, or fruity flavors, they will probably have a bean that meets your preferences. You might be surprised by what you learn. For example, if you have a sweet tooth, you might enjoy some Brazilian coffees or Jamaican Blue Mountain coffees, which often have a chocolate flavor.

When you brew your coffee, you get to experience a unique aroma and taste. While you might not want to stray from your norm all the time, just the occasional change to your morning routine will appeal to your unique Aquarian sensibilities. Why wait until pumpkin spice season to treat yourself to a new coffee flavor!

Collect Wish Dolls

Wish dolls are tiny, personalized creations that can hold your hopes and dreams and help them come true. Aquarius can appreciate all sorts of knowledge and power, and wish dolls can help the universe hear and act on your dreams.

You can make your own wish doll by wrapping a square of fabric over a large cotton ball. (The cotton ball will be the doll's head and the remaining fabric will drape down to create the body.) Then, roll a small, rectangular piece of fabric into a straight line to become the doll's arms. Use a length of yarn to wrap the two pieces together into a doll shape. Once your doll is complete, whisper a wish to it every night and sleep with it under your pillow for forty days. This magical doll might just help make your wish come true!

Listen to Mozart

You've probably heard of Wolfgang Amadeus Mozart, but did you know he was also an Aquarius who followed his own path in life, choosing to be essentially a freelance musician instead of remaining a composer for a particular royal court? Inviting this fellow Aquarian's music into your life can help you feel more relaxed, centered, and connected to the universe.

Mozart was a musical genius at a very young age—he began playing public concerts before he was six. He then had a meteoric rise to fame, playing multiple instruments and eventually composing his own operas and symphonies.

Like other Aquarians, Mozart was brilliant and hardworking—and ahead of his

time. Cue up his *Symphony No. 41* (also called *Jupiter*) and let the music wash over you.

Ride a Unicycle

Exercise is an important component of self-care for all signs, and Aquarius in particular is known for his excellence in athletics. Try getting your blood moving in a unique way by riding a unicycle.

Learning to ride a unicycle requires strong leg and core muscles and a commanding sense of balance—challenges that Aquarius can meet because this activity is so fun to do; it doesn't feel like work. It's also a great way to get out of an exercise funk while burning calories and taking your mind off your worries. After a few classes, you'll be proficient enough to start wowing your friends with cool tricks.

Go See Neon Light Art

Neon lights are best known for announcing whether a store or restaurant is open or closed, but they can also become amazing works of art too. Whether shaped into recognizable objects like lips or words, or arranged into cool patterns, neon light art is a stylish, innovative take on modern art.

Your local art museum might have a visiting exhibit of neon light art, or you might want to take a trip to a large city to see some. Wandering around checking out the unique colors and shapes will open your mind to the myriad ways to see and enjoy art around you every day.

Put a Penguin Stuffed Animal on Your Bed

Stuffed animals aren't just for kids anymore! Put a cute plush penguin on your bed to make you smile and laugh every time you see it. Penguins are ruled by Uranus, Aquarius's ruling planet, and are a perfect example of individual ingenuity in service of the collective—they often huddle together in large groups to stay warm.

Look for a stuffed penguin at your local toy store, or purchase one from a charity that is working to protect their habitat. To spread the love, buy a second one and donate it to a children's charity in your area or give it to a child you know.

Become Inspired by Lightning

Your Aquarian mind works like lightning—offering powerful bolts of amazing ideas, innovative theories, and sparkling creativity. Remind yourself of your infinite potential for greatness by adorning your work area with an image of a lightning bolt.

You can look for a sculpture-like lightning bolt decoration, a stunning nature photograph of real lightning, or a neon light lightning bolt if you're feeling adventurous. Every time you glance at the lightning, you'll be motivated to come up with your next brilliant idea.

Grow Hydroponic Vegetables

Taking good care of your body starts by being mindful of what you put in it. Organic and freshly grown vegetables are the foundation of a healthy diet. Try growing your own vegetables at home in an environmentally friendly way—hydroponically.

Hydroponic gardening is the process of growing food without soil. This method produces high-quality food, takes up less space than soil-based gardens, and is easy to set up in urban or small settings. To get started, do a lot of research on what is involved, and ask your local nursery or other experts for resources for growing your own hydroponic vegetables. Leafy greens are typically an easy crop for beginners to try.

Watch a Science Fiction Movie

There's something exciting and a little scary about space and science fiction movies—they push your imagination to the limit and encourage you to ponder all the possibilities of the universe.

All astronaut, science fiction, and space movies are Aquarius-ruled, so make some snacks and settle in to watch a movie in this genre. Whether you opt for time-honored classics like *Alien* or *2001: A Space Odyssey* or a newer thriller like *Interstellar* or *The Martian*, you'll find yourself thinking about the plot long after the end credits. Aquarius likes to let his imagination run wild, and these types of movies will help you do just that.

Tap Into the Power of Lapis Lazuli

Crystals and gemstones have the power to help you fulfill your dreams and restore your inner balance. Lapis lazuli is a brilliant blue stone that's especially effective for Aquarius. It's known to help you discover your purpose and live whatever dreams your imagination thinks up.

Carry a piece of lapis lazuli in your left pocket (you receive energy through your left side and release it through your right), or place a chunk of it on your desk at work. Whenever you touch or see it, you'll be reminded of the astounding abilities you were born to showcase.

Listen to Electronic Music

Traditional instruments offer beautiful sounds, but electronic options really kick music up a notch energy-wise. The unusual and unexpected notes and sounds you hear in electronic music keep you guessing—and dancing.

Look online for electronic music that speaks to you, or visit a local club to listen to some live. Or—even better—pop into a recording studio, or get some software, so you can compose your own electronic song! Whether it has a percussive base or a cool remix patched in, you'll find yourself moving to the beat of your own sound.

Fight Seasonal Blues

In cold weather months, the lack of strong sunlight (or any sunlight!) can start to wear on you after a while. But there are things you can do to lift your spirits in the dreary winter months. Why not use this time to plan a trip to a tropical spot—either now or in the near future. Also, don't forget to keep up your exercise routine, even if you would prefer to snuggle on the couch. Get outside for a walk when you can; it is sure to lift your spirits. And though you may feel like hibernating, make sure to keep up regular plans with your friends.

If you are feeling low and lethargic on an ongoing basis, reach out to your doctor to discuss using light treatment therapy to alleviate your symptoms.

Hang Up a Photo of Your Planet

Your ruling planet of Uranus is stunningly beautiful. This gas giant, which resides almost two billion miles away from the sun, spins on its side, and is a lovely blue color (thanks to the methane gas in its upper atmosphere, which reflects blue light).

Hanging a photo of your planet near where you work will inspire you to follow your own path—just as Uranus spins in a different direction than any other planet in our solar system. It will also remind you to persevere in difficult times, since Uranus spins that way because of a series of collisions with a huge object billions of years ago. The planet withstood the blows and carried on, spinning in its own unique way.

Display Blue Cornflowers in the Summer

Cornflowers, which are native to Europe but now found in many places in North America, come in a brilliant blue shade that is Aquarius's color. They sometimes grow like weeds, so take a walk around your neighborhood and see if you can gather any. (If not, consider cultivating cornflowers yourself—they germinate quickly and are easy to grow.)

Display a bunch of cornflowers in a simple vase that lets the flowers shine. They don't last long after you cut them, so enjoy their cheerful color while you can!

Bring Back Ragtime Music

Ragtime's unmistakable syncopated rhythm is infectious and joyful. Though ragtime isn't one of the most popular music styles out there today, don't let that stop you from enjoying it. Search online for a classic ragtime composition, like the "Maple Leaf Rag" by Scott Joplin (the King of Ragtime), or look for more modern acts that feature ragtime, like Bob Milne. The beat will soon have you bouncing around, forgetting your worries, and savoring the unique sounds.

Hang Up an Octagon-Shaped Mirror

This type of mirror is as unique as you—what a perfect décor item for Aquarius. Hang an octagon-shaped mirror by your door so you can check your look before you head out. Arrange it over a small table or shelf that can hold your keys, mail, and other essentials, and you've got a useful and distinctive entryway design. The mirror's unusual shape will also surprise your guests and encourage them to check it—and themselves—out.

Invest In a Home Weather Station

The winds on Aquarius-ruled planet Uranus can be quite formidable, blowing at up to about 560 miles per hour (roughly 900 kilometers per hour). Though we thankfully don't experience that sort of extreme weather on earth, we do see our share of interesting storms and forces of nature—both of which probably pique your curiosity.

Consider buying a high-tech, Wi-Fi-enabled home weather station so you can keep track of weather patterns (like temperature, rain amounts, and humidity) and stay abreast of potentially dangerous storms in your area.

If you live in the country, try to watch storms from a safe place where you can take in the vast horizon. If you live in the city and it's safe, head to a skyscraper to view interesting weather rolling in. Let the awesome power of nature remind you of your place in our infinite universe.

Relax with a Blue Ice Cocktail

Since blue is Aquarius's color, this fun cocktail is a perfect way to unwind after a busy week. Add 1 shot vodka, 1 shot blue curaçao, ½ cup (4 fluid ounces) soda (such as Sprite), and a large handful of ice cubes to a blender. Combine until slushy, and serve in a martini glass. The electric blue color of the curaçao will make you feel like you're on a warm beach somewhere. Close your eyes, and hear the sound of the waves crashing and feel the sand in your toes.

Be Grateful for Good Friendships

Reflecting on the good friendships you have is a great way to show gratitude and appreciation for the role they play in your life. It's easy to get busy and accidentally take friendships for granted, so take a few moments to really think about yours.

Try a concentration exercise: As you sit comfortably and breathe slowly and deeply, contemplate how grateful you are for your friendships. Whether it's a longtime friendship that dates back to your childhood or a new friend you just met at work, these connections make you happy, keep you entertained, and offer support at difficult times. Friendships bring out the best in humanity, and reminding yourself of that is a wonderful way to see all the good in the world.

Wear Clothes with Patterns

Aquarius tends to be passionately individual, and your clothes should reflect your personality. Take a look at your closet and drawers, and make sure you have plenty of outfits with patterns and style. A periwinkle-blue gingham checked shirt, a scarf with neon zigzags, colored pinstriped pants, a sheer skirt with metallic thread to wear over leggings—no design is off-limits for Aquarius, and the brighter the colors, the better. Update your clothes periodically, and visit thrift stores or consignment shops for great deals on pieces that are unique and one of a kind—just like you!

Unwind with Frankincense

Most people only know frankincense as one of the gifts the Three Wise Men brought to baby Jesus after he was born. But it is also a powerful essential oil that you can burn as incense to create a special atmosphere in your home. Frankincense has a warm, woodsy scent and can soothe anxiety, minimize insomnia, and improve memory.

It creates a calming atmosphere for meditation or just to help you transition from a busy day to bedtime. You can look for incense sticks at your local health or New Age store or online.

Listen to Raga Music

Raga is a classical musical custom that originated in India to create a peaceful mood. Its name comes from the Sanskrit word *raga*, which means "color" or "to color," implying that the music colors the feelings or disposition of the audience. There are many types of raga, ranging from shorter pieces like songs to lengthier, more involved pieces that can incorporate a musician's improvisation. Look online for various forms of raga music until you find a style that speaks to you. Then play it when you want some quiet, reflective time for yourself.

Give Your Car a Makeover

Say the word *Aquarius*, and people are likely to quote the famous "Aquarius/Let the Sunshine In" song by the band The 5th Dimension. But the other lyrics in that song are just as important—they describe a world where everyone lives in harmony and is guided by love above all else. Show your allegiance to the Age of Aquarius by decorating your car with psychedelic stripes or designs, so everyone will know you are a hippie at heart—meaning, one who appreciates and respects all kinds of people, cultures, and lifestyles.

Play the Bells

A gorgeous set of silver bells featuring different tones can clear your space of unwanted or negative energy. Plus, their pure sound and decorative appeal make them a great addition to any home. Look in antique or music stores for bells, and be sure to play them before you purchase. You want a bell with an inviting, vibrant sound, not a piercing one.

If your home feels stifling, tense, or unsettled, ring one of the bells several times in each room. The vibration of the bell will renew and refresh your home's energy—and you get to enjoy the lovely sounds.

Hang Multicolored Mobiles

When a gentle breeze blows, allow your body, mind, and spirit to be renewed by not only the fresh air but also the lazy motion of a mobile. A double-helix shape works perfectly for this avant-garde sign. You might hang it on your front porch or near a window that's often open to get maximum benefit.

Look for mobiles that are brightly colored and visually interesting, so they're especially fascinating to look at. Don't forget to share the joy with the little ones in your life, too—find an appropriate spot and hang a mobile securely and safely out of their reach and let kids sit under it and experience the whimsical entertainment.

Chill Out with Some Popular Music

Exploring new sounds and music styles is important, but it's also perfectly fine to enjoy songs that are well known. Artists who are true to themselves, unique, and energetic are good fits for Aquarius. In particular, Justin Timberlake, Shakira, Alicia Keys, and Adam Lambert offer songs you can dance to, both for exercise and to take your mind off your day. The reggae beat of Bob Marley classics is fun for a change of pace. If you're in the mood for upbeat country, throw on some of Garth Brooks's rollicking favorites. If you'd rather hear some glam rock, turn on the inimitable Alice Cooper.

Photograph a Flock of Migrating Birds

Aquarius rules group efforts, and what better natural display of a group effort than a majestic flock of migrating birds? Each bird knows their role and plays a part in the greater good. They stay together and help each other get to their destination. Witnessing this amazing skill is a humbling sight indeed. Capture the moment forever by taking high-quality photos of the flock.

Find a spot that's comfortable while you wait for them to go by, and remain unobtrusive to other plants and animals around you. When the time is right, snap the pictures, and later hang a large version of one in your home to remind you of your ability to help your group (be it family, work, or another type) get where it needs to go.

Perform a Marionette Show for Kids

Puppet shows are a perennial favorite for children (and adults)—the quirky characters, the funny dialogue, and the simple sets lend themselves to an unforgettable show. Purchase or create some puppets and then think of a few short stories to tell with them. The stories don't need to be intricate—the props themselves are a big part of the show! Express your unique creativity through the puppets' tales of rousing mischief, sidesplitting tomfoolery, sensational victories, and hilarious failures. Create silly voices for each, and then find some young audience members to delight with this old-fashioned entertainment.

Consider a Pet Cockatoo

Dogs and cats are favorite domestic pets, but a bird might be a better fit for your Aquarian personality. In particular, mynahs and cockatoos are spirited, intelligent birds that can learn to speak. These types of birds can be wonderful companions and will help keep a smile on your face and love in your heart. You may find that you buoy each other's mood and look forward to seeing each other. Cockatoos are even known to dance—join in the fun and dance along with yours! But, if you've never had a pet bird before, it is best to start small, perhaps a parakeet. Just make sure to get expert advice on adopting (and properly caring for) your chosen bird from a local animal shelter before you commit.

Incorporate Curry Powder Into Your Diet

Curry powder is a blend of spices, many of which hold health benefits. Turmeric, coriander, and cumin are just some of the spices typically found in curry powder. Turmeric might have the power to help reduce inflammation, lower cholesterol levels, ease headaches, and alleviate symptoms of depression and arthritis. And the combination of spices in the curry powder can help improve your digestive system. Plus, it's delicious, and it provides the perfect excuse to try out some new curry recipes. There are many different blends of curry powders—in mild, medium, and hot strengths—so check the ingredients for a combination that appeals to you. Or experiment to create your own personalized blend that's as individual as you are, Aquarius!

Play a Kazoo

Aquarius is an air sign—which means proper breathing is especially important to your health and well-being. Practicing slow, deep breaths through meditation is one great way to reduce stress and renew your energy levels, but another—louder and perhaps more fun way—is to play the kazoo.

That's right—the silly kids' toy is a great relaxation tool for you too. Whether you just make sounds or try to play an actual song, the kazoo can help Aquarius consciously exhale and let go of worries. Whistle a familiar tune or just see how loud you can make the sounds—you'll soon realize you're laughing and have forgotten about your cares.

Plant Blue Hydrangeas

If you're looking for a large, flowering bush to fill out a garden or walkway, look no further than the beautiful blue hydrangea. Its giant flowers are stunning to behold and add unique color to a garden. Ask your local nursery which varieties would grow well in your area, as well as for soil recommendations for how to keep the flowers looking blue, and then get planting. The fullness of the flowers does a lovely job of filling a low vase, so be sure to cut a bunch to brighten the inside of your home as well.

CHAPTER 18

Self-Care for Pisces

Dates: February 19–March 20
Element: Water
Polarity: Yin
Quality: Mutable
Symbol: Fish
Ruler: Jupiter, Neptune

Pisces is the last water sign and the twelfth and final sign of the zodiac. She is a mutable sign, ushering in the spring season. In astrology it is said that Pisces marks the beginning of the return to spirit. The intangible, feeling world is Pisces's home, rather than the everyday material world. She is sensitive and psychically tuned in, seesawing between compassionate care for others and the tendency to always have her head in the clouds.

Pisces is one of the most spiritual signs. Her symbol is the two Fish tied together, and in many depictions one fish is above the water and in the light of day, while the other is under the sea and in darkness.

Pisces's imagination and artistic abilities come from these underwater depths. Emotional sensitivity is the hallmark of all water signs, but in Pisces it is especially acute. Pisces needs more rest and downtime than other signs do. Reality is often too abrasive, and she needs to recoup her energies often to stay happy and balanced.

In ancient times when astrologers first began observing the stars, there were only seven planets visible but twelve zodiac constellations. At that time Pisces was ruled by Jupiter, who is also Sagittarius's ruler. Jupiter is called the Greater Benefic, and both Pisces and Sagittarius are blessed by his protection. The bountiful generosity of Jupiter and the desire to help humanity is part of the Piscean nature. In 1846 the planet Neptune was discovered, and after observation, astrologers assigned this misty planet as Pisces's second ruler. Mist is a good metaphor for Pisces, who enjoys an inner world where there is a constant pink haze of emotion and creativity.

Neptune is also a planet that symbolizes spiritual hopes and dreams. In ancient mythology Neptune (known as Poseidon in Greek) was the god of the sea. The symbol for the planet Neptune in astrology is similar to the trident Neptune carried. Navigation in ancient times was precarious, and the changeable nature of Neptune held the fate of sailors in his hands. Would they reach dry land or be cast adrift into the depths? Such uncertainty could also be applied to Pisces. There is something elusive and a bit absentminded about Pisces that can be very endearing, yet some may feel they don't quite understand her. If Pisces is in touch with her soul's purpose and evolvement, she understands compassion more than any other sign does. If Pisces is adrift, however, then she tends to languish in her sensitivities and desires. These tendencies are also symbolized by the two Fish: one reaching upward toward the outside world, and the other downward, toward dreams and the inner self.

As a mutable sign, Pisces is flexible and goes with the flow. Instead of making a decision, Pisces may say "whatever." Decisions will creep up on her before she realizes what she is going to do. This passive approach has some drawbacks for her self-care: It may be too easy for her to float along, rather than guide the ship. Pisces may also have trouble with time schedules. She rarely wears a watch and has to be in the rhythm of something before she can get to appointments on time.

Self-Care and Pisces

The first action in self-care for Pisces is to create comfort, order, color, and cleanliness in her home. Pisces is a natural at organization; this may be her way of creating a world on dry land that feels secure and controllable. Pisces can easily become overwhelmed by oceans of feelings, so knowing exactly where everything is soothes her.

A facet of the Pisces character that may be counterproductive to good self-care is that she can be easily swayed by the opinions of others. Unless she was raised with good nutrition and health habits, she takes a while to understand that taking care of herself requires effort and planning. She is particularly lax about eating regularly and though she is a water sign (and many water signs often tend to prefer salty over sugary flavors), she can develop quite a sweet tooth. Additionally, Neptune, Pisces's ruler, also rules all drugs and alcohol. Any of the signs can have a tendency toward overindulgence, but Pisces's sensitivity and desire to retreat from the world can lead her to seek solutions or comfort in alcohol or other vices.

A far better way for Pisces to handle life's stresses is through a commitment to natural and alternative health practices. The first step is to straighten out her diet and fill in any holes in her vitamin or nutrient needs with supplements. Self-care regarding diet is necessary for everyone, but due to Pisces's especially sensitive system, she needs to take special care in good nutritional habits.

Another essential self-care practice for Pisces is to set aside "space out" time. This can be with music, meditation, or a walk in the country, or by coloring abstract designs in a coloring book. Pisces needs a controllable place to go for relaxation. While some signs flourish when spending a lot of their time socializing, Pisces quickly runs out of steam. To recoup her energies, she needs to be alone and in an unchallenging environment.

Pisces usually enjoys exercise as long as the surroundings are pleasant. She does well in sports because she has a natural sense of rhythm. Water sports are a great activity for her. She also enjoys horseback riding and aerobic dance, which also involve rhythm. In fact, some of the greatest ballet dancers throughout history have been Pisces. Tai Chi and gentle martial arts also appeal to her. Exercise such as this is where Pisces can effortlessly go with the flow.

Psychological self-care is also crucial for Pisces. Learning to articulate her feelings, such as through visits with a therapist, helps her move those feelings from silent worry to a definitive problem she can then solve. A sympathetic therapist who is in tune with Pisces's sensitivity will ensure counseling has a good effect.

Pisces Rules the Feet

Pisces rules over the feet. As the sign most connected to spirituality, Pisces needs her feet to be healthy in order to stay grounded on the earth. Comfortable shoes are a number one self-care item. For a

Pisces woman, high heels are the enemy; eventually her feet will suffer long-term effects. Choose comfort over glamour, and consider orthotics if your feet are especially prone to soreness.

A weekly foot rub is a very good self-care practice for Pisces. She should also consider trying reflexology. Targeting specific organs in the body through different pressure points on the feet, reflexology is a simple practice that can ease many aches, pains, and negative emotions. Pisces should also pamper her feet with regular pedicures. The goal here is for Pisces to feel as comfortable on the ground as she does in the imagination.

Pisces and Self-Care Success

A potential pitfall to Pisces's continuing self-care is her forgetfulness. Pisces just might forget what her program is, or become lost in a poem until hours have passed and she has missed dinner. A beeper clock or watch, or a special alarm on a smartphone, is a great solution. Pisces can also get a lot of use out of a smart watch that can be programmed to send out reminders. Besides keeping Pisces on schedule, a smart watch can keep track of how much of her time was spent doing certain things that day. This will help orient Pisces and give her an idea of how her daily schedule is working out.

A second pitfall to good self-care is dependence on drugs or alcohol. Ruled by Neptune, Pisces is prone to indulgence that can turn into dependence. She should be very mindful of how much she drinks, et cetera. By keeping track of this, she will be able to understand how often she turns to these substances and why. Working with a doctor can also be helpful if Pisces feels she is unable to determine whether she is using drugs or alcohol responsibly. The tendency to overuse drugs or alcohol is not due to a weakness in Pisces's character. In fact, it is the strength of her sensitivities in a world that does not always value feelings that can push Pisces toward these substances. By using her own sensitive feeling mechanism, Pisces can discover better ways to manage and express her individuality.

Lastly, for those Pisces who are actively involved in caretaking professions such as nursing, social work, or counseling, it is easy to become overinvolved with other people's problems. Not only is Pisces an effective caregiver, but she absorbs the energies of the person she is working with, which depletes her own energies over time. Learning to release the lingering thoughts and feelings after work ensures that Pisces practices the self-care that she preaches to others.

Pisces offers the final gift of the zodiac with her compassion and service to others. When Pisces learns that serving herself can magnify her ability to both help others and feel good all around, she provides a perfect model of self-care for friends and family. So let's take a look at some restorative self-care activities designed especially for Pisces.

Relax with a Pedicure

Pisces rules the feet, so it is especially important for her to practice personal wellness routines that include foot care. Healthy, happy feet will keep Pisces well grounded. A frequent pedicure is a must; you can invest in trips to a spa, or get your own foot spa for easy home use.

Give your feet plenty of time to soak in the warm water and expel dirt and oils. Then use a pumice stone and natural lotions to remove dead skin cells and hydrate your skin. If you wish, go one step further and apply an aqua blue nail polish. This shade will look elegant, while also displaying your special connection to the ocean.

Savor Seafood Chowder

Pisces is quite the daydreamer. Constantly moving between creative ideas and deep emotions, she easily becomes lost in her own inner world. While this sets the stage for many of the things that make her so special, Pisces should also practice living in the moment. Root yourself in the present once in a while with a delicious experience.

If you like fish, a warm seafood chowder is the perfect meal for you, Pisces.

Hearty and bursting with different flavors, this chowder is a tasty blend of comfort food and Pisces's astrological home, the ocean. Focus completely on the different ingredients of the meal as you eat, feeling the dish ease both mind and body into a peaceful, centered state. Savoring your food will also benefit your digestive system, which can get upset by fast eating. A healthy gut is a happy you.

Open Your Third Eye with Amethyst Décor

Pisces has a unique insight into the metaphysical realm; in fact, many people call her psychic. The perfect crystal for her to have on hand is an amethyst geode or small cluster. This eye-catching purple mineral can promote a higher level of consciousness by opening your third eye chakra.

Located on the forehead, the third eye chakra is an energy source that connects you to insight and subconscious knowledge. By opening this chakra, you can tap into a higher awareness of what drives you, your loved ones, and your community. Keeping an amethyst cluster or large geode crystal in your home—Pisces's haven—will help you turn creative ideas into actionable plans for the future.

Amethyst can also be used to balance your emotions. As you release negative feelings, the powers of this sparkling purple stone will draw a sense of happiness and optimism to you. Display it in a central part of your home, where you are sure to pick up its positive energies.

Put Those Feet Up!

Because Pisces rules the feet, a footstool would be a great addition to your décor or gift for a fellow Pisces. Pisces is often susceptible to problems with her feet, so having a soft spot where she can put them up, take some of the pressure off, and relax is right in line with her needs. For perfect Pisces style, look for fabrics in oceanic blues and greens, and the cozier and plusher the fabric, the better. Pisces loves the cozy factor!

Cuddle Up in Chenille

Pisces is known for being sensitive, and so is drawn to soft textures that soothe her soul and comfy surroundings that make her feel safe. Because of this desire to feel comfortable and cozy, Pisces tends to decorate her home in fabrics that elicit that feeling. Chenille fits this bill perfectly for Pisces. The feathery fabric is soft and silky with an almost velvety touch, perfect for wrapping around yourself and cuddling in. Invest in some chenille blankets for your home and your Pisces nature will thank you!

Play with Bubbles

Pisces is playful, without a doubt. She loves fantasizing about imaginary realms and sees the world with the same delight as a child. So why not indulge your childlike side and play with some bubbles? Buy a bubble gun and amuse yourself and any nearby kids with a flood of beautiful bubbles. Enjoy the soapy watery texture, watch the calming peaceful orbs float up to the sky, and create fantastical stories of where they might be going and who they might meet. Immerse yourself in the pure, simple joy of bubbles.

Enjoy a Cup of Cocoa

Sometimes Pisces just needs to have a little alone time. What better way to spend a chilly evening than under your favorite blanket with a nice cup of hot chocolate? Add a spoonful of hazelnut spread or some vanilla extract, or top your mug off with some mini-marshmallows; you can personalize your mini-hibernation treat however you like! It's really about enjoying some relaxing time inside when it's too cold to be outside. This chilly night in will be the perfect chance to unwind. Put on your favorite playlist and just sit back and sip that chocolaty goodness.

Watch Your Favorite Tearjerker

It's okay to be emotional, Pisces. Every now and then, you just need a good, cathartic cry. You can achieve such a release in a private space by setting up your very own movie night or Sunday afternoon matinee.

This gives you the chance to relax on your couch and have a good cry—with plenty of Kleenex and snacks within reach. Whether your melancholy mood has you queuing up a classic or a recent release, it's time to turn off the lights and turn on the waterworks. Allowing yourself the opportunity to express your emotions is important for your overall well-being. Being able to do it while enjoying your favorite movie stars act is a win-win.

Collect Sea Glass

Sea glass at a literal level is just pieces of glass that have been washed back onto the shore, but symbolically it is so much more than that. Sea glass begins as something discarded and broken, deemed useless. But then it is weathered, its sharp edges are worn away and smoothed out, and it is reborn again on the shore as something different. This rebirth from the sea resonates deeply with Pisces and her affinity to the water. It also sparks her empathetic personality and reminds her of how interactions with others can shape her in ways that she may never have thought possible.

Collect some sea glass next time you are by the shore, and display it in a clear glass bowl in your home. Place it somewhere the light can shine through it and illuminate the myriad colors, a reminder of how you, too, can weather a storm and emerge as something beautiful.

Decorate with Mermaids

Pisces likes to have her love of the sea reflected in her home décor. It wouldn't be uncommon to see images of seashells, starfish, corals, the ocean, or other aquatic themes in her home. So, when decorating your bathroom, bring a bit of the sea into the room with some mermaids. Mermaids are particularly good for decorating a bathroom where you get ready in the morning, because they represent independence, confidence, and the power to look deeper into a situation. These powerful sea guardians represent not only the beauty of the ocean but also its fierce strength, a fitting motivation for Pisces as she gets ready to tackle her day.

Illuminate Your Home with Stained Glass

Pisces loves stained glass windows, and this is fitting considering this sign rules faith and churches. Bring this element of your sign into your home by buying a panel of stained glass. A form of stained glass that can hang in a window—or some other place that can catch the natural light and filter it into your home—would be the best, as opposed to a stained glass lamp or other ornamentation. When the sun hits the glass, beams of color will burst into your home, filling it with a magical glow. Look for glass panels with aquatic themes to bring your water nature into your décor.

Embrace Your Duality in Your Décor

One of the symbols of Pisces depicts the two Fish tied together but swimming in opposite directions, signifying the duality of this sign. Pisces is very adaptive and can make herself at home in almost any situation and with any group of people. She can often be a mediator between two different sides, and her dual nature allows her to see both sides of a situation. Embrace this dual nature of your sign by decorating with things that represent both your affinity to the sea and your life on land. Try images of mermaids on land, the shore where the ocean meets the sand, or waterfalls cascading down mountainsides.

Enjoy Liqueur-Filled Chocolate

Like the sea, there are many layers to complicated Pisces. She loves to look beneath the surface and discover that not everything is as it seems. That's why when looking for the perfect chocolate confection for your sign, you should try a liqueur-filled chocolate. Though many water signs may prefer fewer sweet flavors, Pisces can often get a hankering for sugary treats (just another layer to her complicated personality). Sweet on the outside with a little kick within, liqueur-filled chocolates perfectly suit your Pisces nature. Plus, they are delicious and indulgent, and what Pisces wouldn't love that?

Add a Scarf

Pisces is known for her flowy, soft, and comfortable style. She is not up for the ordinary in terms of fashion and is usually on the lookout for unique and artsy accessories that are still on the simple, sophisticated side. A fabulous scarf would be an ideal piece for Pisces as it perfectly suits her romantic and dreamy taste. In spring go for a bright scarf draped casually around your neck, and in the wintertime go for a comfy cowl scarf, which also appeals to Pisces's love of warmth and coziness.

Try Some Poppy Seeds

Not only does the poppy flower symbolize imagination, a concept near and dear to Pisces, but the seeds of the flower may have tremendous health benefits for Pisces (providing she is not allergic to poppy seeds). Poppy seeds contain a unique combination of calcium and manganese that may prove beneficial for muscle function and bone health.

In addition, poppy seeds may help improve mental health by regulating neurotransmitters that can improve cognition. So get more poppy seeds into your diet. Try them on bagels, in muffins, or in salad dressings, or added to dishes such as chicken salad or oatmeal. Be aware, though, that consumption of poppy seeds before a toxicology screening can result in a false positive test.

Try a Taste of Caviar

Pisces loves the wildly romantic and often indulges her cravings. Champagne and caviar? Yes, please! But caviar is more than just a decadent treat for Pisces. It also resonates with her love of all things related to the salty sea, and it is a food that can help her mental state as well. Pisces, because of her empathy and compassion, is often susceptible to depression. Historically, caviar was once prescribed to alleviate depression. In fact, recent studies show that caviar has high doses of omega-3 fatty acids, which may improve mood. So find your happy place, quite literally, with caviar.

Revel In a Velvet Coat

Pisces loves the feeling of coziness, and in wintertime would rather stay in her cavern of soft warm blankets than venture out into the cold air. But as she can't remain a hermit all winter long (although wouldn't that be nice!), Pisces should indulge in a velvet jacket when she does brave the brisk weather. The plush and luxe fabric of velvet matches perfectly with Pisces's love of opulence, and its softness and warmth resonate with her love of the cozy and comforting. So, if you must go out into the cold of winter, wrap yourself in velvet and feel the luxury of this distinctively soft fabric.

Spice Up a Meal with Star Anise

Many Pisces enjoy the flavor of star anise. Though many water signs tend to avoid spicier foods, Pisces can take a bit of heat, and a small amount of a spice like star anise is just the thing to inspire her creativity without knocking her watery nature out of balance.

Not to be confused with anise seed (and not Japanese star anise, which is actually poisonous), Chinese star anise is often used in Asian cooking and provides a warm, licorice flavor to dishes. Star anise appeals to Pisces's love of the exotic, and it is also filled with antioxidants and antibacterial properties that benefit her health as well. Include some in your favorite muffins or soup recipe.

Get Out on a Boat

It's no surprise that Pisces loves the water and that the ideal spot for her to unwind would be on a boat. Got a special occasion coming up that you want to celebrate with family and friends? Hire a yacht for a night of luxury and fun on the seas. A yacht not in your budget? How about renting a canoe from a livery for a trip with friends? No matter how you do it, getting out on the water in a boat is an ideal activity for this water sign and one that will make you feel relaxed and in your zone.

Take a Houseboat Vacation

Contact with the water is essential for Pisces. Not only does she find it peaceful and relaxing, but it helps ground her and gives her an inner feeling of contentment. So next time you are planning a vacation, why not consider renting a houseboat? From a houseboat you can better enjoy the serenity of the water you are on, and you get to experience the lake, river, or sea firsthand. In addition, the rocking sensation of the water under the boat is soothing for Pisces, and can be just what she needs if she is having sleeping problems.

A houseboat also perfectly suits Pisces's escapist personality. If she gets bored of her current location or the people in it, she can start the engine and venture off to another destination.

Find Luck with Seahorses

The seahorse is a sacred symbol to Neptune in Roman mythology, and with just cause. The seahorse has long been considered a symbol of good luck, and stories from ancient times told of how seahorses would safely guide drowned sailors to their places in the afterlife. In fact, sailors would often use images of seahorses as good luck charms. Known as a calm and patient creature, the seahorse reminds you to enjoy who you are and be patient with yourself. Try adding seahorse motifs to your home

for beauty and luck, and if you ever find an actual seahorse, that is especially lucky!

Pick Up a Piscean Book

As an emotional and reflective sign, Pisces needs plenty of time alone to relax and recharge her batteries. One of the best ways to unwind is by reading a book. Pisces will delight in getting lost in a great story, setting her many thoughts aside for a few hours and refocusing them on an intriguing plot. But what books will Pisces enjoy?

Pisces is a romantic and nurturing sign, so she loves tales of love—from passionate affairs to the bond between a parent and child. With her special gift of insight, she is also unafraid to explore themes that will make her think. The masterful works of Pisces authors such as Victor Hugo and Amy Tan may top her list.

Ground Yourself with Bach's Clematis

Dreamy Pisces always has her head in the clouds. While this is great for sparking new ideas and creating moving works of art, sometimes a little extra focus is in order. Clematis essence is the perfect nature aid for gently bringing you back to reality so you can concentrate on the here and now.

The essence of this simple white flower can be found diluted in the original Bach Flower Remedies. Try adding a couple of drops of Bach's clematis remedy to a glass of water (follow the directions on the bottle) and drinking slowly throughout the day. (The Bach Flower Remedies are available online.)

Try Hypnotherapy

Pisces is connected to the subconscious. A great way to tap further into your subconscious is through hypnotherapy. Hypnotherapy facilitates access to this part of the brain by quieting your consciousness so that those deeper thoughts and feelings can be heard. A trained hypnotherapist will use calming techniques to move you into a completely relaxed state, where you can dive into your subconscious. By discovering your deepest drives and fears, you can then move toward managing them in ways that aid your overall growth.

In fact, hypnotherapy may help relieve many ailments, from anxiety and insomnia, to chronic pain and addictive habits. If you are considering hypnotherapy, ask your doctor for local recommendations.

Strike a Fish Pose

The Fish Pose is the perfect yoga position for Pisces, as it connects her to her astrological symbol, the Fish, and also increases flexibility while opening up the heart chakra. The heart chakra is responsible for emotions and your connection to others. As a compassionate sign, Pisces benefits from balancing her feelings and being mindful of the give and take within her relationships. Make sure to ask your yoga instructor for direction on performing this yoga pose.

To do this pose, lie on your back with your knees bent and feet on the floor. Lift your pelvis slightly off the floor, sliding your hands, palms down, under your rear. On an inhale, with slightly bent elbows, press your forearms and elbows firmly against the floor and begin to lift your chest, creating an arch in the upper back. Draw your shoulder blades into your back and lift your upper torso and head away from the floor. Tilt your head back, resting it lightly on the yoga mat. Pause for three breaths. Inhale and slightly raise your head off the floor. Then gently lower your torso and head back onto the floor as you exhale.

Keep It Candid

Pisces puts her feet to good work, always being on the move. While you don't want life to pass you by, you should also take a moment to capture it. A great way to stay true to your artistic spirit while on the go is by taking quick candid photos throughout the day. Don't bother posing or waiting for the perfect setup—capture the moment *in* the moment. You could even start a social media account dedicated to these photos. While it may seem a little silly, it's giving you the opportunity to see everything you do from a different perspective. These quick snapshots of your daily life will be an artful mosaic for you to reflect back on.

Share Your Signature Cocktail

Pisces loves sharing both her time and favorite treats with her friends and family members. Slip off to an oceanside oasis, and bring your loved ones along with you, with the sea breeze cocktail. This tropical refreshment is a delicious companion to any cookout, beach gathering, or dinner party. It will quickly become watery Pisces's signature libation.

To mix up some sea breezes for you and your loved ones, simply add 1 cup (8 fluid ounces) vodka, 2 cups (16 fluid ounces) cranberry juice, and ¾ cup (6 fluid ounces) grapefruit juice to a cocktail shaker filled with ice. Shake well, and then pour into a chilled glass and garnish with a frozen lime wedge.

Find a Muse

As an artistic sign of the zodiac, Pisces often uses mediums such as painting, drawing, and poetry to express her many intense emotions. It's important that you have things that feed your inspiration. To avoid creative dry spells, seek out a muse that encourages your artistic side. To find your muse, consider what speaks to your creative soul. This can be a person, a place, or even an activity that sparks expression. What ignites your passion? Is there a place you have visited that made you feel inspired? Is there someone you look to for motivation?

Magnetize Love with a Special Potpourri Potion

Pisces is a sign of love in every form. From romance to friendship, she is a role model for passion and care. If you find yourself losing a bit of that loving feeling, whether it is in the wake of a bad experience or due to stress, draw affection to you with a potpourri love potion. A love potion uses both natural elements and your inner energy to evoke love, typically of a romantic nature.

You can make your own by mixing simmering fresh water with spices, such as cinnamon and clove, and dried petals from flowers that symbolize love, such as roses, lilacs, or lavender. As you mix the potion, focus on your goal, envisioning it becoming a reality. Your home will be filled with the fragrance of love, drawing affection back into your life!

Enjoy a Glass of Red Wine

Red wine is a Pisces favorite. As a romantic sign, Pisces appreciates the seductive scent and taste of a great glass of red wine. It is also a classic touch in an intimate dinner for two, pairing perfectly with a pair of glowing candlesticks and a delicious meal. Set the mood, or romance yourself a little, by sipping your favorite red wine.

Be sure to savor it through all five senses—maybe even pretend you are leading a sophisticated wine tasting (from the comfort of your own home). Delight in the satisfying pop of the wine cork, and then take in the different scents and appearance of the wine once it is poured into your glass. Next, slowly sample the flavors and note the feel of the wine as it warms your throat. For an extra-romantic twist, try a sparkling wine with fresh fruit garnishes.

Accent Your Spaces with African Violets

African violets are the perfect natural accent for the Pisces home and work space. These beautiful purple flowers symbolize deep, everlasting love. As a romantic water sign, Pisces is fueled by the strong relationships she has with partners, friends, and family members alike. Just like Pisces, the African violet is also linked to water and feminine energy, including passion and creativity. Keeping an African violet plant in spaces where you work or create will inspire your special gift for artistic expression.

Listen to Lute Music

Lute music is very soothing, and Pisces loves calming sounds. The soft, often playful notes of the lute can balance Pisces's many emotions. This instrument is also rooted in history as a source of entertainment for nobility, beginning in ancient Egypt—a touch of artistic sophistication that Pisces will enjoy. Bring lute music into your home, specifically to spaces where you relax and recharge. A playlist of lute music on a low volume provides the perfect backdrop for your home oasis, helping you feel fully at peace and ready to dive into your many creative hobbies.

Visit a Reflexologist

As you know, Pisces rules the feet. What you might not know is how much your feet rule the rest of your body. According to reflexology, the different areas of your feet correspond to different areas of your body—from your nose and sinuses to your knees and intestines. If there is something that is ailing you or you feel unbalanced, book yourself an appointment with a recommended reflexologist. The reflexologist will realign your chi, or life force, by working the pressure points on your feet. The eyes may be the windows to the soul, but your feet could be the key to soothing that sore throat, relieving your back pain, and more.

Wrap Up in Silk

Silk offers a smooth, watery feel that can calm the mind and help you feel relaxed. As an emotional and compassionate sign, Pisces can often absorb the feelings of those around her, leaving her feeling overwhelmed or scrambling to solve everyone's problems. Wearing a silk robe is a simple way to ease stress through the powers of touch. This timeless addition to your lounging wardrobe will be your ticket to some luxurious alone time. Choose colors that promote peace and a happy mood, such as light blue or yellow.

Peer Into a Crystal Ball

Pisces is a sign of deep insight—not just into her own subconscious, but into the subconscious of the entire world around her. A crystal ball isn't just a fabulous addition to the Pisces home or work space. It also promotes strong Pisces insight, and delights her love for magic. Sometimes even psychic Pisces has difficulty seeing through the fog. Struggling with a decision? Unsure of the answer to a current dilemma? Simply peer into your crystal ball when your intuitive powers need a little boost.

Feel Connected with Ylang-Ylang

Pisces is a sign of reflection and daydreams—but it is just as important that she have an open flow of communication with people in the physical world. As a compassionate water sign, she feels balanced when her relationships are strong and well cared for. An ingredient found in many perfumes, ylang-ylang promotes social connections and a feeling of intimacy in your relationships. You can diffuse ylang-ylang essential oil in a communal space such as your living room so everyone can benefit from this unifying scent.

Promote Calm with Lotus Flowers

The lotus flower is the perfect image for Pisces to include in her home or office. As a sign filled with emotions and ideas, Pisces can become overwhelmed by everything racing through her head. Simple yet eye-catching, the white Japanese lotus encourages calm, and it can be useful in refocusing your mind and quieting all of the thoughts and feelings that you are experiencing. Frame a photograph of a lotus to place on your desk or hang in your home, or purchase other lotus accents to decorate spaces you frequent each day.

Sip Black Tea

Black tea is the perfect daytime beverage for Pisces! Black tea contains caffeine, as well as an amino acid that can help you stay focused. Daydreamer Pisces can sometimes use this extra dose of concentration to get things done. Black tea is also full of antioxidants and may promote a healthy gut, reduce blood pressure, and boost heart health!

Take a little time to mull things over as you sip the tea before that energy boost kicks in. You can find many different types of black teas, from Earl Grey to Darjeeling, so do a little experimenting to find your favorite.

Learn about Edgar Cayce

Ruled by misty Neptune, Pisces is a sign of special insight that some would call psychic. Reconnect with your metaphysical talents by reading about fellow Pisces, Edgar Cayce. Born in 1877, Cayce was a clairvoyant and became America's most well-known trance medium healer.

During his trances, Cayce would provide readings for people, including cures for numerous ailments, insight into an individual's past lives, and predictions of the future. Over fourteen thousand of his readings can be found on record at the Association for Research and Enlightenment in Virginia Beach, Virginia. His connection to the metaphysical will both resonate with and fascinate Pisces.

Give Someone You Love an Orchid

Orchids are Pisces-ruled. With their vibrant colors and exotic appearance, orchids have a long-standing association with love. Share them with a special someone! It will brighten both of your days. Compassionate Pisces places great importance in deep, strong bonds, so she will delight in this simple way of showing someone how much she cares.

The color of your orchid will also say a lot about your feelings. Go for yellow when gifting an orchid to a friend, pink for a romantic partner, orange for that office crush, and purple for someone you greatly admire.

Share the Wonder of Animals

As an emotional and intuitive sign, Pisces often has a gift when it comes to animals. In fact, some people believe you can communicate with animals on a deeper level. Pisces's compassionate soul also finds sharing with others very rewarding. As a Pisces, your gentle spirit works especially well with children, so share your bond with animals with a child! Whether you take them to a petting zoo or a nearby farm or a shelter to spend time with animals, it will be an invaluable experience for both you and the child—not to mention the animals you visit.

Use a Love-Focused Mantra

Caring Pisces values deep relationships with those around her. When she feels disconnected from a loved one, it creates an imbalance that leaves her unsure. This feeling of instability can cause Pisces to flee to the metaphysical world and avoid communication with others. Fortunately, you can ground yourself and gain back confidence in your relationships by reciting a special mantra.

A great mantra for Pisces is "Love and compassion will help us all." Use this mantra to steady yourself and prevent that urge to flee when you feel uncertain of a current relationship.

Affirm Your Instincts

Pisces has a special gift of insight that those around her admire. But sometimes unexpected things happen, regardless of how vigilant she is in reading situations. These bumps in the road can cause Pisces to doubt her intuition. If you feel that self-doubt creeping in, you can give yourself a much-needed confidence boost through the use of an affirmation. An affirmation, written down and revisited as needed, will serve as a reminder of your abilities.

The perfect affirmation for Pisces is "I trust in my intuition, and incorporate it in my daily life." There is a reason people often say Pisces has a sixth sense. But even the most insightful Pisces is not responsible for predicting every turn life takes you through; this doesn't mean your intuition is wrong, though, and you should stop listening to it. Instead, use your affirmation as a reminder of that fact.

Pin a Guardian Angel to Your Collar

As a sign connected to the psyche, Pisces is tuned in to the powers that be. This includes the intangible forces and past people who may be watching over you throughout your life, offering guidance and aid. Pin an angel to your coat collar or carry it with you in your bag or car as a reminder that you are not alone in your journey. There is protection, guidance, and support waiting for you whenever you may need it.

Grow a Bonsai Tree

Creative and nurturing Pisces loves helping things grow and flourish in beautiful ways. Grow a bonsai tree! This miniature, eye-catching plant is the perfect hobby for exercising both your artistic and caring sides. Bonsai trees are also a part of feng shui, which uses nature and placement to bring balance and positive chi to your home. You can find bonsai kits online, as well as in many garden centers. Be sure to follow instructions on care, and invest in a small pair of scissors for shaping your tree as it grows.

See *The Little Mermaid*

The mermaid is Pisces's finny sister—and not just because they are both linked to the element of water. In fact, though Pisces lives in the physical world, she is often compared to this mythical being, due to her misty planetary ruler, Neptune. Pisces, like a mermaid, has a similarly misty allure, deep intuition, and connection to the metaphysical realm.

Visit Copenhagen, Denmark, where you can find *The Little Mermaid* statue. Made of bronze and posed on a rock along the Langelinie Pier, this special statue was created in honor of the Hans Christian Andersen fairy tale. Unable to travel for a while? You can also stream the animated movie for a burst of mystical inspiration (and childhood nostalgia).

Visit a Monastery

Ruled by Neptune, Pisces is deeply connected to the metaphysical world. Nourish your spirituality by visiting a monastery. One of the oldest types of spiritual centers in the world, a monastery is the living quarters and place of worship for a group of monks or nuns. Monasteries are part of many spiritual traditions, including Buddhism, Christianity, and Hinduism. You can visit one of thousands of beautiful monasteries across the globe, or take a quick trip to one closer to home to meditate or pray where countless individuals have before you. In Europe, some monasteries also offer inexpensive accommodation for travelers, so check out the possibilities!

Create a Self-Care Retreat

For Pisces, the home is where she can truly be herself. As an emotional and reflective sign, she requires a lot of alone time to recharge her batteries and enjoy fun solitary hobbies such as reading and drawing. It is no coincidence that many of her self-care acts are best performed at home. Create a special space within your home that will serve as the perfect retreat (away from family members and housemates) for when you are in particular need of self-care. Store those items especially relevant to your self-care practice there: your favorite silk robe, a gratitude journal, your healing crystals, or a meditation book perhaps.

This space should incorporate calming blue accents. Also, be sure to add plenty of cozy seating options and blankets. Create a self-care oasis within your home oasis!

Adorn Your Bed with Pillows

Pisces is a sign of relaxation and comfort. Nestle into soft surroundings by purchasing pillows of all sizes for your bed. Your comfy nest won't just be for sleeping; it will also be your hub for creativity and relaxing solitary hobbies.

Try to include both soft pillows for resting and firmer pillows for leaning against when enjoying some alone time. This mix of support will help prevent backaches and slouched postures. Be sure to also provide a variety of enjoyable textures to your oasis, such as velvet, silk, and fleece.

People-Watch

Pisces spends a great deal of her time within her thoughts. She loves to reflect, in memories or daydreams, and it is often from these inner thoughts that she gains insights into both herself and the outside world. Feed that natural urge for thought by people-watching. People-watching is a simple pastime that involves sitting back to observe the activity of those around you, often in a bustling public space. You can take a trip to the local coffee shop for an afternoon, or spend the day at a popular park taking in all of the sights and sounds (and some nice fresh air as well).

Take a Fishing Trip

Symbolized by the element of water and the Fish, Pisces shares a bond with this natural substance and its scaly inhabitants. Nourish this connection with a fishing trip! An adventure on either salt or fresh water is just the thing to rejuvenate Pisces. The waves will feel like a second home as she seeks out her astrological symbol. Make it a full-day affair by packing a delicious lunch and bringing along a book or other relaxing activity to pass the time as you fish. How many types of fish can you spot?

Buy a Witch's Hat

Mystical Pisces has an affinity for all things supernatural, including witchcraft. In fact, it is often believed that Pisces exists in two realms at once: the material and the metaphysical. This is represented by her astrological symbol of two fish tied together, swimming in opposite directions.

Tap into your magical side by buying a witch's hat (or full costume!). In need of some inspiration, or perhaps a reminder of your abilities? Put on your hat and feel the divine powers of the witch course through you. You may even be compelled to cast a spell or two.

Index

About the Author

Constance Stellas is an astrologer of Greek heritage with more than twenty-five years of experience. She primarily practices in New York City and counsels a variety of clients, including business CEOs, artists, and scholars. She has been interviewed by *The New York Times, Marie Claire*, and *Working Woman*, and has appeared on several New York TV morning shows, featuring regularly on Sirius XM and other national radio programs as well. Constance is the astrologer for *HuffPost* and a regular contributor to *Thrive Global*. She is also the author of several titles, including *The Astrology Gift Guide, Advanced Astrology for Life, The Everything® Sex Signs Book*, and the graphic novel series Tree of Keys, as well as coauthor of *The Hidden Power of Everyday Things*. Learn more about Constance at her website, ConstanceStellas.com, or on *Twitter* (@Stellastarguide).

BRING THE WISDOM OF TAROT INTO YOUR DAILY
SELF-CARE ROUTINE

PICK UP OR DOWNLOAD YOUR COPY TODAY!

adamsmedia
An Imprint of Simon & Schuster
A CBS COMPANY